Stifled Progress – International Perspectives on Social Work and Social Policy in the Era of Right-Wing Populism

Jörg Fischer
Kerry Dunn (eds.)

Stifled Progress – International Perspectives on Social Work and Social Policy in the Era of Right-Wing Populism

Verlag Barbara Budrich
Opladen • Berlin • Toronto 2019

All rights reserved. No part of this publication may be reproduced, stored in or introduced into a retrieval system, or transmitted, in any form, or by any means (electronic, mechanical, photocopying, recording or otherwise) without the prior written permission of Barbara Budrich Publishers. Any person who does any unauthorized act in relation to this publication may be liable to criminal prosecution and civil claims for damages.

You must not circulate this book in any other binding or cover and you must impose this same condition on any acquirer.

A CIP catalogue record for this book is available from
Die Deutsche Bibliothek (The German Library)

© 2019 by Verlag Barbara Budrich GmbH, Opladen, Berlin & Toronto
www.barbara-budrich.net

   ISBN 978-3-8474-2252-5
   eISBN 978-3-8474-1323-3

Das Werk einschließlich aller seiner Teile ist urheberrechtlich geschützt. Jede Verwertung außerhalb der engen Grenzen des Urheberrechtsgesetzes ist ohne Zustimmung des Verlages unzulässig und strafbar. Das gilt insbesondere für Vervielfältigungen, Übersetzungen, Mikroverfilmungen und die Einspeicherung und Verarbeitung in elektronischen Systemen.

Die Deutsche Bibliothek – CIP-Einheitsaufnahme
Ein Titeldatensatz für die Publikation ist bei der Deutschen Bibliothek erhältlich.

Verlag Barbara Budrich GmbH
Stauffenbergstr. 7. D-51379 Leverkusen Opladen, Germany

86 Delma Drive. Toronto, ON M8W 4P6 Canada
www.barbara-budrich.net

Jacket illustration by Bettina Lehfeldt, Kleinmachnow –
   www.lehfeldtgraphic.de
Typesetting by Anja Borkam, Jena – kontakt@lektorat-borkam.de
Printed in Europe on acid-free paper by paper&tinta, Warsaw

Table of Contents

Kerry Dunn & Jörg Fischer
Social Work and Social Policy in the Era of Right-Wing Populism –
an Introduction 7

What Is Right-wing Populism, and why Is It Gaining Power?

Alexander Häusler
Forms of Right-Wing Populism: The Example Alternative for
Germany (AfD) 17

Samuel Salzborn
German Right-Wing Extremism and Right-Wing Populism:
Conceptual Foundations 33

Christoph Richter & Matthias Quent
Democracy Under Stress: Right-wing Success at the German
Parliamentary Elections: Socio-economic and Political-cultural
Influences 41

Fabian Virchow
Globalization, Crisis, and Right-Wing Populism in Context 59

Birgit Meyer
The Discreet Charm of Populism: The Role of Gender and Female
Politicians in the AfD and Front National/Rassemblement National 71

Why Should Social Workers Be Concerned?

Tomasz Kaźmierczak
Social Work and Social Services in Polish Illiberal Democracy 89

Olga Borodkina
Social Policy and Social Work under Pressure in Russia 99

Christiane Leidinger & Heike Radvan
Anti-feminist and Familyist Positions in Gender and Sexual Politics:
Right-wing Populist Challenges for Social Work 115

Kurt Möller
Right-wing Populism in Germany: Challenges for Social Work 133

Michael Reisch
Social Work under Trump: Experiences from the USA 147

What Can Social Workers Do to Move Forward?

Julika Bürgin
Social Work in Germany: Civic Education and the Concept of
'Bildung' 169

Kerry Dunn
Social Work in Post-Factual Times 179

Chery A. Hyde & Claire Galpern
Human Rights Based Social Work and New Right Populism 191

Barbara Schäuble
Remaining Professional, Taking a Stance: Social Work Strategies
for Countering the Influence of Right-Wing Populist Politics 205

Kerry Dunn & Jörg Fischer
Conclusion: Right-Wing Populism as Continuing Challenge to Social
Work 219

Authors 225

Index 227

Social Work and Social Policy in the Era of Right-Wing Populism – an Introduction

Kerry Dunn & Jörg Fischer

Populist movements are gaining momentum worldwide and pose a challenge to social work due to the profession's commitment to democratic principles, social justice, and human rights. For a long time, there has been an increasing political and social polarization in Western democracies, which has been worsening since the financial crisis of 2008 and the migration crisis of 2015 (Milbradt, Heinze, & König, 2018, p. 4). Anti-democratic tendencies may express themselves differently across national contexts. However, social work is facing similar challenges, particularly the need to clarify its position in response to right-wing populism. The question of how to respond to today's challenges touches on a deeper question, the definition of the profession itself. Is social work just a service provider that develops technologies in all forms of state action to offer minimum forms of individual security and social cohesion? Or does social work understand itself as part of the political-social system and advocate of its own professional values?

Social work is per se political. The only question is whether social work consciously gets into it and tries to proactively control political processes or eludes its own positioning and leaves the interpretation processes to other social and political forces. The example of the US shows that recent changes in the social policy agenda are not coincidental and cosmetic in nature, but represent a basic component of populist politics. In this respect, these policies affect all aspects of social work, from working with clients, to engaging with the political system, to understanding one's own profession. The impact of a policy influenced by a nationalist agenda does not just require adaptation to changing conditions. Rather, professional social work practice is fundamentally challenged in its foundations.

For social workers, the rise of right populism is troubling because the ideas its leaders espouse fly directly in the face of liberal democratic values and institutions, with which our profession is deeply connected. Moreover, the values that guide our profession – which for example in the US include service, competence, integrity, dignity and worth of the person, social justice, importance of human relationships – seem to have no place at the table in political discourse shaped by right-wing populism. As a result, we may feel thrown off balance as we struggle to figure out what our role is in this new political terrain.

This volume was created in order to provide some grounding for social work educators and practitioners. The authors dig deep into the impact of right-wing populism on political systems, policies, and discourses in the US and Europe. They also provide concrete strategies to help us move forward, push back, and work together to protect our profession and those most at risk of harm.

We have organized the chapters into three sections – what right-wing populism is and why its power is growing, the challenges it is creating for social work, and how social workers can respond. While most of the chapters cover all three topics, we grouped them based on their primary goal or focus.

What Is Right-wing Populism, and why Is It Gaining Power?

Populism is a political philosophy and set of strategies that aims to challenge the power of political and economic elites to support the interests of regular people. It is not considered an ideology in the traditional sense, and instead can be used by different ideological groups, meaning there can be both left-wing and right-wing forms of populism.

At its heart, all forms of populism are fueled by critiques of the existing power structure. Much has been written about how right-wing populist leaders have come to power by connecting with people who feel left out of the globalized economy and equality discourses. While many social workers may agree with the critiques populism raises (for example its distrust of corrupt politicians and financial elites), we are alarmed by the solutions it proposes.

The first five articles explore right-wing populism's roots, manifestations, and strategies in contemporary democracies. They help us gain a deeper understanding of how leaders frame diversity, inequality, and belonging, and why these framings resonate with so many people. They show us how similar the strategies and responses are across national contexts, suggesting a need to develop common counter-strategies and international collaboration.

Häusler provides a history of the Alternative for Germany party (AfD) and explains how it transformed into a right-wing populist party. He proposes that the AfD has been successful because it provided a space for feelings of economic and social resentment to be voiced and created a home for a previously separate set of right-wing groups through the use of nationalistic and anti-immigrant rhetoric.

Salzborn lays out the elements of extreme-right political ideology and demonstrates the relationship of right-wing populism to the extreme right. He argues that right-wing populism is best understood not as a separate group or ideology within the family of the extreme right but instead as strategy or set of tools chosen by extreme right groups. These strategies include pushing topics in the media through staged events and a cult of personality, using rhetorical devices that polarize debate, and conjuring opposition between the elites and the people.

Richter and Quent describe results of their empirical research on voter characteristics that explain right-wing populist electoral success in Germany. The AfD was most successful in regions with high unemployment, weaker economies, and high percentages of non-voters but also had support in prosperous regions where there was a local political culture in which disenchantment with democracy and far-right extremism have been become normalized.

Virchow explores the question whether globalization explains the rise of right-wing populism, as some have claimed. After complicating both globalization and populism as concepts, and he connects economic and social insecurity caused by neoliberalism, structural changes and growing inequality to the rise of right-wing populism. He explains that right-wing populism is fear-based, moralizing, polarizing, and exclusive in nature, it has support because it gives people a sense that they can be protected from today's dangers. He proposes that an inclusive, democratic populism should be considered as a way to address people's concerns in a way that increases solidarity and equality.

Meyer argues that in addition to anti-elitism and anti-immigrant rhetoric, attacking gender equality is a core strategy of new right populist parties, particularly by women leaders of those parties. Through analysis of election reports, party programs and public speeches she uncovers how women leaders of right-wing populist parties use traditional women's issues to support right-wing ideals, for example stoking fears of sexual assault to promote anti-immigrant policies. The author proposes that women leaders further the right's agenda in many ways, including by helping soften and normalize hardline policy proposals and positioning themselves as victims who are persecuted for their political beliefs.

Why Should Social Workers Be Concerned?

Right-wing populist leaders have analysts, activists and scholars around the globe worried. Key areas of concern including various threats to democracy; the scapegoating of immigrants and other vulnerable groups; the rollback of hard fought gains against racism, sexism, and heterosexism; and the assault on social work values.

On the whole, social workers who find fault with liberal democracy do so because they want more democracy, more participation, more inclusion. Social workers understand that right-wing populism, while claiming to be the true voice of the people, actually speaks for only some of the people and leads to greater exclusion of some groups. Populism is a cry by those who desire to rise above the messiness of democratic politics. Social workers know the solution is not to circumvent, but to engage directly with, this unavoidable messiness so that our political decisions include more voices.

Social workers are concerned about political polarization, the breakdown in trust between social groups, and the refutation of natural and social science. Both liberal democracy and economy depend on a good dose of trust, not just in people we perceive to belong to the same group but in strangers. Without a willingness to talk to the other and agreement on basic facts, the debate and compromise needed for democracy to work process breaks down.

Right populism frightens us because of its attack on democratic institutions including the media, universities, the branches of government and liberal values. While we may have our own critiques of these institutions, we are afraid of a world without them. Most social workers believe in a public-sponsored safety net through social insurance programs that distribute risk. We know courts can oppress but they are also our best hope for protecting and expanding civil rights. We know legislatures are beholden to lobbyists of corporations and interest groups, but they are also where we can advocate for policies that provide services, protect vulnerable members of society, expand citizenship, and enhance well being. Government, for all its failings, is an institution capable of harnessing mass resources toward public ends. Universities, although a bastion of the class system, also have tremendous powerful for enhancing mobility and participation.

Social workers are also concerned by anti-immigrant rhetoric and policies, increasing violence against minority groups, and attempts to roll back hard-fought women's and LGBTQ rights. In view of a global situation in which the United Nations says there is the highest number of refugees since the end of the Second World War, many countries are affected by a hitherto unknown refugee migration. Even though most of the refugees live in neighboring countries in Asia and Africa and only a fraction reach the West, the arrival of refugees in many affluent countries presents a great challenge. Right populist's refutation of the humanity of migrants and other vulnerable groups, as well as their definition of solidarity as only for a narrowly defined part of society, go directly against social work's mission of inclusion.

We are concerned about the direct assault on concepts like social justice, integrity, human dignity, and human rights and the way that right populists have targeted and corrupted these values. The fundamental rights that should protect all human beings provide a common blueprint for dealing with people who are vulnerable (Staub-Bernasconi, 2007). Concepts like human rights and human dignity are important for the social work profession because help us understand a person's situation, develop advocacy arguments, and intervene in a just manner. They have been important in liberal societies to provide a common language across and within borders around standards of humane treatment of vulnerable groups. When right populists attack not just the standards but the underlying concepts themselves, not only is social work's reason for being called into question but we face a world that is losing its constructed safeguards against atrocities.

Our authors of the next five articles help us understand how these attacks on liberal democratic institutions and values are surfacing in different national contexts and their implications for social work's identity. They make clear that social workers in multiple national contexts are facing new threats to both client wellbeing and core professional institutions.

Kaźmierczak describes social work under the Law and Justice government in Poland. Though there have not been outright attempts to modify the profession, impacts can be seen in policies that impact social work stakeholder groups and threaten social work values. He describes specific policies that are exacerbating economic inequality and hampering the third sector, and explains how social work values are threated by the lack of government intervention when vulnerable groups – immigrant, LGBTQ, and disabled members of society – are attacked and the government's support of conservative, traditional family structures and values.

Borodkina describes how social policy guided by contradictory populist and neoliberal ideals are creating barriers to social work and a disconnect between official claims and practical realities in Russia. She focuses on the example of disability policy. While official rhetoric supports social integration of disabled persons, research shows little progress in actual integration due ongoing barriers and a lack of comprehensive capacities-based policy.

Leidinger and Radvan demonstrate how familyism, or the ideology that promotes the traditional nuclear family as the ideal family form to support the social structure, presents a direct threat to socially-just social work practice in three practice areas: violence against women, reproductive rights and sex education. They posit a key challenge for social work is recognizing the right-wing populists' method of reinterpreting these topics to avoid adhering to destructive right-wing ideas and instead to challenge them.

Möller argues that the biggest challenge posed by right-wing populism the fact that it cannot be countered by arguments alone. Instead of strategies based on the cognitive transfer of knowledge, social workers must find equivalents to those experiences that were instrumental in the adoption of extreme right-wing attitudes and engage people on an emotional level to counter affective and symbolic right-wing populistic metaphors and images.

Reisch focuses on challenges faced by social workers in the US under Trump. He shows that the challenge comes not only from right-wing populism but from historic debates within the profession itself. Although there has been an increase in activism among social workers since the election, we have not seen a mass mobilization of social workers responding to right-wing populist policy due to the dominance of clinical practitioners and licensing concerns within the profession.

What Can Social Workers Do to Move Forward?

The last four articles focus on specific strategies for the profession to respond to right-wing populist rhetoric, climate, and policies. A social work that understands itself not only as an analyzing science, but also as an action-oriented profession, can only do justice to this claim if it succeeds in developing from the analysis of right-wing populism derivations of action that meet professional demands. Social work is called upon to find individual, group and community-level approached to counter right-wing populism. Social work, based on democratic and human rights principles, has a mandate to advocate democratization of society and to address violations of human rights. Challenging people who support inhumane ideologies is not a new experience for social workers, and we already have most of the knowledge and skills we need to do so in the current political environment.

Bürgin argues that social workers to get more involved with civic education projects and explains how we can do so to address the crisis in democracies around the world. The goal of civic education is to create spaces where youth can engage in dialogue about issues that concern them in order to learn how to work across difference to develop solutions. In order to engage in civic education, social workers will need resources to support research, training, conceptual tools, supportive work conditions. They must also engage in democratic political projects themselves to model engagement and continue learning.

Dunn discusses implications of post-fact and post-truth politics for the profession, and how we can use the profession's current skills, values, and knowledge to address the challenges posed. She outlines how elements of the post-fact terrain are similar to traditional social work practice settings. Our experience working with domestic violence and child abuse prepare us to help people and groups understand how information can be used as means of disorientation and control and how to stay grounded in the face of coercion. Our experience working in high-stress environments shaped by complex social dynamics have tooled us with reflection and supervision skills that allow us to maintain connection to our values and our conscience.

Hyde and Galpern describe human rights principles and how they relate to social work values and practice. While social workers involved with efforts that support, protect and empower women, immigrants, unions, people of color and other disenfranchised groups essentially are engaged in human rights based work, in the US there is little effort to explicitly engage in human rights work to counter right wing populism. They argue that the profession has so far failed to analyze or address right-wing populism and name social work concerns as collective human rights issues. A human rights framework would help social workers recognize the grievance narratives of right wing populists, while also challenging the hatred, bigotry and dehumanization inherent in these narratives.

Schäuble explains that the social work profession is deeply tied up with the liberal democratic project, and with debates raging over the value of that project, questions arise about the purpose and goals of the profession. This is not the first time social workers have faced authoritarianism, and we must look at what has and is causing some social workers to capitulate and others to stand firm. Social workers can rely on professionalism, a connection to the hard won battles for social progress of the past, an active framing of the profession, their agency's mission statement, and external advice to shore up their confidence in the face of new right populism's threat to our core values and the rights of the people we serve.

Acknowledgements

This book is the result of a long collaboration with many colleagues in social work in very different countries from the USA, Germany and Poland to Russia. The idea of working together on a product has made it possible to bring together very different discussion groups and to create new forms of professional exchange. Starting with peers involved in the International Social Work and Society Academy (TISSA) with annual conferences at a different Eastern European universities, through partners working with the Institute for Local Planning and Development (IKPE) at the University of Applied Sciences in Erfurt to colleagues who have served as cooperation partners in the International collaboration of the Faculty of Applied Social Sciences at the University of Applied Sciences in Erfurt for a long time.

We would particularly like to mention Prof. Jeffrey Draine of Temple University in Philadelphia, who inspired the implementation of this idea and unfortunately had to withdraw from the project for health reasons. He also came up with the idea of bringing together the two previously unknown publishers and motivating them to cooperate. We, the editors, are very grateful to Jeff for this mediation and would therefore like to express our appreciation to him for making this book possible.

This project could succeed only through the participation of many actors. We would like to thank all contributors for their thoughtful exploration of this challenging topic.

Erfurt/Germany and Fresno/USA, December 2018

References

Milbradt, B., Heinze, F., & König, F. (2018). Politische Bildung in einer Welt des Umbruchs. *DJI* Impulse, 1/18, 4-9.

Staub-Bernasconi, S. (2007). Soziale Arbeit – Dienstleistung oder Menschenrechtsprofession? Zum Selbstverständnis Sozialer Arbeit in Deutschland mit einem Seitenblick auf die internationale Diskussionslandschaft. In A. Lob-Hüdepohl, & W. Lesch, W. (Eds). *Ethik Sozialer Arbeit – Ein Handbuch: Einführung in die Ethik der Sozialen Arbeit,* (pp. 20-54). Paderborn: Schöningh.

What Is Right-wing Populism, and why Is It Gaining Power?

Forms of Right-Wing Populism: The Example Alternative for Germany (AfD)

Alexander Häusler

In the past decades the Federal Republic of Germany had been spared, unlike its neighbours, of strong approval rates of right-wing populist parties. This situation changed with the foundation of the Alternative for Germany (AfD) party. Accompanied by the election success of this right-wing populist party, which is represented in 14 state parliaments as well as in the German Bundestag, the German party system is currently undergoing change. The so-called people's parties are losing their ability to integrate, and a political sullenness is moving more voters to the extreme right. This development is an expression of an increasing shift to the extreme right in German politics whose results are not yet predictable.

The Formation of Right-Wing Populism in Germany

Success of AfD as well as that of some other right-wing parties is based mainly on mobilisation of authoritarian and nationalist passions. As a self-described "voice" of "people's anger," the AFD is giving a resonant space for perceived declassification, disorientation, and resentment. It offers opportunities to express "anger, contempt and devaluation" for a growing number of voters (Zick & Küpper, 2015). The party works as a political modernizer of a deeply-rooted nationalist-authoritarian rebellion. For this reason, factual contradiction and clarification of the extreme right-wing claims of the AfD remain largely ineffective at dissuading some of its supporters; the AfD is chosen in spite of excesses, lies, and scandals because the party provides an outlet for its supporters' emotions.

AFD had success in bundling extreme right ideology into a political party for the German population. This right-wing populist party developed into a home for new-right and racist protest scenes, and it seeks out alliances with other extreme-right forces in Europe. It attempts to copy successful extreme right-wing parties like the French Front National/Rassemblement National and the Austrian FPÖ and to establish contacts with the authoritarian Putin regime.

If one understands right-wing populism as a form of political staging, populist style is used by classically extreme-right parties like the French FN but also parties like the "Swiss People's Party" (SVP), which originated as a conservative party for agricultural interests. In contrast to anti-Muslim parties like the Pro Cologne, Pro NRW, and Pro Germany parties, the political roots of the AfD are not in the extreme right. It rather combined elements of different right movements, from the economically-liberal but nationalist-conservative end of the spectrum to völkisch-nationalist circles.

Table 1 Parteipolitische Achse des europäischen Rechtspopulismus (Beispiele)

Traditional extreme right parties with right populist style	Right populist parties with extreme right relations	Right populists with right conservative or right-liberal origins
• FN • Pro Parties (Pro Cologne, Pro NRW, Pro Germany)	• FPÖ • REP • AfD (after leaving of the Lucke wing)	• SVP • Schill • BfB • AfD in the founding phase (with a focus on extremely right-wing references

After the jettisoning of federal spokesman Bernd Lucke and his followers after his unsuccessful effort to build the AfD succession party ALFA (later renamed "liberal-conservative reformers"), the AFD focused increasingly on the topic of immigration and positioned itself clearly on the extreme right. A look at the extreme-right factions in the European Parliament shows the political development of the AfD moving from a nationalist-conservative direction to the political block of the extreme right. When it secured seven seats in the European Parliament in 2014, the AfD was a member of the EU-sceptical conservatives and reformist faction (EKR-Faction), led by the British Tories. In those days, the majority of the AfD leadership still proclaimed distance from extreme-right parties such as the FN and the FPÖ. After the Lucke's ouster, this changed radically.

While the arm of the AfD which split off under the leadership of Lucke is still a member of the EKR-Faction, the remaining AfD members in parliament lead by Beatrix von Storch and Marcus Pretzell moved to the extreme right. Von Storch went to the right-wing populist EFDD-faction (Europe of Freedom and Direct Democracy) under the guidance of the British UKIP ("UK Independence Party") and Pretzell to the extreme right ENF-faction (Europe of Nations and Freedom). Active groups in the ENF faction include the FPÖ, the FN, and the racist Lega Nord out of Italy. The movement of AfD leaders from EKR to the EFDD and ENF shows that the AfD shifted from an originally eurosceptical, pro-western position to join the extreme right anti-European block.

Table 2 Extreme right factions in the EU Parliament

Europe of Conservatives and Reformists faction (EKR-Faction) (selection)	Europe of Freedom and Direct Democracy (EFDD) (selection)	Europe of Nations and Freedom (ENF) (selection)
• Conservative Party (Tories) • Prawo i Sprawiedliwość (PiS) • Dans Folkeparti (DF) • ALFA/LKR	• UKIP • MoVimento 5 Stelle • Sverigedemokraterna • Tvarka ir teisingumas (Liberal democrats Lithuania) • Beatrix von Storch (AfD; since beginning of 2018 replaced by Jörg Meuthen)	• Front National/Rassemblement National • FPÖ • Lega Nord • Partij voor de Vrijheid (PVV) • Vlaams Belang • Kongress der neuen Rechten (KNP) • Marcus Pretzell (Ex-AfD)

The political approach to the extreme right FPÖ has in this connection a special meaning because of the common language and inherited right-wing framework. This approach manifested itself in February, 2016, when the AfD-chairman of NRW Marcus Pretzell organised a conference in Düsseldorf and federal chairwoman Frauke Petry, FPÖ chairman Heinz Christian Strache, and the member of European Parliament and FPÖ secretary general Harald Vilmsky took part. While it was announced as an event of the conservative EKR-faction of the EU parliament, the conference was in fact just an event of the AfD and the FPÖ. Until the summer of 2015, membership of EKR maintained, at least officially, a strict separation from parties like the FPÖ. That meeting was the first public and official link between AfD and FPÖ, which in Brussels was not a member of the EKR-faction, but belonged to the much more radical faction: "Europe of Nations and Freedom" (ENF). Strache called the invitation for the meeting with the AfD a "historical act." A few days later the chairman of the Bavarian AfD Peter Bystron proclaimed the start of a "Blue Alliance" - inspired by the colours of both the AfD and FPÖ. Bystron completed his press release with a graphic which showed him together with Strache, and between both men there was a map of Germany attached to Austria with the slogan: "The blue alliance is overcoming borders; FPÖ and AfD together for Europe's future!" (AfD Bavaria, 2016).

Developmental Phases of the AfD

It is possible to classify the political development of the AfD into seven phases. The starting point of AfD-foundation was the euro-crisis and the Sarrazin-Debate, which had a key importance to the party during the first phase of development. AfD started to have success because of framing itself as an anti-party against Angela Merkels focused on saving the euro. But the AfD was from the beginning not a one-issue party. In addition to euro-rescue policy, it was the Sarrazin Debate that heavily influenced public discourse in 2010.

During that period, the racist ideas of the former Central Bank board of directors and SPD senator in Berlin, Thilo Sarrazin, about the failure of integration and immigration policy as well as putative genetic and cultural features of Jews and Muslims, opened a gateway for right populism. The Sarrazin Debate encouraged discussion about the chances of a new right wing party: In September, 2010 an Emnid poll predicted 18% of votes for a fictional "Sarrazin"-party (Spiegel, 2010). Before foundation of the AfD, no party to the right of CDU/CSU was able to bundle this set of ideas effectively at the national level.

Sarrazin's success as an author was the intellectual breeding ground of the AfD, and his thesis was reflected programmatically in the demands of the AfD. In his books and interviews the media star and troublemaker stoked anti-Muslim sentiments and strengthened euro-and EU-scepticism among many citizens. Using a populist and new-right tone, he started to fight also against a supposedly left "virtue terror." Sarrazin located the allegedly prevailing restriction of freedom of speech in a "code of the good, true and correct, which dominates big parts of the media class." This "political correctness" emerged as a "transnational phenomenon of the West," which is marked "at least in Europe by the left part of the political range of views" (Sarazin, 2014, p. 35).

Contrary to their own representation as an absolutely new party, it is possible to describe the AfD as a political by-product of some unsuccessful right-wing parties. Former supporters of groups like the CDU, CSU and FDP and extreme-right parties like the "League of Free Citizens" (BFB), the "Freedom Party" (Die Freiheit), the "Republicans" and the "Schill-Party" gravitated toward the AfD as a new sphere of activity. Especially with the BFB–Germanys first anti-euro-right-wing-populist party that dissolved in the late 90s–the AfD had a lot of support during its foundation period (Häusler & Roeser, 2015).

In September 2013 the leader of the unsuccessful anti-Muslim "Freedom party" DF Rene Stadtkewitz asked his colleagues to support the AfD from now on. The AfD also had tangential connections with the political movement of the so-called "new right" (Langebach & Raabe, 2016), because of the support of the weekly Junge Freiheit, which promoted AfD from the beginning, as well as the new-right Institute of State Policy (Kellershohm, 2016). In March 2014 the Patriotic Platform was founded as an association. Here the extreme right wing of the AfD formed for the first time to create inner-party strength. During this first AfD development phase nobody attacked the leadership of party founder Bernd Lucke. But AfD election successes in 2014 in Saxony, Thuringia and Brandenburg the started first inner party transitions and the beginning of the second development phase of the party. This was marked by the significant gain of power of the nationalist-conservative-new-right wing of the party. At the same time arose inner-party discontent over the sole representation of federal spokesman Lucke.

Another political opportunity to reform the AfD as a right movement party was the emergence of the Pegida-Protests in Dresden starting in the fall of 2014, which shaped the third development phase of the AfD and exacerbated the inner-party quarrel. Lucke and former member of the AfD board Henkel stood up for a neo-liberal and pro-western direction for the party and opposed cooperation with racist street protests and the anti-Muslim focus. But this created more inner party conflict. The regional chairmen of Thuringia Björn Höcke and of Saxony-Anhalt Andre Poggenburg initiated the "Erfurt resolution," which united the inner-party right opponents of Lucke under the designation "Der Flügel" (the wing). The result of this struggle was an inner-party shift of power.

The party congress that took place in Essen in July 2015 symbolizes the fourth development phase of the AfD. At this party congress, Bernd Lucke lost the inner-party struggle for the leading role, getting 38% member votes compared with 60% for AfD regional chairwoman of Saxony Frauke Petry. In his greeting to the congress participants, the AfD regional chairman of NRW Markus Pretzell clearly broke from Lucke, proclaiming that the AfD had become not only an anti-euro-party, but also a "Pegida Party" (Steiner 2015). Petry had won against Lucke because she was supported by the right wing of the party. The deciding feature of this phase was the secession of the economical liberal, pro-western wing of the AfD, and the foundation of the organisation "Alliance of Progress and Renewal" (Alfa, later renamed "Liberal Conservative Reformers", or LKR) under leadership of Lucke. This party had no success in the following regional elections.

In late summer 2015, the refugee debate was the dominant public subject, and it became an important political opportunity for the AfD to start a striking series of successes in regional elections. Election polls showed that in that summer, the AfD had only about 5% approval, but this changed massively in its favour during the second half of 2015. Not without reason, the chairman of the AfD of Brandenburg Alexander Gauland described the refugee crisis as a "gift" for his party (Spiegel, 2015). This was the beginning of the fifth development phase of the AfD, in which it turned more into a right-wing-populist-anti-immigration party with German-nationalist rhetoric.

With the so-called autumn-attack, the AfD began to mobilize against the refugee policy of the Federal government. Populist invectives against Chancellor Merkel went hand in hand with an escalating rhetoric against refugees. Since the shift of leadership in summer 2015, the anti-Muslim trend in the AfD increased. The political position "Islam does not belong in Germany" was published in the agenda of 2016, which shows that anti-Muslim propaganda had become a part of the AfD agenda. At the same time, the AfD strengthened its political base in the former East German states using social-populist language with the intention of getting greater numbers of swing voters than the Left and the SPD.

The sixth phase of development of the AfD marks the state of the party before the federal elections of 2017. This phase is characterised by an embrace of the extreme right and another shift in the inner-party balance of power. The creation of an agenda was accompanied by an increasing escalation of the power struggle inside the leadership of the party. On this occasion federal chairwoman Petry, who tried during the federal party congress in Cologne to establish a "pragmatic course (realpolitisch)," suffered a shattering defeat. A new team for the election campaign included the Spiritus Rector of the party, Alexander Gauland, and Alice Weidel, who works in the neo-liberal Hayek Society. The seventh phase of AfD's development begins with its entrance into the German Bundestag (parliament) and the exit of its former chairwoman Frauke Petry. The former chairwoman of the AfD is attempting, together with her husband Marcus Pretzell who is former regional-chairman of the AfD in NRW, to set up a new competitor party to the AfD called "The Blue," an effort which, like Lucke's LKR, probably has few chances of success.

Right-Wing Populist Forms of Expressions

A main feature of right-populist agitation is an "anti-establishment orientation" (Decker, 2011; Kohlstruck ,2008; Priester, 2012), in which a constructed battle between "the people and the elite" serves as the "basis-story" of right populism (Geden, 2007). In this case the term "people" is used in a homogenizing way to describe very different interests of some parts of society in contrast to the "political class", which is selling out "national interests" to the undemocratic, multicultural, and transnational-orientated European Union for its own enrichment (Häusler & Roeser, 2015). The AfD describes "people" as a social-ethnic-cultural-homogeneous unity and separates out segments of the population as not belonging politically, ethnically, and culturally to society. This kind of agitation is based on a policy of fear and the creation of enemy images. Depending on the political situation, AfD leaders change respective enemy images and defame them as a "threat to our people" to show AfD as a protecting and "cathartic" power.

Figure 1 Features of right populism

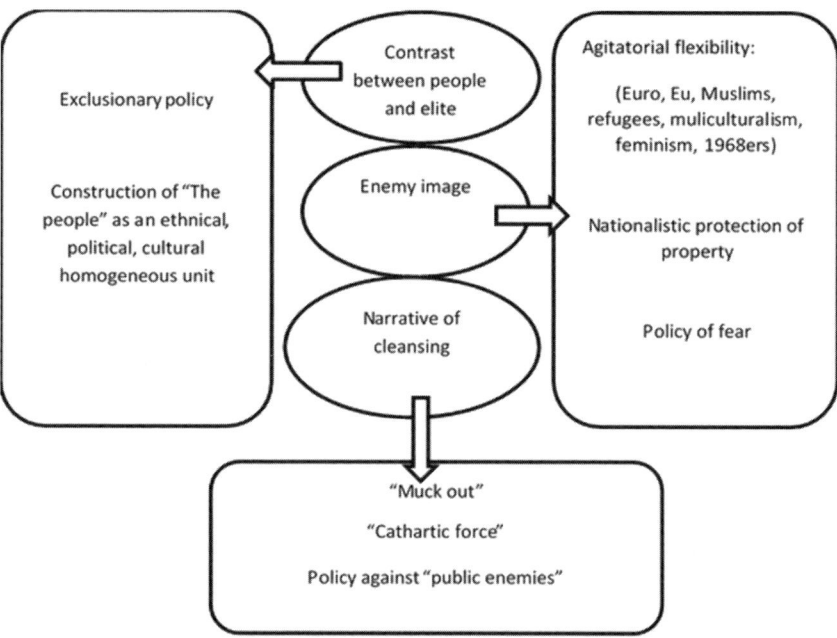

The narrative of "catharsis" serves right-populist parties as a metaphor for an authoritarian uprising against "public enemies." Immigrants, the "corrupt elite" who are hated by right populists as well as emancipative movements, and the established political parties are identified as enemies. The campaign against "the politicians" presents an aggressive challenge to representative democracy. One example is a speech by Markus Forhnmaier, chairman of AfD-youth organisation "young alternative," given at an AfD demonstration in Erfurt on October 28, 2015, in which he said: "I say to left disposition terrorists, to corrupt parties, quite clearly; If we rise to power we will muck out and clean up and after this we will make policy for the people and only for the people – because we are the people, dear friends" (Bernhard, 2015).

Mobilisation to an Extreme Right Cultural War

Domestically the AfD, as a proverbially reactionary party, is fighting a culture war against multiculturalism, pluralism of social life forms, and emancipative social movements. This right cultural war ("Kulturkampf") can be understood as a political fight for images of order. The intention is to establish the normalisation of right-wing ideas about order–regarding the composition of society, values, education, and lifestyle as well as affiliation. One can interpret this cultural war as a reactionary challenge to social-democratizing processes with anti-feminist, homophobic, and racist overtones. The opposition of the AfD to gender-mainstreaming, pluralistic sexual life and family forms, and "early sexual enlightenment," is based on a patriarchal image of society and an assertion of a natural social inequality. The understanding of human inequality as an expression of a "natural order" is the core of the new right's "biologistic idea of man" (Feit, 1987).

Indeed, it is possible to understand AfD's promotion of a "natural human picture and family image" and its rejection of feminism and pluralistic sexual life forms as a means to link different political currents. This linkage is possible because of the "ideology of the natural order of social inequality" (Kemper, 2015, p. 83). For example in the Erfurt resolution of the extreme right wing the AfD seeks to establish itself as a "movement of our people against the social experiments of the last decades" (Gender mainstreaming, multiculturalism, free choice of education styles, etc.) as well as a "movement of resistance against erosion of national sovereignty and identity of Germany" (The Wing, 2015). The cause of this alleged "unnatural" order is emancipative social movements. The AfD-federal speaker Jörg Meuthen explained during the AfD national congress in Stuttgart the political direction of AfD thusly: the forthcoming federal agenda should abandon the "left-red-green" which contaminated 1968 Germany (Meuthen, 2016). Such slogans belonged up to now to the vocabulary of the extreme right.

Social Populism and Völkisch-Authoritarian Populism

Anti-democratic currents of the new right like the new-right Institute of State Policy have been working for several years to establish new political strength for the right. A trendsetting publication by the Institute in 2007 explained: "The political system of the FRG has the chance to diversify only to the right." Simply described, there is for every social class a left and a central party (upper class Green party/FDP, middle class SPD/CDU), and the lower social class is currently represented in Germany only by the Left party/PDS. To fill this gap a half dozen right-populist parties are in competition with each other and with the rather successful nationalists of the NPD. The electoral potential is about 15-20 %. "With such a percentage of votes it is possible to make policy in a political party framework" (Institute of States Policy, 2007, p. 36),

What the NPD, the BFB and the REPs could not provide, the AfD now creates. With the intention to mobilise lower social classes, the party is practising a very specific form of social-populist speech. Right social populism is a form of agitation that attempts, based on right-wing values, a selective engagement of the social-political and economical interests of workers. The intention is to thereby mobilise the working class and at the same time to make right worldviews and ordo-liberal economical opinions attractive. Right social populism instrumentalizes the anger about social and economic injustice in propaganda to support völkisch-nationalist policy approaches. It was the AfD chairman of Brandenburg Alexander Gauland who proclaimed after the first electoral successes in Eastern-German federal states that the AfD is the "party of the small people" (Geis, 2015).

Gauland realised the propagandistic benefit of right social-populist stagings, and he pleads for a break from the former open-neoliberal platform the party supported under Lucke and Henkel. Thus the party changed its position about the minimum wage, which it opposed before. Gauland's strategy was confirmed by the election results of the AfD in Eastern as well as in Western Germany. In Hamburg the party was for the most part not successful in "rich" quarters, but had support in so called "socially weak" neighbourhoods. In Saxony-Anhalt the results were above average in industrial regions, and in Baden Würtemberg the AfD had won direct mandates in both Mannheim and Pforzheim, two industrial towns with a formerly SPD-dominated constituency. Shortly afterwards the elections in Baden-Württemberg, Gauland explained in an interview with the Stuttgarter Zeitung: "The AfD will not leave behind the people at the bottom of the social scale."

His party must "attempt to create as much social justice as possible" (Pichler, 2016). Allegiance to this kind of populism is declared in the "confidential strategy paper" of the AfD. There was a recommendation to avoid too detailed statements.

> For election success of the AfD it's furthermore not helpful to figure out nuanced preparations and technically ambitious solution models to central subjects and to publish results, which are interesting just for some specialists in the political class but overwhelm the voters… [It is] more important to put the finger on the wounds of the established parties than to get tangled in an expert's discussion about solution proposals (AfD, 2016a).

Typical right scapegoats are alternately presented. As the AfD extreme-right-politician Björn Höcke explained at a AfD demonstration in Schweinfurt:

> The social question of the present is not primarily the distribution of people's fortune from top to bottom, bottom to top, young to old or old to young. The new German social question of the 21th century is the question of the distribution of people's fortune from the inside to the outside (Höcke, 2016a).

Such populist statements are examples of a völkisch-authoritarian uprising rhetoric. The term "völkisch-authoritarian populism" helps to describe exact tendencies, ideologies, and agitation patterns which are dominating the AfD today, including right-populist staging, mobilisation of authoritarian passions, and the use of völkisch-nationalist ideology and terms. Arjun Appachrai (2017) describes the right attack on the liberal democracy as a new form of "populist authoritarianism" (p.17), whose central feature he interpreted as the "translation of questions of economic sovereignty into questions of cultural sovereignty" (p. 32). In the propaganda of the AfD, authoritarian populism is enriched with völkisch-nationalist elements. According to party researchers Niedermayer and Hofrichter (2016) the piece of the AfD agenda about "culture, language, and identity" is influenced by a "völkisch-nationalist tone." The preamble of the party agenda of June 2016 ("we want to be Germans and we want to remain Germans") shows the "primacy of the national." The scientists also see "connections to the extreme-right" with Thuringian AfD-chairman Björn Höcke, because he "talks in a way about the reproductive behaviour of Africans and Europeans which is definitely racist" (Niedermeyer & Hofrichter, 2016, p. 277).

Saxony-Anhalt's AfD chairman André Poggenburg also earned public attention with a Christmas message from his regional association. Here he declared that it was now time to think about "responsibility for the people's community" (Volksgemeinschaft). Criticized because of this word choice, he complained about not being allowed "to use some completely unproblematic and even very positive terms." He further explained, "We won't put up with that because real freedom starts with freedom of language!" (AfD Sachsen-Anhalt, 2015).

During one of the demonstrations in Saxony-Anhalt's election campaign Poggenburg defined his party as a "genuine German-nationalist party" (AfD State Parliament, 2016). The last party in Germany which used the term "German-national" in its name was the German-Nationalist People's Party (DNVP) which was founded in the Republic of Weimar at the end of November 1918. It was national-conservative, anti-Semitic, and anti-republican; supported the Kapp-coup in 1920; and later collaborated with the Nazi Party.

AfD as a New Unifying Movement of the Extreme Right

More and more connections between AfD members and extreme-right-movements are becoming apparent. Thus the chairman of the "Patriotic Platform" within the AfD demanded: "We wish a close collaboration between the Identitarian movement and the AfD because AfD is an Identitarian movement and also the Identitarian movement is an alternative for Germany" (Patriotische Plattform, 2016). Groups like for example the "One percent for our land" initiative, supported by AfD politician Hans-Thomas Tillschneider, illustrates organizational connections between AfD politicians and extreme-right movements. This initiative is an attempt of extreme right forces out of the Identitarian movement, the new-right Institute of State Policy (IFS), and the extreme-right conspiracy magazine "Compact" to collect organisational and financial resources for anti-refugee initiatives and to establish a right resistance movement against current policy. Connection to the immigration-hostile Pegida movement is intensifying. By January 2015 about 90% of Pegida followers admitted to voting for AfD in the national elections (Geiges, 2016, p. 142).

In the AfD, forces using a nationalist uprising rhetoric are gaining power. In a lecture at the new-right Institute of State Policy (IFS) in November 2015 the AfD chairman of Thuringia Björn Höcke defined the AfD as a "fundamental opposition movement party." It is the "actually last peaceful chance for our country" (Höcke, 2016b). Höcke illustrated the right uprising rhetoric at the second meeting of the extreme-right members of the AfD around a group called "Der Flügel" near the Kyffhäuser memorial, where he described the current political situation as a national "turning point" and explained: "The patience of our people is over and already the Romans knew the legendary furor teutonicus. Dear friends, we will not allow them to eliminate us! We started this turning point, we want to make this turning point and we will make it!" (Höcke, 2016c). Grounded in nationalist rhetoric, the election successes of the AfD are producing a restructuring of the extreme-right-spectrum.

Until a few years ago the debate about the danger posed by the right was largely limited to distinct extreme-right-manifestations on the right spectrum. The electoral successes of traditional right-wing parties, the marches of neo-Nazi groups and their acts of violence, and the public appearance of extreme-right subcultures dominated understanding of the right danger. The grey area of the "New Right" (Langebach & Raabe, 2016) led a niche existence in Germany for some decades in a pre-political zone. With the rise of the AfD and some other new-right players, perception of the danger posed by the right has changed.

Figure 2 Restructuring of the extreme right spectrum

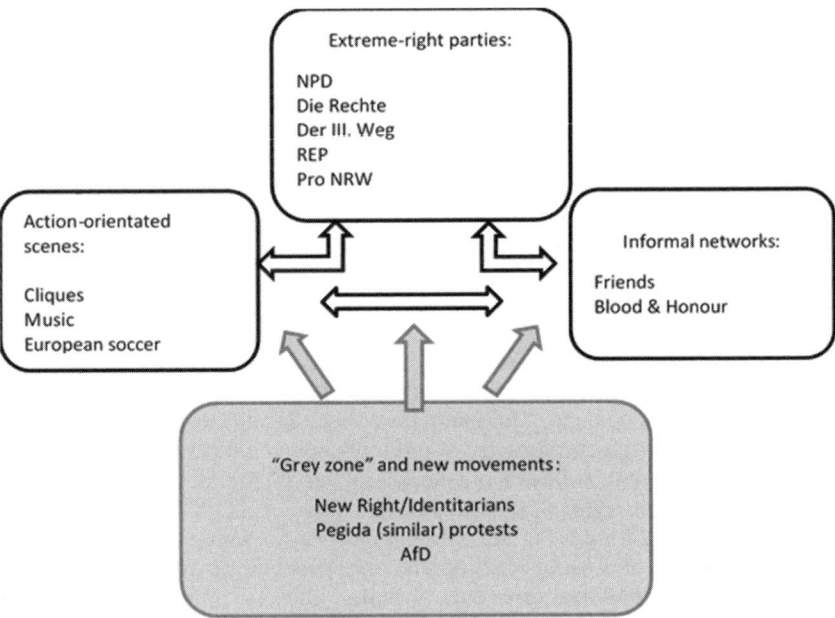

At the same time the increasing influence of these new players in real-life policy caused a change within the extreme right. Because of the increasing influence of this new player on a new right culture of protest, we see a greater social and organizational mix of groups formerly separated from each other in protest scenes. This presents a new and urgent challenge to right-wing extremism research, because the danger is real that "regressive modernisation and post-democratic policy will led to an authoritarian movement that destroys the liberal principles of our society" (Nachtwey, 2016, p. 233).

References

AfD/Alternative für Deutschland (2016). »Demokratie wieder herstellen – Dem Volk die Staatsgewalt zurückgeben - AfD-Manifest 2017 – Die Strategie der AfD für das Wahljahr 2017« vom 22.12.2016. www.weser-kurier.de/cms_media/module_ob/2/1389_1_AfD-Strategie-2017_58a5b0701d8dd.pdf, p. 9 (Abruf: 4.4.2017).

AfD/Alternative für Deutschland Bayern (2016). AfD und FPÖ beschließen Zusammenarbeit, vom 18.2.2016. www.afdbayern.de/afd-und-fpoe-beschliessen-zusammenarbeit/ (Abruf: 27.2.2016).

AfD-Landtags-TV (2016). André Poggenburg: Die AfD ist einfach nicht mehr aufzuhalten!, vom 27.01.2016. www.youtube.com/watch?v=YYwTWkiZYgs&feature=youtu.be (Abruf: 28.1.2016).

AfD/Alternative für Deutschland Sachsen-Anhalt (2015). Liebe Bürger und Mitstreiter, vom 24.12.2015. www.facebook.com/SachsenAnhalt.AfD/photos/a.384418898339525.1073741828.363842953730453/898617830252960/?type=3 (Abruf: 27.2.2016).

Appadurai, A. (2017). Demokratiemüdigkeit. In H. Geiselberger, H. (Ed.): Die große Regression. Eine internationale Debatte zur geistigen Situation der Zeit. Berlin: Suhrkamp.

Bernhard, H. (2016). AfD-Kundgebung in Erfurt. Retrieved from https://www.deutschlandfunk.de/afd-kundgebung-in-erfurt-wenn-wir-kommen-wird-aufgeraeumt.1773.de.html?dram:article_id=335345.

Decker, F. (2011). Demokratischer Populismus und/oder populistische Demokratie? Bemerkungen zu einem schwierigen Verhältnis. In. F. Hartleb, & F. Wielenga (Eds.): Populismus in der modernen Demokratie. Die Niederlande und Deutschland im Vergleich. Münster: Waxmann.

Der Flügel (2015, April 29). Erfurter Resolution.

Feit, M. (1987). Die "Neue Rechte" in der Bundesrepublik. Organisation – Ideologie – Strategie. Frankfurt/New York: Campus.

Geden, O. (2007). Rechtspopulismus. Funktionslogiken – Gelegenheitsstrukturen – Gegenstrategien, SWP-Studie 17. Berlin: Stiftung Wissenschaft und Politik.

Geiges, L. (2016). Nach dem Hype. Drei Entwicklungen von Pegida seit dem Winter 2014/2015. In. K.-S. Rehberg, F. Kunz, & T. Schlinzig (Ed.): PEGIDA. Rechtspopulismus zwischen Fremdenangst und »Wende«-Enttäuschung? Analysen im Überblick, Bielefeld: Transcript.

Geis, M. (2015). Alexander Gauland: Populist mit Stil. In Die Zeit 27.

Häusler, A., & Roeser, R. (2015). Die rechten »Mut-Bürger«. Entstehung, Entwicklung, Personal und Positionen der Alternative für Deutschland. Hamburg: VSA-Verlag.

Höcke, B. (2016a). Die neue soziale Frage (Schweinfurt, 28.4.2016). Retrieved from www.youtube.com/watch?v=flBQo7WDao&feature=share.

Höcke, B. (2016b). Asyl. Eine politische Bestandsaufnahme – Vortrag beim IfS. Retrieved from www.youtube.com/watch?v=ezTw3ORSqlQ.

Höcke, B. (2016c). Rede auf dem 2. Kyffhäusertreffen der AfD-Gruppierung Der Flügel. Retrieved from: https://www.derfluegel.de/2016/06/06/video-rede-von-bjoern-hoecke-beim-kyffhaeusertreffen-2016/.

Institut für Staatspolitik (2007). Parteigründung von rechts. Sind schlanke Strukturen möglich? Wissenschaftliche Reihe – Issue 10, Arbeitsgruppe 2: Politische Kultur Schnellroda: IfS.

Kellershohn, H. (2016). Risse im Gebälk: Flügelkämpfe in der jungkonservativen Neuen Rechten und der AfD. In A. Häusler (Ed.): Die Alternative für Deutschland. Programmatik, Entwicklung und politische Verortung. Wiesbaden: Springer VS.

Kemper, A. (2015). Antiemanzipatorische Netzwerke und die Geschlechter- und Familienpolitik der Alternative für Deutschland. In. A. Häusler (Ed.): Die Alternative für Deutschland. Programmatik, Entwicklung und politische Verortung. Wiesbaden: Springer VS.

Kohlstruck, M. (2008). Rechtspopulismus und Rechtsextremismus. Graduelle oder qualitative Unterschiede? In R. Faber, & F. Unger (Eds.): Populismus in Geschichte und Gegenwart. Würzburg: Königshausen & Neumann.

Langebach, M., & Raabe, J. (2016): Die »Neue Rechte« in der Bundesrepublik Deutschland, in: F. Virchow, M. Langebach, & A. Häusler (Eds.): Handbuch Rechtsextremismus. Wiesbaden: Springer VS.

Meuthen, J. (2016). Rede auf dem AfD-Bundesparteitag von Jörg Meuthen am 30.04.2016. www.youtube.com/watch?v=WcU2eLwVNsc (Abruf: 15.5.2016).

Nachtwey, O. (2016). Die Abstiegsgesellschaft. Über das Aufbegehren in der regressiven Moderne. Berlin: Suhrkamp.

Niedermayer, O., & Hofrichter, J. (2016). Die Wählerschaft der AfD. Wer ist sie, woher kommt sie und wie weit rechts steht sie? In Zeitschrift für Parlamentsfragen 2, Baden-Baden 2016: Nomos.

Patriotische Plattform (2016): Wir sind identitär, http://patriotische-plattform.de/blog/2016/06/14/wir-sind-identitaer/ (Abruf: 14.06.2016).

Pfitzner, F. (2016, February 14). Schulterschluss der Rechtspopulisten, In Neue Westfälische. Retrieved from: http://www.nw.de/nachrichten/regionale_politik/20709041_Schulterschluss-der-Rechtspopulisten.html.

Pichler, R. (2016, April 25). Interview mit AfD-Bundesvize Gauland - Die AfD will als Partei der kleinen Leute punkten, In Stuttgarter Zeitung. Retrieved from http://www.stuttgarter-zeitung.de/inhalt.interview-mit-afd-bundesvize-gauland-die-afd-will-als-partei-der-kleinen-leute-punkten.f915c96e-4687-4f28-9b5c-596fbc15cf2b.html.

Priester, K. (2012). Wesensmerkmale des Populismus. In Aus Politik und Zeitgeschichte 5–6. Bonn: bpb.

Rathcke, J. (2016, February 13). Treffen unter Freunden. In Rheinische Post. Retrieved from: http://www.rp-online.de/politik/deutschland/afd-und-fpoe-in-duesseldorf-treffen-unter-freunden-aid-1.5766055.

Roeser, R. (2016, February 15). Dammbruch nach rechtsaußen, blick nach rechts www.bnr.de/artikel/hintergrund/dammbruch-nach-rechtsau-en.

Sarrazin, T. (2014). Der neue Tugendterror. München: DVA.

Spiegel online (2015). Umfragehoch: AfD-Vize Gauland sieht Flüchtlingskrise als Geschenk. www.spiegel.de/politik/deutschland/afd-alexander-gauland-sieht-fluechtlingskrise-als-geschenk-a-1067356.html.

Spiegel online (2010). Sarrazin-Debatte: Umfrage sieht großes Potential für Protestpartei, n: www.spiegel.de/politik/deutschland/sarrazin-debatte-umfrage-sieht-grosses-potential-fuer-protestpartei-a-715751.html (Abruf: 20.02.2014).

Steiner, T. (2015, June 7). Die AfD stellt sich neu auf: "Wir sind die Pegida-Partei." In Badische Zeitung.
Wildt, M. (2017).Volk, Volksgemeinschaft, AfD. Hamburg: Hamburger Edition.
Zick, A., & Küpper, B. (2015). Wut, Verachtung, Abwertung. Rechtspopulismus in Deutschland, In Friedrich Ebert Stiftung (Ed.). Berlin: Dietz.

German Right-Wing Extremism and Right-Wing Populism: Conceptual Foundations

Samuel Salzborn

What is right-wing extremism? At first glance, the question would seem easy to answer. But it involves various dimensions that are not immediately obvious, because it actually covers two complexes that need to be systematically differentiated before an answer can be formulated. On the one hand, it obviously involves identifying the factors and aspects informing a particular worldview and/or conduct that would justify calling someone or something right-wing extremist. This would cover the basic elements of the far-right worldview and its resulting political practices; in other words, investigating the relationship between theory and application in right-wing extremism, analyzing what characteristics distinguish the far-right worldview conceptually, and examining how these ideas and attitudes lead to specific social and/or political actions. On the other hand – and this is less obvious – the investigation must also consider how the term "right-wing extremism" has come to be applied when categorizing particular political phenomena, be it as an additional label or an essentialist one; in other words, whether, when, and why one chooses to speak of right-wing extremism, or alternatively right-wing populism, neo-fascism, neo-Nazism, or the radical right.

While the term "right-wing extremism" has now become established as an overall label within German scholarship, politics, and media, this has certainly not always been the case (for example, in West Germany until the early 1970s, public debate was dominated by the terms neo-Nazism and neo-fascism, while the 1990s also saw intensive debate on whether the preferred term should be "right-wing extremism" or "right-wing radicalism"; Salzborn, 2015). Even now, there are still multiple terms competing for the status of overarching label, so that the question of "What is right-wing extremism?" must also involve an examination of not only the descriptive label, but also of what exactly is being described (on the question of terminology, see Hempel & Oppenheim, 1948).

At the Core: An Ideology of Inequality

When elements of a purportedly right-wing extremist worldview are discussed within German sociological debates, there are clearly differences of opinion (cf. Birzer ,1996; Holzer, 1994) about what exactly is to be counted as part of this "multidimensional attitudinal complex" (Borrmann, 2012, p. 162) and "heterogeneous mixture of the most diverse argumentative frameworks and viewpoints" (Stöss, 2010, p. 20, translated by the author), and at what point one can speak of a cohesive right-wing extremist worldview (on this, see also Pfahl-Traughber, 2014). It must also be emphasized that far-right groups need not always espouse every element in the relevant spectrum in order to be considered far right, but simply need to draw from the same basic toolbox, while not necessarily all adopting the same tools: for example, a paramilitary traditionalist group that cultivates the ideological heritage of the SS would emphasize military aspects to a much greater extent than an intellectual group that pays homage to the thinkers of the Weimar Era's conservative revolutionary movement, who were the chief ideological forebears of the Third Reich. Nonetheless, militarism is certainly not incompatible with the fundaments of the conservative revolution, and both streams share something in common: they always prioritize authoritarian/military solutions over democratic/diplomatic ones in handling conflicts (Virchow, 2006).

In one of the most popular definitions of right-wing extremism, Heitmeyer (1990) highlights the relationship between an ideology of inequality and an acceptance of violence or force (both terms correspond to the German concept of "Gewalt"). This approach is a sound one in general terms, although it can also sometimes lead to uncertainties, such as in the question of where violence actually begins: Does it already exist in the publication of a racist and dehumanizing article in an alt-right forum, or does it only start with a knife attack by a skinhead? While both are forms of violence, the media often reduces far-right violence to the physical aspect only, thereby forgetting that the fundamental root of right-wing extremism is found not in the practical application of physical violence, but in the underlying mental framework that accepts the use of force.

At the ideological heart of far-right thought is the assertion that human beings are unequal, and thus should be treated unequally. Right-wing extremists thus deny the basic tenet that all persons are equal. They believe that human beings have specific immutable characteristics (whether mental or cultural) that result from their provenance (whether biological or cultural, the latter represented by "culturalist" discrimination). Based on this alleged inequality, right-wing extremists divide human beings into ostensibly disparate groups (e.g. "races," "ethnicities," or "peoples") that are each to be kept homogeneous, meaning they should not "mix." The common denominator of right-wing extremist thought is the ideology of inequality, which in conceptual terms is an expression of structural violence in its sorting of human beings into essentialist collectives that are allegedly "natural" and immutable. This means that at the heart of far-right ideology lies a clearly distinguishable ethnonationalist/racist worldview (Zuber, 2015), which is "prototypical for a *naturalizing of the social*" (Jäger & Jäger, 1999, p. 174, emphasis in original).

The spectrum of far-right variants thus ranges from explicitly racist positions rooted in a model of biological difference and aligned to the Nazi tradition, to homogenizing ethnonationalist conceptions that envision a regionally/ethnically segmented Europe under an ethnopolitical framework, to notions of an "ethnopluralism" (primarily springing from France's *Nouvelle Droite* scene) based above all on assumptions of cultural difference (Müller, 1994; Salzborn, 2005; Salzborn, 2016; Terkessidis, 1995). Although the concrete argumentation of essentialist difference may vary, these models are nonetheless similarly conceived.

Ethnonationalist and "Culturalist" Thought

What ethnonationalist conceptions have in common is the quashing of subjectivity and the prioritizing of the collective over the individual. In right-wing extremism, ethnic identity does not function as an individual chosen identity but as a collective coerced identity, involving both an internally binding component and an externally segmenting one (Luhmann 1998), and thus a coerced inclusion and a coerced exclusion. This means that, at its root, right-wing extremism is always antidemocratic and structurally anti-liberal, as well as anti-individualist. Following on the ideas of Helmut Fröchling (1996), it is in anti-individualism and anti-liberalism that one finds both the key foundations and primary thrusts of far-right ideology, because its argumentation is targeted in principle against the free and self-determined individual; it thereby opts against a political order that takes the liberty, equality, and fraternity of the French Revolution as its conceptual starting point, one that insists on these values as universally applicable human rights, which in the shape of participatory rights granted to every citizen are to be counted among the inalienable norms of the liberal democratic constitutional state.

Hans-Gerd Jaschke (1994) similarly sees the terms "Volk" ("folk," in the sense of people, nation and ethnonation) and "nature" as representing the "axiomatic fundamental principles" of German far-right ideology (p. 55). Nature (along with naturalness) is contrasted against society as an independent existential reality, and is framed as being eternal, superhuman, and/or divine. Nature and naturalness are thus seen in far-right thought as "an inescapable regulator for the way that humans live together" (p. 55, translated by the author). This mystification and glorification of the "natural" serves as the conceptual core of antidemocratic thought, in which the primacy of reason and rationality is negated; this in turn provides the theoretical justification underlying the ideology of inequality. Here, the "Volk" functions as both historical subject and political object, vouching for the homogeneity of the group and standing as its highest authority. In the understanding of the German far right, the individual is a "servant of his Volk," to which he is irrevocably bound in ethnonationalist and cultural terms (Jaschke 1994, p. 56). Right-wing extremism therefore covers the entire range of political agendas, ideologies, ways of conduct, and modes of articulation, along with concrete actions, regardless of the degree of formal organization, that

> take for granted the racially or ethnically determined social inequality of human beings, demand the ethnic homogeneity of Völker [pl. of Volk], and reject the equality dictated by the Universal Declaration of Human Rights; that emphasize the primacy of the community over the individual, take for granted the subordination of the citizen to the national interest, reject the pluralism of values within a liberal democracy, and want to reverse the process of democratization (Jaschke, 1994, p. 31, translated by the author).

One of the main strategies of right-wing extremist campaigning is to challenge individualism through an anti-modern and anti-liberal lens, striving to replace it with an ethnonationalist worldview geared towards an ostensibly homogeneous collective. The ideology of inequality thus aims internally at ethnic/ethnonational homogeneity and externally at ethnic separation. As a result of these twin premises, European right-wing extremism includes both centralist movements as well as regionalist ones, federalist movements as well as imperialist ones (Salzborn & Schiedel, 2003). The important thing here is that right-wing extremism always rests upon on elements of geopolitical thinking and territorial ordering (or reordering), because a "Volk" and its territory are considered together – and not in the democratic sense of a *demos*, meaning an accidental, changeable, and evolving society of individuals living together within a state's sovereign borders, but in the sense of an *ethnos*, meaning an essentialized, static, and homogeneous collective tied to an existentially understood territory (whether already inhabited or yet to be "settled").

Antisemitism is an essential component of the ethnonationalist worldview, because in what it considers to be Jewish, it sees the fundamental opposite of what it wants: in the eyes of the far right, Jews symbolically stand for modernity and the heritage of the Enlightenment, for liberalism and socialism, for democracy and pluralism, for urbanity and intellectualism (Salzborn, 2014). Such antisemitism is expressed in very diverse ways. The explicit ones include denying the Shoah and underestimating the number of Jews murdered by the

Nazi regime in order to downplay Nazi crimes, in addition to vandalizing memorial sites and committing violent attacks against Jews (whether actual or only presumed). Antisemitism can also be expressed in less obvious ways, such as in challenging Germany's historical compensation payments to Israel, or in questioning the Israeli state's right to exist. Other common antisemitic codes include a denial of any responsibility for the Holocaust, criticism of corresponding appraisal and commemoration efforts, and the deluded belief in a "Jewish global conspiracy" (as particularly seen in propaganda alleging Jewish control of finance and the media).

The conspiracy trope is a fundamentally antisemitic one, in both historical and systematic terms. However, conspiracy fantasies can take numerous forms in today's right-wing extremism: beyond the paradigmatic and still dominant antisemitic ones, there are also those that warn against the ostensible Islamization of Europe. This includes occasional claims that ostensible "elites" are trying to weaken the "ethnically pure Volk" by deliberately encouraging Muslim immigration. Going even further, there are also allegations that "Islam" itself has a master plan for the invasion of Germany, Europe, and/or "the West" in general (see Salzborn. 2016 for a more detailed analysis).

In summary, it can be said that right-wing extremist thought is sustained by an ideology of inequality, one that denies the individuality and subjectivity of human beings while aiming to reverse the achievements of emancipation and the Enlightenment. Against the model of an open, pluralistic society, the far-right worldview advocates an ethnonational, homogeneous community – alleged to be a "natural" collective, sometimes defined in racist terms, sometimes in culturalist ones. The rejection of pluralism, democracy, and individual freedom leads to a hierarchized political understanding, as expressed in antisemitic sentiments, alongside racist, anti-liberal, patriarchal, anti-feminist, homophobic, elitist, social Darwinist, and authoritarian ones.

Right-Wing Populism as a Strategy of Right-Wing Extremism

The term "right-wing populism," although commonly used by the German media, has been the subject of intense debate among social scientists, focusing on the central question of whether right-wing populism is an independent political phenomenon that is separate from right-wing extremism, or simply a strategic political option within right-wing extremism. In the context of European comparative studies, political organizations and parties from different countries are often lumped together into ideological "families," categorized according to shared ideological features that transcend national borders (Salzborn, 2012).

In regards to the broad family of "(neo-)Fascist, (neo-)Nazi, right-wing extremist or right-wing populist parties," it has recently been argued that "right-wing populist" parties represent their own distinct subgroup within this family. This argument is firmly rejected here; in fact, one can argue that there is generally little point in labeling particular parties from the far-right spectrum as "right-wing populist" solely because of their chosen political strategy (for an overview of the relevant debate, see Backes & Moreau, 2012; Heinisch & Mazzoleni, 2016; Lazaridis, Campani & Benveniste, 2016; Pirro, 2015). The "right-wing populist" label is simply a particularizing one that points to the strategy chosen by a specific right-wing extremist stream.

Populist right-wing extremists are simply those that make use of populist tools and strategies. They try to agitate the public by choosing particular topics and pushing them in the media, especially through the use of staged events and a personality cult (as lately exploited by Donald Trump), with the goal of inserting themselves into established public discourses; here, they pick up on current topics of debate, and polarize the discussion through targeted polemics. A central strategy is to conjure up an ostensible opposition between the political elite and "the people," with the far right purporting to advocate for the latter. Far-right populists claim that they are fighting against the alleged Establishment. As seen from Trump's election to the American presidency, this strategy can even allow a central figure of the economic elite to present himself as an enemy of the elite.

Proponents of populist right-wing extremism will often try to avoid using explicitly fascist and/or Nazi vocabulary. Although Austria's FPÖ is an example of a far-right populist party for which this does not apply, and Germany's AfD has begun to openly argue for the rehabilitation of Nazi expressions like "völkisch" and "Volksgemeinschaft," words that promote "ethnonationalist" concerns and the "ethnonational community" (Grigat, 2017; Salzborn, 2017b). However, a closer examination of the underlying political substance, meaning the core ideological foundations, reveals no significant differences between populist and non-populist forms of right-wing extremism. Populism is therefore no more than a strategic option for right-wing extremists: after all, the historical Nazis used the same rhetoric to set themselves up as defenders against the alleged political and media elites of the Weimar Republic, wielding words like "Volksverräter" and "Lügenpresse" ("betrayer of the Volk" and "the lying press") in the battle against democracy itself – words that are now being deployed again in the present day.

References

Backes, U., & Moreau, P. (Eds.). (2012). The extreme right in Europe: Current trends and perspectives. Göttingen: Vandenhoeck & Ruprecht.

Birzer, M. (1996). Rechtsextremismus: Definitionsmerkmale und Erklärungsansätze. In J. Mecklenburg (Ed.), Handbuch deutscher Rechtsextremismus, (pp. 72–83). Berlin, Germany: Espresso.

Borrmann, S. (2012). Rechtsextremismus: Facetten eines Begriffs. Ost-West: Europäische Perspektiven, 3, pp. 162–238.

Fröchling, H. (1996). Die ideologischen Grundlagen des Rechtsextremismus: Grundstrukturen rechtsextremer Weltanschauung; Politischer Stil, Strategien und Methoden rechtsextremer Propaganda. In J. Mecklenburg (Ed.), Handbuch deutscher Rechtsextremismus, (pp. 84-123). Berlin, Germany: Espresso.

Grigat, S. (Ed.). (2017). AfD & FPÖ: Antisemitismus, völkischer Nationalismus und Geschlechterbilder. Baden-Baden, Germany: Nomos.

Heinisch, R., & Mazzoleni, O. (Eds.) (2016). Understanding populist party organisation: The radical right in Western Europe. London.

Heitmeyer, W. (1990). Jugend und Rechtsextremismus: Von ökonomisch-sozialen Alltagserfahrungen zur rechtsextremistisch motivierten Gewalt-Eskalation. In G. Paul (Ed.), Hitlers Schatten verblaßt: Die Normalisierung des Rechtsextremismus, 2nd ed. (pp. 101–133). Bonn: Dietz.

Heitmeyer, W. (2008). Die Ideologie der Ungleichwertigkeit: Der Kern der 'Gruppenbezogenen Menschenfeindlichkeit.'" In Deutsche Zustände, 9th installment, edited by Wilhelm Heitmeyer, 36–44. Frankfurt.

Hempel, Carl G., & Oppenheim P. (1948). Studies in the Logic of Explanation." Philosophy of Science 15: 135–175.

Holzer, W. (1994). Rechtsextremismus: Konturen, Definitionsmerkmale und Erklärungsansätze." In Handbuch des österreichischen Rechtsextremismus, rev. ed., published by Dokumentationsarchiv des österreichischen Widerstandes, 12–96. Vienna.

Jäger, M., & Jäger, S. (1999). Gefährliche Erbschaften: Die schleichende Restauration rechten Denkens. Berlin.

Jaschke, H.-G. (1994). Rechtsextremismus und Fremdenfeindlichkeit: Begriffe, Positionen, Praxisfelder. Opladen.

Lazaridis, G., Giovanna C. & Benveniste, A. (eds.) (2016). The Rise of the Far Right in Europe: Populist Shifts and "Othering". London.

Luhmann, N. (1998). Der Staat des politischen Systems: Geschichte und Stellung in der Weltgesellschaft. In Perspektiven der Weltgesellschaft, edited by Ulrich Beck, 345–380. Frankfurt.

Müller, J. (1994). Mythen der Rechten: Nation, Ethnie, Kultur. Berlin.

Pfahl-Traughber, A. (2014). Das Zehn-Stufen-Modell der 'Extremismusintensität': Kategorien zur Analyse und Einordnung politischer Bestrebungen. Jahrbuch für Extremismus- und Terrorismusforschung 8: 7–36.

Pirro, A. L. P. (2015). The Populist Radical Right in Central and Eastern Europe: Ideology, Impact, and Electoral Performance. London.
Salzborn, S. (2005). Ethnisierung der Politik: Theorie und Geschichte des Volksgruppenrechts in Europa. Frankfurt.
Salzborn, S. (2012). Demokratie: Theorie, Formen, Entwicklungen. Baden-Baden.
Salzborn, S. (2014). Antisemitismus: Geschichte, Theorie, Empirie. Baden-Baden.
Salzborn, S. (2015). Rechtsextremismus: Erscheinungsformen und Erklärungsansätze. 2nd ed. Baden-Baden.
Salzborn, S. (2016). "Vom rechten Wahn: 'Lügenpresse,' 'USrael,' 'Die da oben' und 'Überfremdung.'" Mittelweg 36 6: 76–96.
Salzborn, S. (2017a). Kampf der Ideen: Die Geschichte politischer Theorien im Kontext. 2nd ed. Baden-Baden.
Salzborn, S. (2017b). Angriff der Antidemokraten: Die völkische Rebellion der Neuen Rechten. Weinheim.
Salzborn, S. & Schiede, H. (2003). ‚Nation Europa': Ethnoföderale Konzepte und kontinentale Vernetzung der extremen Rechten. Blätter für deutsche und internationale Politik 10, 1209–17.
Stöss, R. (2010). Rechtsextremismus im Wandel. Berlin.
Terkessidis, M. (1995). Kulturkampf: Volk, Nation, der Westen und die Neue Rechte. Cologne.
Virchow, F. (2006). Gegen den Zivilismus: Internationale Beziehungen und Militär in den politischen Konzeptionen der extremen Rechten. Wiesbaden.
Zuber, J. (2015). Gegenwärtiger Rassismus in Deutschland: Zwischen Biologie und kultureller Identität. Göttingen.

Democracy Under Stress: Right-wing Success at the German Parliamentary Elections: Socio-economic and Political-cultural Influences

Christoph Richter & Matthias Quent

Introduction: AfD's Election Success–An "Odd Critique of Affluence"?

In the small town of Pirna in Eastern Germany, the right-wing populist and, in part, far-right extremist party "Alternative für Deutschland" (Alternative for Germany–AfD) managed to take 35.5% of the secondary votes cast in the 2017 German parliamentary elections. During a street survey conducted by a radio station in the town the day after the election, one passer-by cited the government's current pension policies as the reason why he cast his vote for the far-wing populists. His parents had worked their entire lives and were now only receiving the very minimum pension payment. In previous elections, he had voted for the Christlich Demokratische Union (Christian Democratic Union–CDU). Another AfD supporter explained that he had formerly checked the box for the Sozialdemokratische Partei Deutschlands (Social Democratic Party of Germany–SPD), but stated that the party had not been social for some time now. Both interviewees admitted that they voted for the right-wing populists as a form of protest.

This part of Germany was long considered to be a stronghold for the right-wing extremist party Nationaldemokratische Partei Deutschlands (National Democratic Party of Germany–NPD), and neo-nazis in the region still make use of well-established structures. Attacks against refugees and their supporters are a common occurrence here. At the same time, this county is one of the most important tourist regions in the state of Saxony, and, with an unemployment rate of 6.4%, it is not exactly one of the most economically disadvantaged areas in this part of Germany. Just as a comparison: The unemployment rate in the city of Münster in Western Germany stands at 5.5%, a place where the right-wing populists counted their worse election results in all of Germany, only mustering 4.9% of the votes.

In the radio interview mentioned above, an employee at a charitable organization in Pirna described an "odd critique of affluence" that had driven people in this region to vote AfD. Many voters that chose the right-wing populists due to dissatisfaction have a house, a regular income, and some even have several cars. Is this a contradiction? Support for right-wing populist and extreme right parties generally tends to be ascribed to the so-called "left-behind," the losers of modernization. An analysis of the German federal election results by the Institute for Democracy and Civil Society (2017) shows that right-wing populists have not only been successful in mobilizing voters in relatively disadvantaged regions but also in those that are economically strong. It also suggests that the relevant reasons for the AfD's success in the elections can primarily be ascribed to the political culture of the electoral districts: AfD proved to be more successful in districts where a significant portion of the population had either completely abstained from the democratic process in 2013 or exhibited support for extreme right parties, as compared to electoral districts with a lower portion of non-voters and voters for the extreme right NPD party.

The first part of this text presents an inventory of right-wing populist successes in mobilizing voters. Where and why was the party especially successful? Which economic, demographic, and political-cultural factors provided a favorable environment for this success? Secondly we take a look at the special circumstances leading to the huge electoral gains of the right-wing populists in Eastern Germany, in comparison to the western states. Based on these findings, we address the consequences for social policy when gains are made by right-wing populist parties, as well as the need for pursuing sustainable and on-going engagement in response.

Electoral District Analysis of the 2017 German Parliamentary Election

The state of research on right-wing populist and extreme-right electoral behavior is extensive and empirical findings vary greatly across countries, research methods, and areas of focus. According to Peter Lösche (1993, p. 22), new parties establish themselves on the basis of various social conflict lines that are pertinent in their respective contexts. Two relevant conflict lines that shaped public and academic discussion during the period prior to the 2017 German parliamentary elections, both in general and in regard to the AfD, were social-economic in nature, on the one hand, and cultural-political, on the other (Inglehard & Norris, 2016). While right-wing populist parties have been part of the political landscape for quite some time in many European countries, up until 2017 a diverse array of parties at the right-wing fringes in Germany were unable to overcome the five-percent hurdle needed to enter the German parliament–even despite experiencing considerable wins, especially in eastern states. As such, it was surprising when the right-wing populist party AfD gained 12.6% of the vote in the German parliamentary elections in September 2017, particularly at a time when the country was enjoying very good economic conditions, at least when considered from the view of economic average values. Several explanatory theories have been proposed to explain the AfD's electoral success.

Socio-economic theories (often "losers of modernization" theories) make reference to people's economic life situation. It is assumed that real or feared economic deprivation leads to disappointment and anger, which manifests itself in a turning away from established parties and towards the alleged solutions offered by populist and extremist parties. According to this view, social groups with less access to education and lower incomes and those affected by unemployment or precarious working conditions, in particular, are exposed to the pressures of deprivation and competition caused by the processes of modernization. Frustration about their material and social condition is said to make them increasingly turn to populist and extremist promises for a solution (Lipset, 1984; Betz, 1993; Anastasakis, 2000; Spier, 2010).

While many studies across Europe confirm such effects in accordance with theories of the socio-economic losers of modernization (Lubbers et al. 2002; Arzheimer/Carter 2006; Spier 2010; Werts et al., 2013; Dippel et al., 2017), the findings for AfD in Germany exhibit differing outcomes. Some studies point to lower income and educational value among potential voters (see Brähler et al., 2016; Brenke & Kritikos, 2017), while others tend to situate the party's voters in middle to higher levels of income and among those with relatively few socio-economic concerns (Bergmann et al., 2016; Lengfeld, 2017). In order to arrive at verifiable theses in light of these quite divergent findings, we first test the assumptions of the losers of modernization theories, specifically that higher levels of unemployment, a lower gross domestic product (GDP), and falling incomes lead to greater electoral victories for the AfD in the respective electoral districts. The variables of education, age, and the demographic structure serve as controls for the socio-economic and political-cultural variables. Based on the variable of population density, we assess the assumption that right-wing populist are more likely to gain high popularity in low-population areas than in urban regions (Quent & Schulz, 2015).

A second line of popular explanatory approaches refers to *political and cultural value orientations* and their transformation. According to these, a decisive factor for party preferences can mainly be found in political and cultural attitude patterns. One especially popular explanation is the *cultural backlash thesis*. Liberalization and a move towards flexibility and global mobility in the wake of structural changes brought about by modernization processes give rise to new conflict lines in relation to normative value orientations (Götz, 1997;

Binder, 2005; Gabriel, 2000; Inglehart & Norris, 2016). People who feel left behind or those who stand in conflict with more liberal views on topics such as family, sexuality, or national identity mobilize as a form of cultural counter-movement against liberal and cosmopolitan value orientations.

In the aggregate data available for the period directly after the German parliamentary elections, no variables can be found that directly reflect cultural or political characteristics. However, in order to be able to test the effects of the political-cultural dimension on voting preferences, we refer back to the vote share of NPD secondary votes and the portion of non-voters in the electoral districts from the preceding German parliamentary election in 2013. We do so because many studies show that the extreme right NPD party and the right-wing populist AfD are the most closely related across the spectrum of parties in terms of the attitudinal dimension. The greatest commonalities among voters from both parties, although different, can be found in relation to their rejection of immigration (Bergmann et al., 2016) along with their authoritarian, anti-democratic, and chauvinistic attitudes (Brähler et al., 2014).

In general, the AfD exhibits greater potential for far-right extremism as compared to other parties (Kroh & Fetz, 2016; Brähler et al., 2016). We investigate whether and to what extent the share of NPD secondary votes points to a specific political-cultural climate in the parliamentary elections of 2009 and 2013, one which proves favorable to the AfD's success in the elections within the respective electoral districts. As the investigation does not target individual voting behavior among NPD voters or possible shifts in voting to the AfD, the portion of NPD voters in 2013 is deducted from the AfD votes in 2017 in the final regression model. In so doing, we verify the assumption that increased popularity for far-right extremist parties can serve as an indicator of a general climate marked by an estrangement of democracy and anti-democratic sentiments that crosses individual voters and groups of voters. We may suppose that the NPD certainly does influence political culture locally despite its insignificance in the federal parliament itself. Around 360 NPD elected officials are strongly rooted in eastern communities in particular in terms of their political function at the city and municipal council level as well as among county councils. In such areas, where far-right extremist issues supported by the NPD have found resonance in the social discourse for a long time, we may assume that processes of normalization and relativization go hand in hand with lowered resistance to far-right extremist positions within daily political discourse to a much greater degree.

The portion of non-voters in the 2013 parliamentary elections is investigated as another variable within the political-cultural conflict lines. Findings as to the reasons and background for non-participation in elections are extremely disparate (see Neu, 2012; Eilfort, 2001; Güllner, 2013; Schäfer, 2013), rendering it impossible to consider non-voters as a homogeneous group or suggesting that they have a generalized affinity for the right-wing vote. However, it would seem more reasonable to consider the portion of non-voters in the electoral districts as an indicator of political estrangement. In this context, political estrangement can assume extremely diverse manifestations, without necessarily being accompanied by a proclivity for anti-democratic attitudes or actions. As many electoral districts with a high percentage of non-voters are, at the same time, economically disadvantaged regions, we may assume a high level of social exclusion among non-voters.

The fact that a portion of those excluded from social participation tend to be more open to authoritarian opportunities for participation (in the case of the AfD party manifesto platform, this entails exclusive cultural and nationalist policies to a far greater extent than material-economic ones) seems quite relevant since the policy offering of the AfD strongly targets populist critiques of the existing "elite" and the party's alleged function as mouthpiece giving voice to the quiet, non-included "people." Based on these considerations, we expect that an increasing portion of NPD votes and/or non-voters in the 2013 parliamentary elections will be reflected in a greater degree of success achieved by the AfD in the 2017 parliamentary elections.

Differences in Voting Behavior in Eastern and Western Germany

During the German parliamentary elections in 2017, the AfD received around twice as many votes (proportional to the number of voters) in the newly-formed Eastern German states (former GDR states) than in the Western German states. By now, the image of the "far-right East" has become familiar in public discourse. In the wake of the neo-Nazi violence during the 1990s and the electoral success of extreme right-wing parties such as the NPD who were deeply anchored in the local and state parliaments (until today), the electoral gains of the right-wing populist AfD in Eastern Germany seemed hardly surprising.

Sociological explanations for this are manifold (e.g., Gabriel, 2000) and still controversial: a collective education in authoritarianism and obedience under the former East German dictatorship, which had many connections to right-wing ideology through its mixture of socialist and nationalist identity (Poutrus et al., 2000); the anti-fascist state doctrine of the GDR, which has preceded a more consistent denazification, but barely processed the national socialist history in an open, critical, and comprehensive way, externalizing the past by accusing the West of "clerical-fascism" and thereby marginalizing the extreme right-wing tendencies of its own population (Poutrus et al., 2000); a neo-Nazi subculture that already existed in the GDR, but was ignored and concealed by the regime, which attacked in pogrom-like fashion migrants, asylum seekers, and leftists before, but in particular, directly after the German reunion (Pfahl-Traughber 2000); and finally, the disappointment of proclaimed hopes after the German reunification and the non-recognition of the lifetime achievements of former East German citizens, resulting from the mass closures of businesses in the former East German states, high unemployment rates, and the feeling of being second-class citizens in the reunified Federal Republic. For parts of the population, this feeling lead to strong exaltation of an "East German identity" which is immune against criticism and feelings of inferiority and in which their own "strength" is defined by depreciating the "other" and those perceived as "weaker."

Obviously, there is a confluence of factors that must be taken into account when trying to explain the significantly higher degree of support for right-wing populism and extremism in Eastern Germany. However, based on the available data, it was necessary to focus on aspects of economic deprivation and disenchantment with democracy or anti-democratic attitudes. In the context of the developments after the German reunification period, a strong connection between economic, social, and political exclusion processes can be assumed. The East German revolution brought significant changes in social structure to the newly-formed state. As a consequence of numerous shutdowns and restructurings of industrial enterprises, as well as the complete loss of entire industrial sectors, large parts of the population have lost material security as well as social recognition and participation. From 1987 to 1991, industrial employment declined by around a third (Heimpold, 2010). Overall, a limited number of quite successful social advancements in the post-reunification period were offset by a variety of social downsides, such as the loss of professional status or the loss of a job (Hofmann, 2010). Against this backdrop, Vogel (1999) describes the east's post-transition employment situation as a two-third society in which only about a third managed to integrate and established themselves under the conditions of the new labor market, while the remaining two-thirds where working under precarious conditions, either fearing or facing job losses.

The extent of these social changes cannot be measured in terms of material consequences only. The large traditional, proletarian, and lower middle-class social culture played a central role for social integration into the propagated "working class-society," which created meaning and identity, and which suddenly disappeared in the wake of reunification. Many years after the fall of the Berlin Wall, when the euphoria of the German unification was dissolved in the face of increasing social insecurity, did the extreme right-wing party NPD achieve notable electoral success (Stöss, 2000; Dippel et al., 2017).

Even decades after reunification, a significant discrepancy between East and West in terms of the actual and perceived material life conditions causes feelings of backwardness and disadvantage for those who did not benefit from the East German Revolution as they expected. These feelings of disappointment and frustration have lead to a departure from the established party system. Thus, especially in the newly-formed German states, there are strong connections between negative perceptions of the economic situation and low levels of satisfaction with democracy (Stöss, 1996; Gabriel, 2000). The authors of the 'Thüringen Monitor' have use the term "Ostdeprivation" ("East Deprivation") to describe this perception of personal and/or collective discrimination. In doing so, they show that this perception of social disadvantage correlates strongly over time with right-wing extremist attitudes in the former East Germany (Best et al., 2015).

Methods

Using a multivariate analysis, we estimated ten multi-level models relating to the influence of diverse variables in the socio-economic (unemployment rate, GDP, disposable income), socio-demographic (age, level of education, population density, portion of immigrants), and political-cultural context (NPD secondary votes and portion of non-voters in the 2013 parliamentary elections) across all 299 electoral districts. The data we used for this includes information from the Election Commissioner along with publicly viewable information from the regional statistical offices.

The multivariate regression analysis allows us to simultaneously test numerous independent variables within the model in terms of their collective effect on a dependent variable. Additionally, using a hierarchical multi-level model, we are able to consider the circumstance that the single observations (electoral districts, in the present case) are sorted into groups (German federal states, in the present case). In relation to federal states, these can also be divided into Eastern and Western German states. Using this method, we can calculate a single intercept for each of the 16 federal states. Assigning the individual observations to particular groups in the statistical model not only improves the quality of the estimate, as a general rule, but hierarchical structuring of the data is also necessary in order to preclude distortions in the estimates (Barr et al., 2013, p. 2). In addition to the intercepts, the last model also considers differences in the gradients of the regression lines among the groups (random slopes). These so-called mixed-effects models, in which all possible variations are permissible, allow for the maximum degree of model specification and are best suited for arriving at generalizable results in terms of the influence of the independent variables on the dependent variables (Barr et al., 2013, p. 11). Data was analyzed using SPSS, the R Programming Environment, car and lme4.

We took a step-by-step approach for the multivariate analysis of the AfD's electoral success. Here, the dependent variable (y) comprises the (logarithmic) portion of secondary votes for the AfD in the 2017 parliamentary elections. The independent (z standardized, partially logarithmic) variables (x) are the socio-economic, socio-demographic and political-cultural indicators, which are implemented into the model step by step. First, we estimate a so-called zero-model (Model 1: only intercepts), which serves as a reference for the subsequent models. We then include the variables West_East (Model 2: variables that classify the federal states into eastern and western federal states), the socio-economic variables (models 3-4), the socio-demographic control variables (models 5-7) and the political-cultural variables (model 8) into the model in this order. In order to emphasize that this investigation is not aimed at individual voter behavior, but rather at the analysis of the political-cultural realm, the secondary votes for the NPD during the 2013 parliamentary elections were excluded from the election results for the AfD in 2017 (models 9 and 10). Finally, models which encompass all variables are estimated twice. Whereas in model 9, only random intercepts for controlling the hierarchical data structure are included, in model 10, there is an additional control for the impact of a variation in the effect of the independent variables among the federal states (random slopes).

The variables applied in this analysis qualify electoral regions as social spaces and not as either individual social conditions, party preferences, or specific demographic groups. We may assume that relevant interrelations exist between the social space and those living within it. Connections pertaining to social spaces shape and influence the life worlds of the individuals living and interacting within them and, as such, contribute to the formation of political opinions. The relatively functional electoral district classifications as a social space do not constitute significant points of reference for individual orientations. Nevertheless, electoral districts as aggregated social spaces certainly do lend themselves to comparison at the county and municipal level–along which daily life worlds are oriented. It is, however, important to only interpret aggregate data as such.

Findings

The socio-economic assumptions put forth by the losers of modernization theory are initially confirmed to a large extent by our electoral district analysis. The AfD saw its greatest wins in districts with high unemployment rates and lower levels of GDP. Especially in comparison with the 2013 parliamentary elections, the party proved to be more successful in economically disadvantaged regions in 2017. However, there were also electoral districts with medium and high levels of income in which the AfD was successful as well. The results show that the voter structure of the right-wing populists in the electoral districts is, on the whole, socio-economically heterogeneous in relative terms, even if it was comprised of economically weaker regions to a greater extent in the 2017 parliamentary elections.

The results also indicate that electoral districts with a high portion of NPD voters and of non-voters are most affected by economic deprivation as compared to all other parties (CDU/CSU, SPD, GRÜNE, LINKE, FDP). The loss in votes among the largest popular parties and the rise of the AfD exhibit a relevant socio-economic component as one of the causal factors. An uneven distribution of economic strength, disposable income, and access to the labor market continue to ferment significant divisions in Germany: most apparently between Eastern and Western German electoral districts, but also along the north-south axis and within the federal states themselves (such as the obvious urban-rural divide). The AfD was certainly able to benefit from this and achieve electoral successes in economically weaker regions in particular. Yet, the explanatory power of the socio-economic indicators is rather weak in its own right. In general, the socio-economic indicators are subject to large regional fluctuations and also partly display contrary effects in relation to the assumptions proposed by the losers of modernization theory.

In view of the socio-demographic indicators, the analysis shows that an increase in the average age of voters in the electoral districts (especially within the group between 35 and 59 years of age) correlates to votes for AfD. Decreasing population density leads to a significantly greater number of votes for the AfD: the party proved more successful at mobilizing voters in rural areas than in large cities.

At the political-cultural level, the results indicate that a greater portion of NPD voters and/or non-voters in 2013 relate to a clear and significant increase in success on the part of the AfD in the 2017 parliamentary election. These two indicators exhibit the greatest explanatory power among all other variables, by far. Here, the NPD connection across all federal states proves to be the strongest; the non-voter connection, on the other hand, is notably weaker and also does not apply to all electoral districts. This implies that the relevant factors that account for the AfD's success in the elections, at least until 2013, even stretch back to the 2009 parliamentary elections in relation to the NPD effect. This supports the thesis that the AfD was particularly successful in places where, for years, a greater portion of the populace had either completely detached from the democratic process or supported far-right extremists. This is an effect that can be found across all federal states, both those in the east as well as in the west. In order to stress that this is not an effect of voter migration, the secondary vote portion for the NPD in 2013 was deducted from that of the AfD in 2017.

Around half of the significant margin between east and west in the AfD's electoral success can be explained by the analyzed indicators: A greater portion of NPD secondary votes in many eastern electoral districts, a high number of non-voters in 2013, and a large socio-economic divide in comparison to the western electoral districts are important reasons for the AfD's extraordinary results in many parts of Eastern Germany. At the electoral district level, the portion of non-voters in Eastern Germany is 12% above the nation-wide average, and the portion of NPD secondary votes is even 100% higher. In view of economic and demographic indicators, the differences remain significant. The unemployment rate is around 34% and the share of individuals entitled to welfare benefits is 37% above the national average. Disposable income, on the other hand, is 14% below the average of all electoral districts and overall economic strength is 23% below average. However, the socio-economic argument of the economically disadvantaged in the east falls short upon closer investigation.

The strong positive connection between deprivation and AfD electoral success correlates, in part, to the stark socio-economic differences between Eastern and Western Germany. In some Eastern federal states, for example in Saxony, we find that comparatively high economic performance can also be accompanied by high AfD approval. Conversely, in Western states such as Bremen or North Rhine-Westphalia, we discover positive correlations between the electoral support for the AfD and socio-economic deprivation. While the explanatory power of the socio-economic situation among the individual eastern states obviously does not contribute much to the explanation, a measurable influence arises in comparison to the socio-economic situation of constituencies in Western Germany. At the constituency level, this finding could be cautiously interpreted as the previously described phenomenon of "East Deprivation." More important for the mobilization success of right-wing populists in Eastern Germany than the current economic situation seems to be the real and/or perceived inequality and deprivation in comparison to the Western states, on the basis of past experiences of social dislocation and feelings of inferiority after the German reunification. In addition, the significant higher number of non-voters and NPD secondary votes, which are also exposed to significant levels of deprivation, point to a strong intermeshing of economic disadvantage and disenchantment with democracy in Eastern Germany.

Discussion

We can assert that the political-cultural dimension offers the strongest explanation for the AfD's electoral success when compared to the other indicators. The explanatory power of the socio-economic and socio-demographic indicators amounts to around 25% while the remaining 75% result from the inclusion of the political-cultural indicators. On their own account, the unemployment rate, GDP, and income only account for the AfD's mobilization success to a limited degree. At the same time, we can see that the AfD also experienced gains in electoral districts with higher levels of income. An exclusively socio-economically based deprivation theory hits upon its limits here: there are clearly also strong ideological motivations behind voting for right-wing populist parties that are independent of an economically fragile situation.

Overall, there are many indications that the relevant dimension behind the electoral success of the right-wing populists can, indeed, be found in the mobilization of voters along the political-cultural conflict line, one which runs between an open, liberal, and pluralist conception of society as opposed to a homogeneous, authoritarian, and nationalistic worldview. The successful exploitation of this conflict seems to be the key to the electoral success achieved by right-wing populists; based on this, the party was able to appeal to and mobilize socio-economically deprived as well as more affluent constituencies to a much greater extent than the NPD had ever done. The socio-economic heterogeneity of the voters and the impossibility of constructively binding them together economically or socio-politically gives us cause for concern that the party will continue to exploit this political-cultural conflict line in order to bridge the socio-cultural divides among its voters.

The division of the socio-economic and the political-cultural levels proves to be methodologically and conceptually wise for analyzing the two most prominent lines of argumentation separately. However, it should also be remembered that, in reality, both dimensions overlap and interact with one another. Structural weaknesses, democratic estrangement, and a greater willingness to vote for far-right extremist parties do, in fact, go hand in hand in many regions and significantly favor the electoral success of the right-wing populists. The fact that the most economically deprived electoral districts in particular host the highest portion of non-voters and votes for the far-right extremist NPD party suggests that there is an intimate interconnection between exclusion from social and economic participation and a withdrawal from democratic culture, even going so far as forthright rejection through a vote for a far-right extremist party.

The democratic and the social questions are correspondingly closely related to one another, as well. Speaking of equality without creating equal opportunity will push at least part of the population towards far-right extremist parties that purport to resolve this contradiction through nationalist and racist egoism, anti-pluralism, and the negation of democratic promises for equality. However, the strong influence of the political-cultural indicators also cannot be exhaustively explained on the basis of socio-economic conditions: the effect of the NPD and non-voters remains quite strong even when controlling for the moderating effects of income, unemployment, GDP, population density, migration, age, and education. This indicates that the political-cultural climate constitutes a strong autonomous aspect. Both in Eastern and Western Germany, particularly in economically disadvantaged but also in prosperous regions, the AfD has been able to benefit from a local political culture in which disenchantment with democracy and far-right extremism have become normalized. Overall, it is clear that we are dealing with a long-term process that neither appeared overnight nor can be stopped with a mere "Keep on going!"

Causes and Motives for the Shift to the Right

Within media and political discourse, the so-called immigration crisis was quickly portrayed as the central cause driving the success of the AfD. The immigration movements were said to overstrain municipal capacities and lead to insecurities, feelings of a loss of control, and fear of competition, through which AfD was able to accumulate political capital. Unfortunately, it is in the very nature of public political controversies to recur in cycles and exhibit a limited capacity to recollect previous debates or events. It is often the case, as in the present debates, that long-running and continuous processes are only able to break through the threshold of public attention once they manage to force the public to pay attention by way of extraordinary events (such as significant electoral gains or a marked increase in right-wing acts of violence). One is quick to forget that Europe has experienced a prolonged continuity of right-wing mobilization even after 1945. Without a doubt, the immigration crisis offered right-wing populists and far-right extremists a welcome occasion to pursue an event-related mobilization on the basis of longstanding fears and resentments. However, occasion and cause are often confounded in the public debate.

Many studies (e.g., Heitmeyer, 2012; Zick & Klein, 2014; Brähler et al., 2014, 2016) have investigated far-right extremist and group-focused enmity at regular intervals and generally highlight the relatively high potential for group-focused enmity across all of society. These attitude patterns serve as the basis for AfD to successfully mobilize its constituents, as this study also shows. Over the long term, the AfD's success in the 2017 parliamentary elections has drawn from a climate marked by disenchantment with democracy and even openly anti-democratic sentiments as well as the persistence of socio-economic inequalities. In this context, the public culture of discourse, in which only extraordinary events are able to breakthrough into the collective consciousness, proves problematic being that it ignores the continuity of far-right extremist and group-focused enmity that exists across social strata. When such long-term influential factors are ignored, occasions are quickly transfigured into causes, leading the democratic discourse to run the risk of becoming the driving force for right-wing populist discourse strategies. On occasion of the present situation, we can observe that the interpretation of the "refugee crisis" as the cause behind AfD's success covers up the danger of a shift to the right across the entire political party landscape. As the AfD's electoral success is, in most cases, exclusively attributed to the "refugee crisis" within public discourse, almost all parties including the social democrats, the liberals, and the conservatives are increasingly resorting to more restrictive approaches to immigration rather than pursuing a sustainable debate on the causes of group-focused enmity and how to deal with it. These developments are allowing right-wing populist parties to benefit most of all.

The AfD on a Socio-Political Trajectory: Challenges for Social Policies

In comparison to the previous parliamentary elections in 2013, the AfD was able to mobilize constituents to a much greater extent in regions with high unemployment rates, weaker economic strength, and high portions of non-voters in the 2017 elections. The rapid process of radicalization that the AfD went through the past years (Kroh & Fetz, 2016; Brähler et al., 2016: Goerres et al., 2017) therefore also corresponds to a transformation in the socio-cultural profile among some segments of the electorate. This is no coincidence but rather is the result of the party's strategic orientation, especially in the wake of the strengthening of the national-socialist wing that has pushed a social-populist trajectory and benefited from the weaknesses of the neo-liberal powers within the party since the departure of Bernd Lucke in 2015. With the electoral success of the National Front in France, which, since 2012, has exclusively reformulated the social question on the basis of nationalism and aggressively promoted it in elections (e.g., Schmidt, 2014), the model adopted by the extreme right has been taken as a recipe for success to win over new and ever-larger electoral groups. The AfD has also seized upon this strategy. "For we will increasingly attend to the needs of the ordinary people and defend the social achievements from 150 years of the workers' movement against the destructive powers of predatory capitalism!" declared AfD Thuringia state party chairman

Björn Höcke this past year, therewith outlining the social-populist promise of his growing wing within the AfD (Roeser, 2017).

Prior to the parliamentary elections, the party consciously sharpened its electoral campaign to more deliberately target less well-off groups of voters, as an AfD strategy paper on the parliamentary elections also reveals (AfD Manifest, 2017). The potential target groups named in this strategy paper included liberal-conservative middle-class voters, protest voters, and EU skeptics along with non-voters and citizens with below-average incomes. The results from the electoral district analysis show that the AfD was highly successful in mobilizing groups of voters in line with this social-populist orientation.

What to Do? Integrating Non-voters

Post-election surveys show that around one quarter of AfD voters stem from the group of previous non-voters (Infratest Dimap, 2017; Election 2017 Research Group, 2017). In quantitative terms, the AfD electorate stands in comparison to a much larger group of non-voters in the 2017 parliamentary elections. With a figure of around 23%, the latter constitutes the largest group, behind former CDU voters, and therefore represents around of quarter of total eligible voters. Considering the relatively greater degree of economic and material deprivation in electoral districts with a higher percentage of non-voters, it is necessary for parties to develop strategies to once again integrate non-voters into the democratic discourse through social and material participation.

In line with the results of our investigation, findings from a study by the Bertelsmann Foundation show that the AfD succeeded in decreasing the social divisions in its voter turnout as the party was able to mobilize people from socio-economically precarious milieus as well as former non-voters (Verkamp & Wegschaider, 2017). Even more worrying than the number of total non-voters is the clear socio-economic pattern that electoral districts with a higher portion of non-voters exhibit: higher levels of deprivation correspond to a significantly greater portion of non-voters in the individual electoral districts. This circumstance is alarming because entire groups of voters affected by economic deprivation systematically remain outside of the democratic process. This finding should cause the other parties to look into the extent to which reaching and incorporating these groups of voters has proven successful, or desirable, through party platforms and the focus of election campaigns.

Directing particular attention to the large group of non-voters appears far more promising than orienting policy offerings exclusively to those who have already decided on their vote. Additionally, we must discuss the ever-starker division within society between the socio-economically dependent and the beneficiaries of transformation and modernization processes of the past decades, and how these gropus encounter one another, including in view of the cultural conflict lines. If allowing all segments of the population to participate in the process of modernization and transformation in socio-economic and material terms ultimately proves successful, this may well serve as a foundation for people coming to consider themselves a part of the changing image of society, including in normative terms, and even to embrace open, pluralist, and progressive worldviews.

Conclusion: Progressive Perspectives of Inclusionary Social Policies

In view of the connection between the AfD election results, political culture, and economic status, social debates on how to achieve equality of living conditions must not be ceded to the extreme right. The high portion of non-voters in disadvantaged regions constitutes significant voter potential, which democratic forces should urgently take action to win over. The government must prove that it is capable of regulating and moderating the processes of modernization and globalization. This includes openly addressing and transparently discussing pressing social issues on all political levels, particularly those that affect the direct realities of people, including matters such how to connect rural areas to the global economy, the shortage of skilled professionals, and the risk of poverty among older adults. The public discussion about social grievances must be carried out beyond the framework of ethnic or religious attributions so that politics does not come to pit social groups against one another.

The progressive parties must once again convincingly address social issues and find sustainable answers to economic challenges such as digitalization that inspire confidence, and they must create effective measures aimed at the material and political as well as cultural inclusion of precarious groups and disadvantaged regions. Answers and concepts addressing social transformation that promote solidarity should not remain a topic restricted to academic circles and political think tanks but rather must be developed and discussed publicly, in line with the realities of those affected.

In view of pressing social questions, new concepts for communication and exchange among political actors within the democratic parties and people at the local level are needed, along with new strategies for how people can practically be incorporated into policy making beyond merely casting a vote. Politics that only approach their constituents during election times and shy away from discussing complex issues with people in the context of everyday life will ultimately lose credibility in the short and long term. Against the backdrop of the available data, only a fundamental paradigm shift in social policy can effectively counteract feelings of inferiority and deprivation that have grown over long periods of time, which have also led to a departure from democracy in parts of the population, especially in Eastern Germany. Wherever democratic forces lose sight of entire social groups in socio-political terms and whenever political participation is not actively pursued and promoted, anti-emancipatory, nationalistic, and extreme right forces are sure to gain strength. The 2017 German parliamentary elections represented a turning point that can be seen as opportunity for both a radical redefinition of democratic and social participation and sustainable merging on equal footing of east and west.

References

AfD Manifest (2017). The strategy of the AfD for the 2017 election year. Retrieved from http://www.talk-republik.de/Rechtspopulismus/docs/03/AfD-Strategie-2017.pdf
Arzheimer, K., & Carter, E. (2006). Political opportunity structures and right-wing extremist party success. European Journal of Political Research 45, 419-443.
Barr, D. J., Levy, R., Scheepers, C., & Til, H. J. (2013). Random structure for confirmatory hypothesis testing: Keep it maximal. Journal of Memory and Language, 68, 255-278.
Bergmann, K., Diermeier, M., & Niehues, J. (2016). Parteipräferenz und Einkommen. Die AfD – eine Partei der Besserverdiener? IW-Kurzberichte 19. Köln: Institut der deutschen Wirtschaft.
Best, H., Niehoff, S., Salheiser, A., & Salomo, K. (2015). Politische Kultur im Freistaat Thüringen. Thüringen im 25. Jahr der deutschen Einheit. Ergebnisse des Thüringen Monitors 2015. Friedrich Schiller Universität Jena, Retrieved from: http://www.thueringen.de/mam/th1/tsk/thueringen-monitor_2015/thuringen-monitor_2015.pdf
Betz, H. (1993). The New Politics of resentment: Radical right-wing populist parties in West Europe. Comparative Politics, 25, 413-427.
Binder, T. (2005). Die Wahlerfolge rechtspopulistischer Parteien. Eine Folge von Modernisierungsprozessen? Discussion Papers. Berlin: Wissenschaftszentrum für Sozialforschung.
Brähler, E., Decker, O., & Kiess, J. (2014). Die stabilisierte Mitte - Rechtsextreme Einstellung in Deutschland 2014. Leipzig: Kompetenzzentrum für Rechtsextremismus- und Demokratieforschung.
Brähler, E., Decker, O., & Kiess, J. (2016). Die enthemmte Mitte. Autoritäre und rechtsextreme Einstellung in Deutschland. Die Leipziger „Mitte"- Studie 2016. Gießen: Psychosozial Verlag.

Brenke, K., & Kritikos, S. (2017). Wählerstruktur im Wandel, *DIW Wochenbericht* 29, 595-606.
Dippel, C., Gold, R., Heblich, S., & Pinto, R. (2017). *Instrumental Variables and Causal Mechanisms: Unpacking the Effect of Trade on Workers and Voters.* Retrieved from http://www.anderson.ucla.edu/faculty/christian.dippel/DGHP.pdf
Eilfort, M. (2001). Mobilisierung als Schicksalsfrage? Auch Nichtwähler entscheiden die Bundestagswahl 2002. Konrad Adenauer Stiftung. *Die politische Meinung*, 383, Oktober 2001, 22-28.
Election 2017 Research Group Forschungsgruppe Wahlen (2017) *Bundestagswahl 24. September 2017.* Retrieved from http://www.forschungsgruppe.de/Aktuelles/Wahlanalyse_Bundestagswahl/Newsl_Bund_17092 8.pdf
Gabriel, O., Falter, J., & Rattinger, H. (2000). *Wirklich ein Volk? Die politischen Orientierungen von Ost- und Westdeutschen im Vergleich.* Opladen: Leske & Budrich.
Goerres, A., Spies, D., & Kumlin, S. (2017). The Electoral Supporter Base of the Alternative for Germany (April 3, 2017).
Götz, N. (1997). Modernisierungsverlierer oder Gegner einer reflexiven Moderne? Rechtsextreme Einstellungen in Berlin. *Zeitschrift für Soziologie* 26(6), 393-413.
Güllner, M. (2013). *Nichtwähler in Deutschland.* Friedrich-Ebert-Stiftung. Retrieved from http://library.fes.de/pdf-files/dialog/10076.pdf
Heimpold, G. (2010). Zwischen Deindustrialisierung und Reindustrialisierung Die ostdeutsche Industrie – ein Stabilitätsfaktor regionaler Wirtschaftsentwicklung? *Informationen zur Raumentwicklung* 10/11, 727-743.
Heitmeyer, W. (2012). *Das entsicherte Jahrzehnt. Deutsche Zustände Folge 10.* Berlin: Suhrkamp.
Hofmann, M. (2010). Soziale Strukturen in der DDR und in Ostdeutschland. *Dossier: Lange Wege der Deutschen Einheit.* Bundeszentrale für politische Bildung (bpb). Retrieved from http://www.bpb.de/system/files/pdf/JIEGS0.pdf
Infratest Dimap (2017). *Nachwahlbefragung des Unternehmens 'Infratest Dimap' am 24.09.2017 für die ARD* (91.088 Befragte). Retrieved from https://wahl.tagesschau.de/wahlen/2017-09-24-BTDE/index.shtml
Inglehart, R., & Norris, P. (2016). *Trump, Brexit, and the rise of populism: Economic havenots and cultural backlash.* Harvard Kennedy School faculty research working paper series, RWP16-026.
Kroh, M., & Fetz, K. (2016): *Das Profil der AfD-AnhängerInnen hat sich seit Gründung der Partei deutlich verändert.* DIW Wochenbericht Nr. 34.
Lengfeld, H. (2017). Die „Alternative für Deutschland": eine Partei für Modernisierungsverlierer? *Kölner Zeitschrift für Soziologie und Sozialpsychologe (KZSS).* Wiesbaden: Springer Fachmedien.
Lipset, S. (1984). Der Faschismus, die Linke, die Rechte und die Mitte. In: Nolte, E.: *Theorien über Faschismus.* 6. Auflage, Königstein, 449-491.
Lösche, P. (1993). Kleine Geschichte der deutschen Parteien. Stuttgart, Berlin. Köln: Kohlhammer.

Lubbers, M., Gijsbert, M., & Scheepers, P. (2002). Extreme right-wing voting in West Europe. *European Journal of political Research* 41, 245-378.

Neu, V. (2012). *„Dann bleib ich mal weg" DER MYTHOS DER „PARTEI" DER NICHTWÄHLER.* Konrad Adenauer Stiftung. Retrieved from http://www.kas.de/wf/doc/kas_31915-544-1- 30.pdf?130704105023

Othon, A. (2000). Extreme Right in Europe. A Comparative Study of Recent Trends. *Discussion Paper 3*. London School of Economics & Political Science.

Pfahl-Traughber, A. (2000). Die Entwicklung des Rechtsextremismus in Ost- und Westdeutschland. *Aus Politik und Zeitgeschichte,* B 39/2000, 3-14.

Poutrus, P., Behrends, J., & Kuck, D. (2000). Historische Ursachen der Fremdenfeindlichkeit in den neuen Bundesländern. *Aus Politik und Zeitgeschichte,* B 39, 15-21.

Quent, M., & Schulz, P. (2015). *Rechtsextremismus in lokalen Kontexten: Vier vergleichende Fallstudien.* Wiesbaden: Springer VS.

Roeser, V. R. (2017). AfD: Sozialdemagogie gegen Marktradikalismus. BNR. Retrieved from https://www.bnr.de/artikel/hintergrund/afd-sozialdemagogie-gegen-marktradikalismus

Schäfer, A., Verkamp, R., & Gagné, J. (2013). *Prekäre Wahlen. Milieus und soziale Selektivität der Wahlbeteiligung bei der Bundestagswahl 2013.* Retrieved from http://www.wahlbeteiligung2013.de/fileadmin/Inhalte/Studien/Wahlbeteiligung-2013- Studie.pdf

Schmidt, B. (2014). Wie Marine Le Pen den Front National modernisierte. Bundeszentrale für Politische Bildung (BpB). *Dossier Rechtsextremismus.*

Spier, T. (2010). *Modernisierungsverlierer? Die Wählerschaft rechtspopulistischer Parteien in Westeuropa.* Wiesbaden: Springer VS.

Stöss, R. (1996): Rechtsextremismus. In: Niedermayer, Oskar (Eds.). *Intermediäre Strukturen in Ostdeutschland. Beiträge zu den Berichten zum sozialen und politischen Wandel in Ostdeutschland.* Bd.3.2, Leske und Budrich, 193-215.

Stöss, R. (2000). *Rechtsextremismus im vereinten Deutschland.* 3., überarbeitete Auflage, Bonn 2000. Retrieved from http://library.fes.de/pdf-files/ostdeutschland/00887.pdf

Verkamp, W. (2017). *Populäre Wahlen, Mobilisierung und Gegenmobilisierung der sozialen Milieus bei der Bundestagswahl 2017.* Berlin: Bertelsmann-Stiftung.

Vogel, B. (1999). Arbeitslosigkeit in Ostdeutschland. Konsequenzen für das Sozialgefüge und für die Wahrnehmung des gesellschaftlichen Wandels. *SOFI-Mitteilungen* Nr. 27/1999, 15-23.

Werts, H., Scheepers, P., & Lubbers, M. (2013). Euro-sceptism and radical right-wing voting in Europe 2002-2008. Social Cleavages, socio-political attitudes and contextual characteristics determining voting for the radical right. *European Union Politics* 14(2), 183-205.

Zick, A., & Klein, A. (2014). *Fragile Mitte, Feindselige Zustände.* Friedrich Ebert Stiftung (FES). Bonn: Dietz.

Globalization, Crisis, and Right-Wing Populism in Context

Fabian Virchow

In August 2017, the conservative daily *Frankfurter Allgemeine Zeitung* published an article it its business pages in which the author gave a strong warning on the "unjust consequences of globalisation." She further argued that there is a new certainty around Europe today: "The times when the states continued to reduce their borders and brought the entire world population closer together seem to be over for the time being." In her view, part of that development had also been the rise of populist forces in several European countries (Brankovic, 2017).

Yet, a general usage of the term "populism" for phenomena as different as *Syriza* in Greece (Spourdalakis, 2014) and *Podemos* in Spain (Kioupkiolis, 2016) on the one hand, and *Lega Nord* in Italy (McDonnell, 2006; Huysseune, 2010) and the *Freedom Party* in Austria (Turner-Graham, 2008; Grigat, 2017) on the other, might confuse more than it creates clarity. In fact, it is mainly right-wing populist parties that have gained significant ground in European politics. They are running countries as we see with the *Law and Justice Party* (Prawo i Sprawiedliwos'/PiS) in Poland (Beylin, 2015; Bachmann, 2016) and *Fidesz* (Fidesz - Magyar Polgári Szövetség) in Hungary, and a growing number of these parties have been invited as partners into coalition governments. The increased influence of right-wing populist and extreme right-wing parties raises the question of whether, and if so in what way, this development has been caused by globalization, as the German journalist proposed.

In order to explore this question, I will start with a brief overview of the conceptualization of populism, then turn to the assumption that globalization is one of its root causes, and finally discuss if crisis has contributed to the rise of right-wing populism.

Populism: What Are We Talking About?

Populism is a political term, and a concept in political science since the 1960s. The Latin root *populus* means people, also in the historical-political sense of nation. The term is used for a wide range of historical and political phenomena and its content therefore is contested. It has been viewed as a multifaceted, historically-specific occurrence, as a certain kind of ideology, a technique of rule, a political tactic, or a way of protest and communication, thus making it difficult to come to the one precise academic definition (Heinisch & Holtz-Bacha, 2017; Jörke & Selk, 2017).

In the 19th century populism arose as a political term referring to the partisanship for the ordinary people against the exploiting classes by praising simple life amongst relatives in rural communities. Rooted in the traditional world view of agriculture as the dominant mode of production and living, and facing increasing industrialization, urbanization, and division of labour, diverse expressions of populism emerged, such as the Russian *Narodniks*, who demanded the sharing out of large-scale land-holding and the revival of the traditional rural common-land economy, and the *Populist Party* in the U.S.A., that protested against the deflationary gold standard policy and monopolistic freight rates of the private railway companies (Stock, 1996).

In Latin America populist movements have been mostly nationalist patronage parties with a strong and charismatic leader and a massive support from the marginalized urban lower classes. Most prominent amongst Latin American populist leaders had been Argentina's Juan Perón (1895-1974), Brazil's Getúlio Vargas (1883-1954) and Mexico's Lázaro Cárdenas (1895-1970). Although most of their followers were from the lower classes, they were also supported by middle class professionals. The populist leaders made use of anti-oligarchic and nationalist, meaning "anti-imperialist" as directed against US-domination, discourses. In the economic domain they established expansionary policies often rooted in import substituting industrialization plus price controls and the protection of local industry. Government resources were often awarded according to loyalty of protagonists to the charismatic leader who achieved the image and status of a quasi-messianic figure. Frequently trade unions acted as an extension of the government, e.g. its members mobilized for mass rallies to support the party or the leader. In the 1960s and 1970s military dictatorship tried to eradicate populism by taking power by a coup followed by brutal persecution, mass arrests, and murder of left-wing and trade union activists (Conniff, 1982).

Mudde and Kaltwasser (2013) have made the important distinction between *inclusive* and *exclusive* populism:

> Today, European populism is predominantly exclusive, while Latin American populism is chiefly inclusive. Two factors are crucial for understanding these different regional patterns: on the one hand, the way in which populist actors define who belongs to 'the people' vis-á-vis 'the elite', and on the other hand, the ideological features that are attached to the particular populist ideology of the actors (p.148).

The distinction between "the people" and "the elite" is a moral one: "Whereas the former is depicted as a homogeneous and virtuous community, the latter is seen as a homogeneous but pathological entity" (p. 151) often described as corrupt and aloof. While populism in general makes use of this polarizing, dichotomous, and moralizing approach, there are different perspectives in regard to who belongs to "the people" and "the elite." In addition, populism:

> is not only about attacking 'the elite' and defending the interests of 'the common people'; it is also about the very idea that all individuals of a given community are able to unify their wills with the aim of proclaiming popular sovereignty as the only legitimate source of political power (p. 151).

Priester (2012) has identified additional basic elements of populist thought and argumentation structures such as the denunciation of elites from a perspective of conspiracy theory and the summoning of crisis and decline (p. 42). The definition of populism as a "thin ideology" distinguishes it from other conceptualizations, which describe populism mainly as a political style (Reinemann, 2017) or a strategy "through which a personalist leader seeks or exercises government based on direct, unmediated, uninstitutionalized support from large numbers of mostly unorganized followers" (Weyland, 2001, p. 14).

In contemporary Europe populism is mainly visibly in the form of right-wing populism whose parties have achieved a significant foothold in the electoral systems of a number of European countries. Generally, populist politicians and parties/movements like Heinz-Christian Strache and the *Austrian Freedom Party*, Christoph Blocher and the *Swiss Peoples Party*, Matteo Salvini's *Lega Nord* in Italy, Victor Orbán and the *Fidesz* as well as Jaroslaw Kaczyński's *PiS* and Marine Le Pen's *Front National/Rassemblement National* are seen as the most important populist parties in today's Europe. They all claim to represent the rightful source of political power–which is the people–against self-interested politicians and so called 'politically-correct' intellectuals. Whilst earlier populism in speaking of the peoples-elite antagonism referred to parts of the ruling classes as the elite, today's populism from the right avoids targeting any such section of society but instead holds state institutions and state intervention into politics responsible for mistakes in societal development. What once had been a critical approach to (certain aspects of) the market economy has now become a neo-liberal critique of any state interventionism by the majority of European right-wing populist politicians and political parties. Accordingly, the opposite of elite is now understood as hardworking citizens and businessmen who are not looking for state assistance.

In addition, these populist political parties and movements, claiming to speak for the overlooked majority, put forward an agenda of hostility to taxation, ethnic regionalism, tightening of crime control, and anti-immigration. Not least, the often xenophobic underpinning of right-wing populism picks up the tradition of illiberal nationalism or even far-right political agendas. Often oversimplified solutions are offered for quite complex social and economic problems.

Populism is closely linked to representative politics in a sense that modernity gave rise to the emergence of the institutions of representative politics populism is antagonistic to. Populism calls for more direct democracy that is justified with the assertion that representative politics have failed because there is no direct link between the ruling elite and the large number of voters because of the growing complexity of decision making processes and the multiple government structures the citizen is confronted with when s/he has a matter of concern. Populists argue that politics are dominated by the interests of political parties and interest groups leading to a "special interest state." Instead of what is said to be highly complicated processes of representative politics with its core elements of parties, elections, interest groups and legislative assemblies, populists use the language of popular sovereignty against the institutions of representation and speak up in favour of their models of a charismatic leadership (or at least highly centralized political structures) that is directly linked to the masses by referendums or acclamation.

This paper goes with the concept of populism not mainly as an emotionalizing and polarizing style of politics but as a world view that operates along dichotomies of "Us" and "Them" in which "Us" is "the people" idealized as hard-working and tidy people while "Them" are the elite stereotypical seen as corrupt and aloof; but "Them" are also the "Other," the "Outsider" from a nativist perspective. Therefore, right-wing populism is not only a style of communication (Merkle, 2016), but more importantly a pattern of interpretation that looks at the world in a moralizing way through the dualism of a good people on the one hand and the corrupt elite on the other (Priester, 2016, p. 547), and adds further elements for creating a collective identity by which claims making of the supposed "Other" to political and social rights is denied in favour of what is discursively constructed as a racially or ethnically homogenous people. Especially important are "producerist" mental figures, used to ostracize all those who are successfully labelled as not contributing to the production of material goods and the GDP of a given society (Berlet & Lyons, 2000). Producerism can be turned against groups that are marginalized anyhow such as long-term unemployed, homeless, refugees, and Romani people. In one example, producerism became relevant in Germany when the Eurozone countries in general and the German government particularly decided to run a bailout program to address the Greek crisis (Karyotis & Gerodimos, 2015), and tabloid media discourse accused "the lazy Greeks" for living on German taxpayers money (Bickes et al., 2012). In another, in anti-Semitic worldview producerism is part of the imagination that Jewish people are living in a parasitic relationship to other peoples (Foxman, 2010; Holz & Weyand, 2014).

Right-wing populism presents itself as the "true voice of the people" arguing that it is the sole political force that dares to speak about tricky topics. Yet, this trope runs hand in hand with the devaluation of democratic negotiation processes and their complexities. Models of direct democracy and decision making are often presented as alternatives which rest on the idea that there is the immediate connection between the the "will of the people" and the head of state. Societies with right-wing populist governments have regularly installed authoritarian structures and procedures.

Globalization–What Are We Talking About?

Some twenty years ago, economist John Cassidy described globalization as the slogan of the late 20th century par excellence (Cassidy, 1997, p. 20). In doing so, he referred to the growing importance of a term that stands at the center of numerous political and media discourses as well as scientific debate and theorizing as a symbol of current and historical developments, as a negative cipher of social upheaval, but also as a magical invocation (Liebert, 2003; Badura et al., 2005; Middell & Engel, 2010). Yet the core of what is discursively labeled as globalization is as controversial as its (global) social reach, its manifestations, its temporal location, or the (normative assessment of) impact on a relevant proportion of humanity living on this planet (Bairoch, 2000; Hall, 2000; Kiely, 2005; Wallerstein, 2000). Academic debate in political sciences and sociology is full of controversies and different perspectives on globalization.

Some consider the currently dominant discourse on globalization to be a "gigantic misreading of current reality" (Wallerstein, 2000, p. 250) and point out that the fundamental transformation of the capitalist system can only be understood in the context of the enforcement of the capitalist world economy since the year 1450s as well as the latest Kondratiev cycle, which has been ongoing since 1945. Others criticize the notion and idea of globalization as suggesting "a process of convergence to some single standard" (Hall, 2000, p. 68), whereas world economics is still a long way from being global, transnational corporations are still "national firms with international operations" (p. 66), and in the area of migration, the economies of the North refine their selection criteria and increase the barriers to entry and therefore one cannot speak of a global labor market.

There are also historical investigations that show, for example, that the level of international ties and cooperation at the end of the 20th century is comparable to the level reached shortly before the First World War (Hirst & Thompson, 1996; Sutcliffe & Glyn, 1999) and the international business world still "rests upon rather resilient national bases" (Caroll & Fennema, 2002, p.

414). Therefore, to speak of a transnational business community does not hit the spot.

Bartelson (2000) sees a (non-linear) historical sequence of the conceptualization of globalization, from "transference" to the "transformation" to the "transcendence": "Behind the veil of semantic ambiguity we find the conviction that globalization is *taking place*, without such a conviction constituting common ground, there would be no discourse or debate of globalization" (p. 191, emphasis in original). At the very least, one can speak of a forcefulness and sociological significance of discourses ("the broad acceptance of globalization as a fact is a social fact", Bartelson, 2000, p. 180), which assess globalization as a process in which,

> industrial and commercial companies as well as financial institutions increasingly operate transnationally (…). This goes hand-in-hand with an increase in mergers and the acquisition of industrial, commercial and financial companies, leading to an increase in the global role of large, multinational companies and to a lessening of the role of nation-states. The diminution of the role of states (or of regional governments) has been further accelerated by the shift toward the privatization of public companies (including services) and by deregulation (Bairoch, 2000, pp. 197-198).

In addition, mobility and migration gained importance, and international connectivity and the exchange of culture and media products are intensifying.

In the late twentieth century, in particular, the ideology of neo-liberalism and its paradigm of unleashing the market and invoking individual responsibility for one's well-being and success has fostered extensive structural changes in many states. Governments often argued the TINA-way and pushed through cuts in the social security system and changes in labor regulations by referring to the "forces of globalization" and the increasing global competition. Tax relief for big industry and the rich combined with restrictive spending policies often resulted in the undermining of central tasks and functions of the state. This development not only hit lower-income households and people working in precarious jobs, but also a growing part of the middle class felt more insecure and threatened (Kocher, 2006). These trends have been further reinforced by the financial crisis of 2008, not least because the promise of economic and social advancement, which was significant for the postwar stabilization of the Federal Republic of Germany, has lost its power of persuasion.

Entanglements in Context

The subjectively felt insecurity and loss of control with regards to living conditions (Heitmeyer, 2001, p. 506 ff.; Sauer et al., 2018) often coincide with a serious reduction of confidence in political parties and institutions and can be considered as causally responsible for the development or consolidation of extreme/populist right-wing attitudes and the electoral support of ring-wing populist parties (Betz, 2001; Swank & Betz, 2003; Flecker & Hentges, 2004; Vlandas & Halikiopoulou, 2016).

Recent studies on voters of the nationalist and authoritarian German party Alternative for Germany (Bender, 2017; Häusler, 2018) make clear that the decision to elect the party is less due to an objectively difficult economic situation, but above all correlates with the subjective perception of one's own life situation, which is much more pessimistic than in the population average (Kroh & Fetz, 2016; Bergmann et al., 2017). In addition, AfD voters are often characterized by experiencing a loss of control that is fueled by the sense of being at the mercy of technological innovations and detached political institutions who fail to protect them from immigration and crime. Accordingly, a policy proposal that emphasizes authoritarianism and anti-immigrant positions can be attractive. However, employees whose employment relationships are not subject to a collective agreement or are not characterized by fixed-term contracts are much more willing to vote for the AfD than persons in fixed and collectively agreed employment relationships (Hilmer et al., 2017). Other surveys indicate that people with medium and higher status tend to have a stronger AfD election intent, which could be explained by the party's economic liberal goals (Lengfeld, 2017).

The increase in the trans-border movement of goods and human beings is considered a relevant indicator in regard to the level of neoliberal globalization. Migration and asylum have grown into two of the most important policy fields in the Federal Republic of Germany. There, the ideal of a homogeneous "German people" has only been questioned offensively for a comparatively short time, namely by the Citizenship Act of 2000. In the autumn of 2010, Chancellor Angela Merkel declared "multiculturalism" to be have failed. Immigration and asylum are issued widely discussed along the criteria of whether they threaten the security or are useful for German society. A law allowing immigration beyond the possibility of asylum is still missing today. In this respect, it is hardly surprising that a considerable minority of the population is skeptical or strongly opposed to immigration (Brähler et al., 2016; Zick et al., 2016).

The idea of a homogenous and willing to perform community created by opposing "the strangers", "the unproductive" or "the EU bureaucrats" can subjectively cushion one's own experience of insecurity, loss of control, and the devaluation of biographies. Nationalist and authoritarian policy proposals appear to be plausible solutions to (self-perceived) social exclusion and precarious everyday experiences. Hence, authoritarian and exclusionary political agendas offered by right-wing populist parties are supported.

Large right-wing populist parties represent a program of neoliberal politics to which in some cases social-protectionist claims like supporting the demand for minimal wages are added (Nocun, 2016; Auinger, 2017; Bonvalot, 2017). The political strategy of right-wing populist parties makes strong use of the fear people have (Wodak, 2016): fear of migrants, fear of social decline, fear of violence and criminality, etc. These parties live on fanning those fears, rather than offering a rational view of current societal issues. They are hoping for a deepening of economic and social crisis as crisis is seen as the driving forces of a reactionary rebellion (Virchow & Häusler, 2018). They present narratives with references to "Heimat" (Homeland) or "Abendland" (Occident) in order to give people a sense of belonging and protection (Faber, 2018) in a world that is actually dominated by world views according to which inequality is meaningful and unavoidable: Social positions and affiliation are either considered biologically given or thought to be just results of competitive situations in which people are placed, such as in the labor and housing markets.

Already in the early 1980s, on the occasion of the neoliberal policies of the Thatcher government that has destroyed structures of solidarity and unleashed forces of inequality by its neoliberal program, Stuart Hall emphasized the idea of a democratic populism (1986) as an alternative; recently Moeller (2017) presented an approach in which "the people" would be constituted against the forces of power and the elites but is not conceptualized as a closed and excluding entity around a particular national/ethnic identity. Having this idea work would also mean to reverse a development in which migrant workers have mostly been addressed as Muslims in many European countries instead of fellow workers, thereby undermining the much needed solidarity and joint action in favor of a more egalitarian and diverse society (Yılmaz, 2016).

References

Auinger, H. (2017). Die FPÖ. Blaupause der Neuen Rechten in Europa. Wien: ProMedia.
Bachmann, K. (2016). Rebellen ohne Grund. Ursachen und Folgen des Wahlsieges der PiS. Osteuropa, 1-2, 37-60.
Badura, J., Rieth, L., & Scholtes, F. (Eds.) (2005): Globalisierung. Problemsphären eines Schlagwortes im interdisziplinären Dialog. Wiesbaden: VS Verlag.

Bairoch, P. (2000). The constituent economic principles of globalization in historical perspective. International Sociology, 2, 197-214.
Bartelson, J. (2000). Three concepts of globalization. International Sociology, 2, 180-196.
Bender, J. (2017). Was will die AfD? Eine Partei verändert Deutschland. München: Pantheon.
Bergmann, K., Diermeier, M., & Niehues, J. (2017). Die AfD: Eine Partei der sich ausgeliefert fühlenden Durchschnittsverdiener? Zeitschrift für Parlamentsfragen, 1, 57-75.
Berlet, C., & Lyons, M. N. (2000). Right-Wing Populism in America. Too Close For Comfort. New York/London: The Guilford Press.
Betz, H. (2001). Radikaler Rechtspopulismus im Spannungsfeld zwischen neoliberalistischen Wirtschaftskonzepten und antiliberaler autoritärer Ideologie. In D. Loch, & W. Heitmeyer (Eds.), Schattenseiten der Globalisierung (pp. 167-185). Frankfurt/Main: Suhrkamp.
Beylin, M. (2015). PiS: Vom sozialen zum national-katholischen Populismus in Polen. In E. Hillebrand (Ed.). Rechtspopulismus in Europa: Gefahr für die Demokratie? (pp. 69-76). Bonn: Dietz.
Bickes, H., Butulussi, E., Otten, T., Schendel, J., Sdroulia, A., & Steinhof, A. (2012). Die Dynamik der Konstruktion von Differenz und Feindseligkeit am Beispiel der Finanzkrise Griechenlands: Hört beim Geld die Freundschaft auf? München: Iudicium.
Bonvalot, M. (2017). Die FPÖ – Partei der Reichen. Wien: mandelbaum.
Brähler, E., Decker, O., & Kiess, J. (Eds.) (2016). Die enthemmte Mitte: Autoritäre und rechtsextreme Einstellung in Deutschland. Gießen: Psychosozial-Verlag.
Carroll, W. K., & Fennema, M. (2002). Is There a Transnational Business Community? International Sociology, 3, pp. 393-419.
Conniff, M. L. (Ed.) (1982). Latin American Populism in Comparative Perspective. Albuquerque: University of New Mexico Press.
Faber, R. (2018). Ewiges Abendland? Ein historischer Rückblick aus aktuellem Anlass. In R. Faber, & O. Briese (Eds.). Heimatland Vaterland Abendland. Über alte und neue Populismen. Würzburg: Königshausen & Neumann, pp. 171-199.
Flecker, J., & Hentges, G. (2004). Rechtspopulistische Konjunkturen in Europa – sozioökonomischer Wandel und politische Orientierungen. In J. Bischoff, K. Dörre, & E. Gauthier (Eds.): Moderner Rechtspopulismus. Hamburg: VSA, pp. 119-148.
Foxman, A. H. (2010). Jews & Money: The Story of a Stereotype. New York: Palgrave Macmillan.
Grigat, S. (Ed.) (2017). AfD & FPÖ: Antisemitismus, völkischer Nationalismus und Geschlechterbilder. Baden-Baden: Nomos.
Häusler, A. (Ed.) (2018). Völkisch-autoritärer Populismus. Der Rechtsruck in Deutschland und die AfD. Hamburg: VSA.
Hall, J. A. (2000). Globalization and Nationalism. Thesis Eleven, 1, pp. 63-79.

Hall, S. (1986). Popular-demokratischer oder autoritärer Populismus. In: H. Dubiel (Ed.): Populismus und Aufklärung. Frankfurt/Main: edition suhrkamp, pp. 84-105.
Heinisch, R. C., & Holtz-Bacha, C. (Eds.) (2017). Political Populism. A Handbook. Baden-Baden: Nomos.
Hilmer, R., Kohlrausch, B., Müller-Hilmer, R., & Gagné, J. (2017). Einstellung und soziale Lebenslage. Working Paper 044. Düsseldorf: Hans-Böckler-Stiftung.
Hirst, P., & Thompson, G. (1996). Globalization in Question. Cambridge: Polity Press.
Holz, K., & Weyand, J. (2014). Arbeit und Nation. Die Ethik nationaler Arbeit und ihre Feinde am Beispiel Hitlers. In: S. Voigt, & H. Sünker (Eds.). Arbeiterbewegung – Nation – Globalisierung. Weilerswist: Velbrück, pp. 202-228.
Huysseune, M. (2010). A Eurosceptic vision in a europhile country: The case of the Lega Nord. Modern Italy, 1, pp. 63-75.
Jörke, D., & Selk, V. (2017). Theorien des Populismus. Hamburg: Junius.
Karyotis, G., & Gerodimos, R. (2015). The Politics of Extreme Austerity. Greece in the Eurozone Crisis. Basingstoke: Palgrave Macmillan.
Kiely, R. (2005). Globalization and Poverty, and the Poverty of Globalization Theory. Current Sociology, 6, pp. 895-914.
Kioupkiolis, A. (2016). Podemos: the ambiguous promises of left-wing populism in contemporary Spain. Journal of Political Ideologies, 2, pp. 99-120.
Kocher, R. (2006). Mehr Zustimmung, aber weniger Vertrauen. Frankfurter Allgemeine Zeitung, 21 June 2006, p. 5.
Kroh, M., & Fetz, K. (2016). Das Profil der AfD-AnhängerInnen hat sich seit Gründung der Partei deutlich verändert. DIW-Wochenbericht 34, pp. 711-719.
Lengfeld, H. (2017). Die „Alternative für Deutschland": eine Partei der Modernisierungsverlierer? Kölner Zeitschrift für Soziologie und Sozialpsychologie, 2, pp. 209-232.
Liebert, W. (2003). Zu einem dynamischen Konzept von Schlüsselwörtern. Zeitschrift für angewandte Linguistik, pp. 57-75.
Markou, Grigoris (2017). The Rise of Inclusionary Populism in Europe: The Case of SYRIZA. Contemporary Southeastern Europe, 1, pp. 54-71.
McDonnell, D. (2006). A Weekend in Padania: Regionalist Populism and the Lega Nord. Politics, 2, pp.126-132.
Merkle, S. (2016). Populistische Elemente in der Kommunikation der Alternative für Deutschland. Eine qualitative Analyse von Wahlwerbung und Pressemitteilungen im Europawahlkampf 2014. In C. Holtz-Bacha (ed.), Europawahlkampf 2014. Wiesbaden: Springer VS, pp. 129-152.
Middell, M., & Engel, U. (Eds.) (2010). Theoretiker der Globalisierung. Leipzig: Leipziger Universitätsverlag.
Moeller, K. (2017). Invocatio Populi. Autoritärer und demokratischer Populismus. In D. Jörke, & O. Nachtwey (Eds.), Das Volk gegen die (liberale) Demokratie. Leviathan Sonderband 32 Baden-Baden: Nomos, pp. 257-278.

Mudde, C., & Kaltwasser, C. R. (2013). Exclusionary vs. inclusionary populism: Comparing contemporary Europe and Latin America. *Government and Opposition, 2,* 147-174.
Nocun, K. (2016). *Wie sozial ist die AfD wirklich? Eine Expertise zu Positionen in der AfD bei der Sozial- und Steuerpolitik.* Berlin: HBS.
Opratko, B. (2017). Rechtspopulismus als Krisenverarbeitung. Anmerkungen zum Aufstieg von AfD und FPÖ. *Prokla, 1,* 123-130.
Poier, K., Saywald-Wedl, S., & Unger, H. (2017). *Die Themen der „Populisten."* Baden-Baden: Nomos.
Priester, K. (2012). *Rechter und linker Populismus: Annäherung an ein Chamäleon.* Frankfurt/Main: Campus Verlag.
Priester, K. (2016). Rechtspopulismus–ein umstrittenes theoretisches und politisches Problem. In F. Virchow, M. Langebach, & A. Häusler (Eds.): *Handbuch Rechtsextremismus* (pp. 533-560). Wiesbaden: Springer VS.
Reinemann, C. (2017). Populismus, Kommunikation, Medien. Ein Überblick über die Forschung zu populistischer politischer Kommunikation. *Zeitschrift für Politik, 2,* pp. 167-190.
Sauer, D., Stöger, U., Bischoff, J., Detje, R., & Müller, B. (2018). *Rechtspopulismus und Gewerkschaften. Eine arbeitsweltliche Spurensuche.* Hamburg: VSA.
Spourdalakis, M. (2014). The miraculous rise of the "Phenomenon SYRIZA." *International Critical Thought, 3,* 354-366.
Stock, C. M. (1996). *Rural radicals: Righteous rage in the American grain.* Ithaca, NY: Cornell University Press.
Sutcliffe, B. & Glyn, A. (1999). Still underwhelmed: Indicators of globalization and their misinterpretation. *Review of Radical Political Economies, 1,* 111-132.
Swank, D., & Betz, H. (2003). Globalization, the welfare state and rightwing populism in Western Europe. *Socio-Economic Review, 2,* 215-245.
Turner-Graham, E. (2008). "Austria First": H.C. Strache, Austrian identity and the current politics of Austria's Freedom Party. *Studies in Language & Capitalism, 3-4,* 181-198.
Vlandas, T., & Halikiopoulou, D. (2016). *Why far right parries do well at times of crisis: The role of labour market institutions.* Brussels: ETUI.
Virchow, F., & Häusler, A. (2018). Vom Lob der Krise–Krisenvorstellungen und Krisenpolitik rechtsaußen. In J. Roose, F. Scholl, & M. Sommer (Eds.), *Europas Zivilgesellschaft in der Wirtschafts- und Finanzkrise. Protest, Resilienz und Kämpfe um Deutungshoheit* (pp. 163-179). Wiesbaden: Springer VS.
Wallerstein, I. (2000). Globalization or the age of transition. *International Sociology, 2,* 249-265.
Weyland, K. (2001). Clarifying a contested concept: Populism in the study of Latin American politics. *Comparative Politics, 1,* 1-22.
Wodak, R. (2016). *Politik mit der Angst. Zur Wirkung rechtspopulistischer Diskurse.* Wien/Hamburg: Edition Konturen.
Yılmaz, F. (2016). *How the workers became Muslims. Immigration, culture, and the hegemonic transformation in Europe.* Ann Arbor, MI: University of Michigan Press.

Zick, A., Küpper, B., & Krause, D. (Eds.) (2016). *Gespaltene Mitte–feindselige Zustände. Rechtsextreme Einstellungen in Deutschland 2016.* Berlin/Bonn: Verlag J.H.W. Dietz Nachf.

The Discreet Charm of Populism: The Role of Gender and Female Politicians in the AfD and Front National/Rassemblement National

Birgit Meyer

Social Work is committed to human rights and the protection of fundamental equality between men and women. Social Work serves and supports vulnerable groups in society. It also needs the protection of the state and the support of democratic institutions and civil society. Democratic institutions and the values of social justice and equality are currently under threat by right wing movements and parties, not only in Europe but also worldwide.

Gender equality is a core target of these attacks. "Gender" or what is scornfully called "Gender Madness" ("Gender-Wahn") or "Gender Ideology" ("Gender-Ideologie") serve as hate slogans ("Kampfbegriffe") in right-wing campaigns to discredit the anti-discrimination policies and social movements, which began in the 1960s-1970s. Equality policies under threat include Affirmative Action in the US; Gender Mainstreaming in Europe; and reforms of abortion and family laws to ensure equal opportunities and treatment irrespective of gender, ethnic origin, age, or religious beliefs and to protect the rights of divorced parents, single mothers/fathers and their children, homosexuals, and LGTBI-people. These developments in equality and human rights and the continuing battle against discrimination are major achievements in Western liberal democracies. They reflect, question, and oppose traditional hierarchies, norms, and laws. However, they are not yet secure and well-rooted achievements, and they are particularly under threat by right wing populism today.

Gender equality can serve as a good seismograph for the state of justice and equality in a society, and for the acceptance of diversity and the protection of vulnerable groups within it. By contrast, the denunciation of gender equality is linked to other forms of hostility, such as ethnic racism, anti-Semitism and the denigration of immigrants and Muslims (Zick & Küpper, 2015). Therefore, it is reasonable to describe right-wing populism and its attacks on equality as anti-democratic (put references that were in footnote into citation here). Furthermore it seeks a denial or reduction of rights and the values of the social work profession.

Curiously, right wing populism is also attractive to women. Why are anti-equality slogans, movements, and parties appealing or "charming" i.e. seductive to women? What explains the rising support for populist parties? Women are often in leading positions within right wing parties. How do they succeed in winning supporters? Are the emancipated women at the top of right-wing populistic parties the attractive and modern face (or façade) that helps make palatable policies that attack the achievements of liberal democracies in securing a wide range of rights and liberties for women and other minorities? Are the attacks on Islam or quota policies and equal opportunities officers especially seductive for women and men when they are presented by female leaders? Furthermore, we need to ask whether we will soon have large numbers of people who are attracted by xenophobic and white-male-supremacist ideas in the field of social work?

This paper cannot undertake a critical analysis of the abundant literature on populism. While there exists much about the reactionary policies and divisive strategies of populist movements/parties/leaders, there is little or no mention of populism's views on gender or women's rights. Given this minimal treatment of gender issues, I argue that political programs, speeches, documents and self-presentations need to be properly analyzed in relation to gender (roles) as well as the female leaders themselves. What assets do they bring to populist parties? I argue that women in leadership positions can strengthen them in many ways. I identify in this article five important roles women play for their parties.

I focus on Germany and France, and on gender issues and female politicians to explore: Where are the similarities and the differences in the topics and in the strategies of right wing populism? Which leading female figures are promoted and why? How do they present themselves? Who are the supporters and the voters for the right wing parties "Front National/Rassemblement National" in France and "Alternative für Deutschland" (AfD) in Germany? The core elements of my research are election analysis, party programs and decisions, the public speeches of the politicians, as well as political science studies, media and Internet sources.

Fundamentally, there are numerous differences between France and Germany. Differences occur not only in the structure of the political system and in election procedures or the role of the President or Parliament in both countries, but I focus here on the differences and similarities of female politicians. In 2011 when Marine Le Pen took over the leadership of the FN, feminism and women's rights were seen as topics that could be exploited to benefit the party by dressing xenophobic and racist resentments in pseudo-feminist new clothes. The FN promotes the idea that the rights of white French women ("Francaises de Souches") should be protected against the dangers of Islam and of Islamization of France. One could observe a manipulative use of political conflicts that are central to feminism: sexual freedom and self-determination of women and minorities and protection against violence. In Germany, by contrast right-wing populist movements and parties resent feminism and oppose vehemently the concept of Gender and Gender Studies or policies like Gender Mainstreaming.

I will now very shortly define *feminism* and *populism* because there are so many popular definitions.

Feminism is the "advocacy of women's rights on the basic promise of equality of the sexes" (Oxford Dictionary.com) and it seeks the "political, economic and social equality of the sexes by means of activities on behalf of women's rights and interest" (Merriam-Webster.com). Feminism also advocates and campaigns against a wide range of injustices and inequalities in societies primarily ruled by men. In addition, feminism identifies all kinds of discrimination and exploitation of women in the private and public sector (Meyer, 2002, p. 137). Feminism was Merriam-Webster's "Word of the Year 2017" showing a 70%-increase of use over 2016.

Gender stands for the criticism of (a) assumptions about the "natural" capacities and qualities of women and men and (b) of traditional rules of submission of women towards men.

Gender Studies analyze the various historical national and cultural forms of these rules and, most important, the different expectations, beliefs, and values that are connected with masculinity and femininity in societies.

Right-Wing-Populism refers to a belief in "the people" as an opposite social pole to "the elites" or "the establishment" and to an unspecific "we" against "the others" with a moral exclusiveness (Mudde, 2007, 2017; Müller, 2016). Right-wing populism distorts political issues in order to manipulate and mobilize assault on democratic institutions such as courts, judges, "the establishment", Media, journalists and politicians. Right wing populism mobilizes fear and aggression against migrants and raises specters of sexually dangerous refugees and the Islamization of western societies. Other features are:

- The denigration of human beings who are "different" or non-white;
- Authoritarian law-and-order-policies;
- Nationalism, chauvinism, racism;
- Opposition to diversity and to pluralistic attitudes, arguments, and lifestyles; and
- Emotional rhetoric, hate-speech, and "alternative facts" (Mudde 2017).

Right wing populism refers to feminism and Gender Studies as threats to the traditional family and its role in transmitting traditional divisions of labor, to "civilization" and Christianity, and to male supremacy and heterosexuality (Hark & Villa, 2015).

France: Liberté, Ègalité, Laicité, Parité

A very prominent feature of current French politics is the discourse of French identity and the commitment to "La République" and its core values of liberté, égalité, and laicité. These republican values were forged in the French Revolution and the struggle against the French monarchy, the leading aristocrats, and the religious establishment. Parité is a new achievement. It aims at equality of women in politics.

France is a newcomer in Women's suffrage: the country only implemented it in 1944. Decades later, in 1999, the percentage of female members of Parliament was only 11% (while it was one-third in Germany). The "Law of Parity" ("la Loi de la Parité") introduced in 2000 aims at a 50% representation of women in Parliament on the local and national levels. It has already achieved positive results: there is now a nearly 50-50 division in local Parliaments. While in 2012, there were only 26% women on the federal level in the Assemblée National, there were 39% following the election in June 2017. In contrast to the Quota-policies in Germany where parties are free to decide whether they want to install a quota, it is the *state* in France, which requires the parties by law–facing threat of financial penalties–to secure a 50% quota of each sex on party lists and as MPs. These penalties are light, and some parties, including the Republicans and the FN, have simply paid the fine and continued to ignore the law. The FN has 25% women in parliament. In contrast the newly founded *La République en Marche* of Emmanuel Macron had 50% female candidates and now has 48% women MPs.

The Front National/Rassemblement National

Following its establishment in 1972 by its long serving leader Jean-Marie Le Pen, the FN has been the platform for national-conservatives and right wing extremists.

Xenophobic, anti-Semitic, nationalistic, and aggressive political statements and positions used to mark the public image of the FN. Since 2011 when Marine Le Pen, daughter of the founder and a lawyer by profession, took over the party leadership, the FN has sought to modernize itself. It has become more sophisticated and discarded a lot of ideological baggage. Marine Le Pen has introduced a strategy of "de-demonization" ("Dédémonisation") and "de-diabilisation" ("Dédiabolisation") in order to win new members and voters. Political scientist Nonna Mayer describes Marin Le Pen's manifesto as old cheese put into new packages (Mayer, 2012; see also Kuchenbecker, 2017). The FN under its new female leader is described as still racist and anti-immigrant. "Race" has been displaced by "culture" in their speeches. However, since 2011, the membership of the FN has gone up to 84,000 (from 31,000 in 2011) and the gender gap in voting has closed. In April 2017 at the Presidential Elections in France, Marine Le Pen reached the second round by winning 21.4% of the votes behind Emmanuel Macron with his new Party La République en Marche (LReM). In the final election on May 7, she lost against Macron but received 35% of the total and more than 10 million votes: a remarkable success in the eyes of her followers and the media.

Marine Le Pen's FN profits from a high unemployment rate in France, especially from young people (20-25%), as well as fear of terrorism and frustration of the political establishment among a wide range of the population. The principal political preoccupations of the FN are immigration, social security policies, EU and NATO, Islam, and policies to limit the refugee influx, topics which French women are also very concerned about. Predictably, Marine Le Pen takes advantage of the fact she is a woman, and she addressed particularly women in the presidential campaign, repeating throughout the campaign "I want to defend French women!"

Gender in the Front National/Rassemblement National Program

Family law and gender politics did not play a major part in the FN's political program until Marine Le Pen took over. Violence against women, sexual assaults and the defense of women's rights (against refugees) became major topics in speeches and public interviews. Her website declares: "Free women of France, who have been able to enjoy all their lives the great freedoms and rights which were fought for by their mothers and grandmothers, are now threatened by the migration crisis which brings the beginning of the end of women's rights!"

For the Presidential elections, she needed the support of female voters and particularly addressed them: Le Pen mixed measures against domestic violence with anti-immigration resentments and claimed that violence against women only exists because of the "migrant-crisis" and occurs mainly in multicultural societies.

Dietze (2016) introduces the concept of "Ethnosexism." She considers "'the sexually dangerous Muslim refugee' as a figure of defense against migration and analyses its function in feminist and liberal attitudes for narratives of western superiority" (p. #). The FN combines its traditionalist family policies with an Ethnification of social problems. Deviation from "normality" is in their view morally reprehensible. An essential distinction is made between native French people (Francais de Souches) and others: migrants. Family currently plays a central role in the platform and the speeches of the FN.

According to the FN's current platform, French families should be protected against decadence, egotism, and immigrants. Strong family policies are in the eyes of the FN conducive to national solidarity and serve French identity and values. In France, there is historically a heavy emphasis on national identity and patriotic values.

Emphasis on patriotism, national identity, and "the people" with demonizing rhetoric can win over women as well as men. This may underline the thesis that experience of injustice and inequality does not necessarily lead to solidarity with the weak and marginalized. Discrimination could be externalized to others, to weaker groups in society (Amesberger & Halbmayr, 2002, p. 428).

Eribon (2016) showed that a significant number of the former supporters of the French Communists Party hit by unemployment in the economic crisis in France have now moved over to the FN. The FN got 40% of the worker's vote, and nearly 30% of the unemployed voted for the FN.

The political platform of the FN rejects all unconventional forms of family life, such as same -sex -marriages (which were introduced by law in 2013), divorced persons or non-French couples with or without children or single mothers. The FN asks for a limitation on abortion cost refunds (for non-French persons) and questions the legitimacy of couples in same-sex-marriages having the right to adopt children.

Marine Le Pen called the Gender Pay gap scandalous in an interview, but added that fundamentalist Islam was a much bigger threat for women (Vahabzadeh, 2016).

The FN demands the prohibition of the headscarf in *all* public areas. A headscarf ban has been in force by law since 2004 in schools and universities for staff and students.

In all these issues, we see a divergence between the rhetoric and the lifestyles of the leading figures of the Le Pen family: Marine lives a non-traditional life as a twice-divorced woman with three children who lives with a partner, is a well educated lawyer, and is active in politics as a leading figure. She therefore serves as a role model for French women who are not attracted to the idea of returning to the traditional role of homemaker.

Her niece Marion Maréchal-Le Pen is a militant anti-feminist. She is in her mid-twenties and was a member of the Assemblée Nationale until 2017. She marched in and organized the 2013 demonstrations against abortion and the same-sex-marriage and adoption law ("Manif pour tous" against "Marriage pour tous"), which was implemented under Francois Hollande. She fights against Islam from the standpoint of a strong Catholic, whereas Marine Le Pen advocates laicité.

Marion Maréchal Le Pen did not run in 2017 for personal family reasons and accused Macron of being a "danger to civilization", because he favors a multi-cultural society. She believes that the "danger of Islamic terrorism is inherent in such a society" (Vahabzadeh, 2016). The niece is ambitious: she wants to succeed her aunt in power and is waiting in the political background for her moment.

Germany

In post-war Germany, right-wing parties had trouble getting enough votes to enter local parliaments and did not enter the federal Bundestag before 2017. Moreover, they always had a male profile. Female membership lay continuously below 20%, and the voters also projected the image of a male's party ("Männerpartei"). Voters for the extreme right-wing parties are generally young, male, with middle or low educational background, and irregular employment or low paid jobs (Neu & Pokorny, 2015).

The Alternative für Deutschland – AfD

The AfD was founded 2013, primarily as a party with neoliberal views on economic policy and a skeptical position on Europe. Today the membership is approximately 26,000. A nationalistic right wing of the party dominates today over the neoliberal wing. Political scientists and party analysts increasingly characterize the AfD as nationalistic, right-wing populistic, conservative, authoritarian, and xenophobic (Decker 2006, 2015, 2018). Cas Mudde sees the AfD as a "populist radical right party, because it combines the elements of nativist populism and authoritarianism (Mudde, 2017b).

Some of the party's leading figures like Björn Höcke, André Poggenburg and Beatrix von Storch have been portrayed by the press as having markedly anti-Muslim views.

At the last federal elections to the Bundestag in September 2017, 9% of female and 16% of male voters in Germany elected the AfD to Parliament. They are the third strongest party and send 94 MPs to Parliament. Only 10 (11%) of the AfD MPs are women.

Prominent Women and Gender Policies in the AfD

The most prominent figures are the ex-spokesperson Frauke Petry, the EU-MP and new MP of the Bundestag, Beatrix von Storch and the leader of the election campaign Alice Weidel, an economist and a lesbian who has two adopted children with her partner from Sri Lanka. Similar to Marine Le Pen, these women do not personify the traditional image of the virtuous homemaker and mother of the family. Petry received a PhD in Chemistry and founded a company; she is divorced, has five children of her own, and remarried Markus Pretzel, former AfD-chairperson in Rhein-Westphalia and EU- MP, who has also 4 children with a former wife. Alice Weidel, the co-leader of the AfD-parliamentary group received her PhD in economics and worked in finance. Nonetheless, the official language of the party proclaims an admiration of the traditional (heterosexual) family with three or more kids. Here again party platform and the real lives of leading women in the party contradict each other. Particularly Alice Weidel has been presented as the right-wing-populist party's moderate voice and face.

Putting the spotlight on homosexuality and modern forms of partnership serve as a "façade-modernity" ("Fassaden-Fortschrittlichkeit") (Dietze, 2018) to cover up the intention of re-traditionalizing gender roles and family styles.

At the party congress 2017, the topic of "family" was very prominently discussed.

The AfD warns of the self-destruction and the self-elimination of the German people (and the German family). In addition, it favors active policies to stimulate the birth rate with incentives such as a mortgage-reduction for large families. The AfD demands an end to financial support for abortion and argues against a reckless adulteration of German people („planlose Durchmischung des deutschen Volkes") (Siri & Lewandowski, 2015).

With the slogan "more children instead of mass immigration" ("Mehr Kinder statt Masseneinwanderung" (AfD, 2016, p. 41), the AfD draws attention to the sinking birth rate in Germany and simultaneously demands a halt to immigration. Among the party campaigns slogans before September's general elections were: "Islam has no place in Germany" and "Against the Islamization of Germany" (Guardian, 2018).

Frauke Petry, Beatrix von Storch and right-wing journalists like Birgit Kelle in particular are protagonists of very conservative, right-wing family and immigration policies, which they support with inflammatory populistic rhetoric.

Von Storch presents herself as an opponent of abortion and same-sex-marriage. She kept a low profile on these points during the election campaign of 2017 because of Alice Weidel's candidature and present relationship.

The AfD strongly campaigns against equal rights for women, against quotas in the economy and in politics, and against the EU-concept of Gender Mainstreaming. European laws in favor of equality and the term Gender or Gender Studies are targets of hostility and ridicule. Gender Mainstreaming is accused of denying gender identities and forging early sexualization of children.

Party slogans include: "Stop Gender-craziness! Simple truth: Men and women are different: Alternative for Germany!" "Gender-Wahn stoppen. Simple Wahrheit: Mann und Frau sind verschieden: Alternative für Deutschland" (AfD-Wahlplakat, 2017). Here one can see the simplification of complex political matters.

Summary: Populism against Feminism and Gender in France and Germany

In both countries women leaders at the top are symbols of a new and modern version of their populistic parties. Women's issues have been moved from backstage to the front line.

Right-wing populist movements and parties play in both countries on every area of discontent in the population: social and economic insecurity, mistrust of the governing establishment, EU-skepticism, the presence of foreigners, and the perceived threat to old-fashioned gender roles are addressed in similar ways in the FN and the AfD platforms. Their criticism of (funding) abortion and same-sex-marriage with adoption rights are also similar. However, in Germany the AfD is more open in their attacks on feminism, Gender Studies and Gender Mainstreaming policies.

> Gender Mainstreaming was one of the main battlefields in the struggle against 'gender ideology', right wing actors do not treat it predominantly as a technocratic policy tool for which it is repeatedly criticized by feminist theoreticians. Instead, they understand 'gender' as 'gender identity' of the trans/queer identity politics, and see Gender Mainstreaming as a conscious and conspiratory strategy for spreading this approach (Kovats, 2018, p. #).

The "framing effect" of right wing populistic attacks on gender, feminism, and the achievements of the women's movements, particularly the view of gender as an "ideological concept," is obvious and worrying because these positions have already entered other party's platforms, e.g., the CSU in Bavaria, and the Konrad-Adenauer- Foundation of the CDU, which has workshops with the title: "Gender–an instrument for re-education?" The special edition of the political science journal "femina politica" entitled "Attack on Democracy" exposes the manipulative activity of authoritarian populism. One of the ways it denigrates plurality and diversity in society is to use gender issues. Hark and Villa (2015) suggest the term Anti-Genderismus.

Right wing populism aims to undermine the rule of law and government by stirring up anti-establishment, anti-Islam, and anti-equality emotions, and by creating a backlash against cultural modernization. In France, in particular the FN has many objectives: Marine Le Pen focused on sexual harassment, domestic violence, and the achievements of the women's movement in her election campaign to defend (white) French women against the invasion of Muslims. Maybe there is some genuine concern for the safety of women. However, there are two other objectives: one is to win more support for her party (53% of French voters are women), and the second is to vilify Muslims. Le Pen presents herself as the "Anti-Merkel" and as the "voice of a free Europe."

In the German AfD, the anti-immigration and anti-Islam slogans are similar: On 17 February 2018, there was a "March of Women" in Berlin to the Chancellor's office organized by the AfD where the safety for women was linked to the end of Muslim immigration. In 2017 Frauke Petry asked Angela Merkel in an interview after the New Year's events in Cologne, whether Germany looks "multi-kulti" enough for her taste? In addition, B. von Storch twittered about "barbaric mass-raping, Muslim hordes" in January 2018 (Dietze, 2018).

What Role Do Leading Female Figures Play in Increasing the Appeal of Populist Parties?

The discrepancies between the old-fashioned role models and classic divisions of labor and the modern life styles of most leading women in both the Front National/Rassemblement National and AfD are campaign assets: they can attract a great range of any (female and male) supporters and voters. The modernity of these female protagonists is used to reject accusations of xenophobia, misogyny, or homophobia.

My thesis is that the female leaders have five strategic and presentational roles.

First, the female leaders provide role models, which women admire and want to emulate. Therefore, they have an *identification role* by performing the role of a super modern woman who is omnipotent – a working mother, politician, partner, lover, party leader and election-winner. She seems to combine easily fighting leadership contests, winning election campaigns, and conducting family business. How many women can say that?

Perhaps women are impressed by these self-confident party women who have fought successfully against men. Marine Le Pen succeeded her father and even forced him to leave his party after he did not give in to her criticism of his anti-Semitic statements. Frauke Petry won her battle against the co-founder of the AfD, Bernd Lucke, and forced him 2015 to leave his party. However, she quit the AfD herself after achieving very good results in the September 2017 federal elections where she won 37.4% of the first votes and got a direct mandate. After resigning, she immediately founded a new party "Die Blauen" where she hopes to build up a challenge to the right-wing extremists in the AfD.

Secondly, female leaders have a role as *reconcilers and mediators and* as *softeners* of hard aggressive politics. Ironically, the traditional images and stereotypes of women in politics might help them: Women seem to be less extreme in their political positions and are able to build bridges between those with xenophobic-nationalistic views and those with civil-conservative party-views. Women might also be combative and sharp in their tone, but simply by their presence they appear to soften radical positions. In spite of their sharp attacks on their political enemies, women's looks, outfits, and bodies sugar-coat their positions. Not by chance, they often smile and dress very conventionally: white blouses, classic suits, or dark blazers.

Thirdly, female leaders also have a *role of normalizing* the unthinkable. Through calculated rhetorical slips and denunciations of certain groups in political debates, they contribute to the acceptance of nationalistic, xenophobic, and sexist attitudes in society. They normalize taboos and use the fact of being a woman to turn taboos into accepted norms of behavior. Frauke Petry and Beatrix von Storch demanded the use of weapons at borders, possibly to shoot women and children in order to defend Germany's frontiers against immigrants. The AfD hoped that these demands would slowly leak into mainstream public opinion because even women were asking for them.

Fourthly, female leaders intentionally present themselves as victims; they play the *victim-role*. Often they paint the image of the misunderstood and prosecuted party. They accuse the media, politicians, and elites. In addition, the establishment is said to treat them with hostility. Both the FN and the AfD ask in their programs for changes in the media and cultural institutions. They accuse journalists and academics of painting a very negative image of the country, which they regard as unpatriotic and overly critical of national values and symbols. Only the national and the "suppressed culture" should be sponsored by public funds. Women especially can use their vulnerability as a women or having a female body. Female leaders are using the issue of violence against women and sexual assaults to ask for personal safety as women and protection against violence in partnerships, and in public spaces, especially against male immigrants.

Fifthly, female leaders use their *attractiveness* as an asset. The frequent presence of women in leading positions in the populist parties at press conferences, election meetings, and talk shows serves as "erotic capital." A woman in politics still represents the "other," the newcomer, the trespasser especially when she is young, pretty, and attractive. Her body is an eye-catcher among men at male-dominated gatherings. Media and journalists succumb to these clichéd images. They fall into the trap of the erotic capital set by the parties when they report on hairstyle, dress, style, taste, looks, or charm of the politicians (Meyer, 2009). Physical assets and appeal can, in fact, be strategically deployed in a male-dominated party to reinforce hegemonic masculinity, in politics and beyond (Connell, 1995).

Conclusion

We have to take the new right wing populist movements and parties seriously. They already have unsettled modern democracies and long established patterns of party behavior with their anti-establishment approach and their advocacy of cultural Apartheid – a policy of discrimination and anti-integration, which is based on fear, and mistrust of "the other." Gender, family politics, and equality between men and women feature very prominently in their programs and their public image. Leading female politicians in France and Germany help to give their populist parties a modern appearance in order to promote traditional, even reactionary values. They serve as role models for the electorate and detoxify and tone down policies aimed at re-establishing hierarchical gender roles and a chauvinistic and male dominated society. I have argued that right-wing populism constitutes an effort to return to social inequalities based on perceived natural differences.

After the Brexit-vote, Inglehart and Norris (2016) identified two major developments in western democracies as promoting factors for right wing populism in 32 countries. First, an *economic based explanation*: The resentment felt by the losers in globalization and by neoliberal policies. Those who have lost or fear to lose their jobs and social position are seen as the strongest supporters of the right-wing populistic agenda (Küpper, 2018; Zick & Küpper 2015; Zick, Küpper & Krause, 2016).

Secondly, a *cultural backlash explanation*, which describes the reaction of increasing, numbers of people to the rapid cultural changes that have taken place in Western societies. Those people–mostly male, not highly educated, and older, especially in the US–who oppose what they see as the erosion of Christian values in families, at schools, at universities, and in public. In their eyes, this erosion has been fostered by moralizing "elites," establishment and progressive intellectuals, and last not least by immigrants.

It is necessary to respond to these anxieties and fears by reducing the enormous wealth gaps, poverty, and disintegration by means of effective policies aimed at justice and equality. According to Habermas (2016), it is necessary to build up new confidence in constitutional institutions and in democratic procedures in politics. Radical reforms need to occur in France and Germany, and conflicts and crisis have to be addressed by clear opposition to a brutal neoliberal capitalism, which has opened the gap between rich and poor to an enormous degree.

But if we address what we might call the third factor, the anxieties about new role models for men and women and other cultural changes, we have to find an answer to the modern and attractive female face of two parties, which have much in common despite being in two different cultures and societies. Of course we have to consider different cultural, local, and historical backgrounds to these developments, but both the FN and the AfD use the clever device of having some educated and emancipated women visibly at the top of the party while promoting an anti-emancipation, nationalistic, and xenophobic agenda in their party platforms. A return to patriarchal family structures and anti-immigration policies clearly have consequences for the types of problems likely to be encountered by social workers. In addition, right-wing populist agendas could affect social work as a human rights profession.

One probable consequence of a revival of male supremacy both in politics and in family life would be an increase in psychological and physical pressures on women and children, especially girls in families, and on gender issues and equal opportunities in politics. This would increase the number of people in society in need of social support. This in turn would increase the competition for scarce resources, including the number of available social workers. Social support agencies would need to set new priorities, recruit experienced professionals, and seek increased financial resources to meet the new challenges. The taxpayer would have to meet the increased social costs of these retrograde policies. A major consequence of the rise of these two populist parties has been to force the mainstream parties in their respective countries to adopt a harder line on immigration and security and on welfare claimants. These tighter policies are also bound to have negative repercussions on social work.

References

Amesberger, H., & Halbmayr, B. (2002). Konsequenzen für die (Frauen)Politik-Gegenstrategien zum Rechtsextremismus. In H. Amesberger, & B. Halbmayr (

Eds.) Rechtsextreme Parteien – eine mögliche Heimat für Frauen? (pp. 423-431). Opladen: Leske und Budrich.
Chwala, S. (2015). Der Front National. Geschichte, Programm, Politik und Wähler. Köln: Papy Rosssa Verlag.
Connell, R. W. (1995). Masculinities. University of California Press.
Decker, F. (2006). Die populistische Herausforderung. Theoretische und ländervergleichende Perspektiven. In F. Decker, Frank (Ed.) Populismus. Gefahr für die Demokratie oder nützliches Korrektiv? (pp. 9-32). Wiesbaden: VS Verlag für Sozialwissenschaften.
Decker, F., Henningsen, B., & Jakobsen, K. (Hg.) (2015). Rechtspopulismus und Rechtsextremismus in Europa. Die Herausforderung der Zivilgesellschaft durch alte Ideologien und neue Medien. Baden-Baden: Nomos Verlagsgesellschaft.
Decker, F. (2018). Rechtspopulismus in Europa. Ein Überblick. In K. Möller, F. Neuscheler (Hg.) "Wer will die hier schon haben?" Ablehnungshaltungen und Diskriminierung in Deutschland. (pp. 131-143). Stuttgart: Kohlhammer.
Dietze, G. (2016). Das ‚Ereignis' Köln. In Femina Politica 25 (1), pp. 93–102.
Dietze, G. (2016). Ethnosexismus. Sex-Mob-Narrative um die Kölner Silvesternacht, Ethnosexismus. (Sex-Mob-Narratives around the New Year's Eve in Cologne). In movements, 2, p. 1.
Dietze, G. (2018). Rechtspopulismus und Geschlecht. Paradox und Leitmotiv. In Angriff auf die Demokratie. Themenschwerpunkt der Femina Politica. Zeitschrift für feministische Politik – Wissenschaft. Im Erscheinen.
Eribon, D. (2016a). Wie aus Linken Rechte werden. Teil I. Der vermeidbare Aufstieg des Front National. In Blätter für nationale und internationale Politik 8/2016, pp. 55-63.
Eribon, D. (2016b). Rückkehr nach Reims. Berlin: Edition Suhrkamp.
Graf, P., Schneider, S., & Wilde, G. (2017): Geschlechterverhältnisse und die Macht des Autoritären. In Geschlechterverhältnisse als Machtverhältnisse, Femina *Politica*. Zeitschrift für feministische Politikwissenschaft 26(1), pp. 70-88.
Habermas, J. (2016). Für eine demokratische Polarisierung. Wie man dem Rechtspopulismus den Boden entzieht. In Blätter für nationale und internationale Politik 11, pp. 35-42.
Hark, S., & Villa, P.-I. (2015) (Hg.). Anti-Genderismus. Sexualität und Geschlecht als Schauplätze aktueller politischer Auseinandersetzungen. Bielefeld: Transcript.
Inglehart, R., & Norris, P. (2016). Trump, Brexit, and the Rise of Populism: Economic Have-Nots and Cultural Backlash. Cambridge: Harvard Kennedy School.
Kemper, A. (2014). Keimzelle der Nation? Familien- und geschlechterpolitische Positionen der AfD – eine Expertise. Berlin. Friedrich-Ebert-Stiftung, Forum Politik und Gesellschaft.
Kovats, E. (2018). Conservative counter-Movements? Overcoming Culturalising Interpretations of Right-Wing Mobilizations against "Gender Ideology". In Angriff auf die Demokratie. Sonderheft der Zeitschrift Femina Politica, issue 1/2018. forthcoming.

Kuchenbecker, T., & Le Pen, M. Tochter des Teufels. Vom Aufstieg einer gefährlichen Frau und dem Rechtsruck in Europa. Herder: Freiburg.

Kürschner Volkshandbuch Deutscher Bundestag (2018). 19. Wahlperiode:2017-2021. NDV: Rheinbreitbach.

Mayer, N. (2015). The Closing of the Radical Right Gender Gap in France? In French Politics 13 (4), pp. 391-414.

Meyer, B. (2009). „Nachts, wenn der Generalsekretär weint" – Politikerinnen in der Presse, In Aus Politik und Zeitgeschichte, Beilage zur Wochenzeitung „Das Parlament", (50), pp. 9-16.

Meyer, B. (2002). Feminismus. In M. Greiffenhagen, S. Greiffenhagen (Hg.). Handwörterbuch zur politischen Kultur in Deutschland. Köln: Westdeutscher Verlag.

Mudde, C. (2007). Populist Radical Right Parties in Europe. Cambridge University Press.

Mudde, C. (ed.) (2017). The Populist Radical Right. A reader. Routledge.

Müller, J.-W. (2016). Was ist Populismus? Ein Essay. Suhrkamp:Frankfurt/M..

Neu, V., Pokorny, S. (2015). Ist „die Mitte" (rechts)-extremistisch? In Aus Politik und Zeitgeschichte. Beilage zur Wochenzeitung „Das Parlament". 40/2015. pp. 5f.

Sineau, M. (2012). Les paradoxes du gender gap al la francaise.

Sineau, M. (2012). Une partie de l'électorat feminin a cédé a la tentation lepéniste. in: Elle, 24.4.2012

Siri, J., & Lewandowsky, M. (2015). Alternative für Frauen? Rollen, Netzwerke, geschlechterpolitische Positionen in der Alternative für Deutschland (AfD). Eine Publikation der Heinrich-Böll-Stiftung. Internet: www.weiterdenken.de/de/2015/12/17/alternative-fuer-frauen (1.8.2016).

The Guardian (24.1.2018). Far right German politician converts to Islam.

Vahabzadeh, S. (2016). Abtreibung und anderes Teufelszeug. Auch in Europa rütteln Rechtspopulisten an Errungenschaften der Frauenbewegung. In: Süddeutsche Zeitung 12.11.2016, p. 2.

Wilde, G. (2018). The Authoritarian as Discourse and Practice – A Feminist-Poststructural Approach. In: G. Wilde, A. Zimmer, K. Obuch, & C. Panreck (Hg.): Civil Society and Gender Relations in Authoritarian and Hybryd Regimes. Leverkusen (i.E.)

Wilde, G., & Schneider, S. (2012). Autokratie, Demokratie und Geschlecht: Geschlechterverhältnisse in autoritären Regimen. Einleitung. In Falsche Sicherheiten. Geschlechterverhältnisse in autoritären Regimen. Themenschwerpunkt der Femina Politica. Zeitschrift für feministische Politik – Wissenschaft, 21 (1), pp. 9-16.

Wilde, G., & Meyer, B. (2018). Die Macht des Autoritären und die Gefährdungen für demokratische Geschlechterverhältnisse. Eine Einleitung. In Angriff auf die Demokratie. Themenschwerpunkt der Femina Politica. Zeitschrift für feministische Politik – Wissenschaft. forthcoming.

Zick, A., & Küpper, B. (2015). Wut, Verachtung, Abwertung. Rechtspopulismus in Deutschland. Ed. by Friedrich-Ebert-Stiftung von R.Melzer und D. Molthagen. Dietz: Bonn.

Zick, A., Küpper, B., & Krause D. (2016). Gespaltene Mitte - Feindselige Zustände: Rechtsextreme Einstellungen in Deutschland In Friedrich-Ebert-Stiftung. Dietz: Bonn, pp. 203-218.

Why Should Social Workers Be Concerned?

Social Work and Social Services in Polish Illiberal Democracy

Tomasz Kaźmierczak

Within two years, the governing right-wing populist Law and Justice party (PiS – Prawo i Sprawiedliwość) – in spite of social protests – changed Poland from a democratic state of law into a country that does not meet the basic legal and institutional standards of liberal democracy. This would not be possible without violating the Constitution several times. At the same time, the Law and Justice government has been – and still is – highly active in the area of social policy, which manifests in a series of welfare initiatives, including the flagship Family 500+ (Rodzina 500+) Programme (to be discussed in more detail later on). An opposition journalist referred to these governmental initiatives as a kind of mass anaesthesia, protecting the party against the loss of their high support. If it is indeed pure political engineering, it has proven very effective so far. However, it is undeniable that PiS seems to focus on social policy much more than previous governments that tended to marginalize it, paying more attention to macro-economic indices than indices describing the situation of particular types of households.

PiS needs social policy not only due to their current political tactics, but also in order to carry out their vision of social order: the welfare of conservative-national families, but without liberties such as democracy, and without law and (independent) justice. One could say that the vision of Law and Justice is quite real: liberal democracy has been dismantled, while the standard of living in Poland is higher than ever, as the Polish economy continues to flourish thanks to a good economic situation in Europe – wages keep rising, and unemployment has not been this low in years. In the upcoming years, this vision will probably prove futile. It is a paradox of history that the country ruled by Law and Justice – that manifests its anticommunism so strongly – should be in fact so similar to Poland from the times of real socialism, and PiS to the communist party itself.

In this paper, I would like to demonstrate how the policy of PiS's government up to date has influenced the conditions of social work and the operation of social services. I pay special attention to two matters: the consequences of this policy for different categories of stakeholders of social work/social services, and the legitimization of that work/services. The main part is preceded by an overview of the political background.

Transformation of Poland into an Illiberal Democracy

PiS won the parliamentary elections (October 2015), with the support of 37.5% of the voters. This put an end to the 8-year rule of the liberal-conservative Civic Platform (PO) and the Polish People's Party (PSL) coalition. Although it was not the best electoral result in the last 27 years (that is, since the times of transformation), it was the first time when one party got a sufficient number of seats to form a government on its own. It was due to the fact that many votes (17%) went to parties that did not pass the electoral threshold, which increased the pool of seats for the winning party. So if not the success of PiS itself, the scale of reward gained with this success was due to a coincidence; colloquially speaking, Law and Justice was lucky.

Almost immediately after coming to power, the government of Law and Justice started to implement not only their electoral promises, such as the huge social transfer programme informally called 500+, but also to introduce changes leading to the dismantling of liberal democratic institutions and the state of law, that is: changes in the country's political regime, which were not mentioned in the electoral campaign or in the party's programme. In order to introduce these changes, PiS decided to break democratic rules in two ways: first of all, by adopting unconstitutional solutions; and secondly, by abusing the democratic mandate achieved through electoral victory. The problem is that this success was achieved with low (as it usually happens in Poland) voter turnout (51%), so in reality only 18.6% of eligible voters voted for PiS. This gives sufficient mandate to rule within the existing democratic order, but under no circumstances does it authorize to change this order.

Virtually from the very beginning, the actions and governing style of PiS caused deep and highly emotional political conflict that still remains vivid in both the (still free) public sphere and the private sphere, dividing families and informal groups. At the same time, social scientists undertook the first attempts to conceptualise the processes they observe. According to one of the most eminent Polish political scientists, Radosław Markowski (2017a, 2017b), these processes can be considered a supply-side revolution: a revolution inspired and implemented top-down, resulting in the creation of a new form of democracy on the rubbles of liberal democracy, which is nowadays referred to as illiberal. Markowski identifies its Polish version as clientelistic authoritarianism, similar to the historical Estado Novo of Oliveiro Salazar in Portugal, or contemporary Hungary governed by Victor Orban. Characteristic symptoms of the ongoing revolution include: (1) a fundamental, all-encompassing discontinuation and negation of everything that was done by previous governments, even if it was something rational that made sense and worked well; (2) a far-reaching replacement of elites (high level staff in crucial institutions: public administration and state agencies, the army and the police, the public media, law enforcement and judiciary, as well as state-owned companies), carried out in favour of party members and with disregard for meritocratic criteria; (3) intense historical policy consisting in the reinterpretation of Poland's recent history and sometimes even writing it anew against facts; (4) introducing regulations that increase the power of the central government, while limiting the capacity of local authorities and civil liberties, and subjugating the judiciary to the executive branch.

Nationalist discourse played a paramount role in PiS's electoral campaign, and it still remains an important tool to justify their governing style and the directions of their actions. It consists of emphasising the unique quality of the Polish nation and its links with Catholicism, with the central figure of a Polish catholic. This patriotic and national narrative remains functional for PiS to ensure support of voters who perceive their national and Catholic identification as one of the main sources of identity and (self-)value; and it is also used to justify acts of violation of the state of law with the allegedly higher interest (good) of the nation, and the "will of the sovereign [of the people]".

The nationalist discourse goes hand in hand with a strong anti-immigrant (anti-refugee) narrative. Although the former has not been invented by Law and Justice – national-patriotic organisations promoting xenophobic and even fascist ideas have been gaining power for many years now – PiS has cleverly adopted this discourse, legitimizing it and raising its value to the level of the basic discourse; the latter has been intentionally created by them. The electoral campaign took place at the exact moment when huge waves of refugees from the Middle East and Africa started to reach Europe, and at the time of ISIS terrorist attacks. PiS cynically took advantage of these events, to create a massive feeling of threat (among other things, by convincing many Poles that refugee/immigrant = terrorist), while at the same time assuring these irrationally frightened people (and confirming this reassurance with governmental decisions) that, for the sake of safety, not a single refugee/immigrant will be let into Polish territory. As a result, in spite of many errors committed by PiS and the party's clumsiness, pushy propaganda and image-devastating blunders, their support remains at the "electoral" level; while the number of Poles who believe that Poland should not accept refugees increased 2.5 times between mid-2015 and late 2016 (May 2015: 21%; December 2016: 52%) (CBOS, 2017).

Social work, or – broadly speaking – social services, have never been as politically susceptible in Poland as it has been the case in the most developed welfare states. So, it is not surprising that – at least so far – the current government has also not introduced significant initiatives directly in this area. This doesn't mean, however, that the conditions of social work and the operation of social services have not been modified. The impact of PiS on social work can be identified and analysed in at least two aspects: (a) the consequences of new regulations for various categories of stakeholders of social work and social services; and (b) the problem of legitimization (of social work and services).

Consequences of New Regulations for Different Categories of Stakeholders of Social Work and Social Services

There is no doubt that Family 500+ (Rodzina 500+) is the flagship project of PiS. Introduced during the electoral campaign under the catchy slogan: "500 PLN[1] for every child in your family", it was supposed to attract people from beyond the party's hard electorate, and thus guarantee electoral victory; and, after implementation, to help the party stay in power for at least two terms. The first assumption has proven right; as to the second one, time will tell. In fact, the Family 500+ programme is a bit less generous, but it does broadly what was promised: it gives the right to receive tax-exempt 500 PLN monthly for each child in the family starting from the second one, regardless of family income, while in families who earn less than the specified income threshold, the benefit is also granted for the first or the only child.

The official objectives of Family 500+ are not entirely clear. The programme's legal basis: act on state aid for the raising of children, states that the 500 PLN should be spent to partially cover expenses related to the raising of children (until they reach 18 years of age), including care and subsistence. Governmental statements emphasise that the main objective of the programme is to raise the fertility rate, which is supposed to, at least a little, mitigate unfavourable demographic trends. However, considering our knowledge of the factors that influence fertility rates, the probability that the government's expectations will be fulfilled is rather low. Nonetheless, it is a fact that the Family 500+ programme contributes to the reduction of poverty, which is a quite logical consequence of pumping substantial amounts of money into households. However, the first statistical data available prove that this reduction is smaller than initially expected. The government expected that extreme poverty among children and adolescents would be almost totally eradicated. This did not happen. The scale of reduction differs depending on the number of kids in the family: the smallest improvement took place in one-child families (a reduction by 0.2%) and families with 4 and more children (22%), while the biggest improvement has been observed in families with 3 kids (a 48% drop), although

---

1   500 PLN equals ca. 120 EUR.

the improvement was due not only to the social transfers, but also to the best labour market situation in many years (GUS, 2017).

Along the Family 500+ programme, major changes were introduced to the pre-school and education system that had been built quite consistently for about 20 years. First of all, PiS reversed initiatives of the previous government that (1) had made school obligatory from the age of 6 (PiS reversed it to the age of 7); and (2) had introduced obligatory pre-school education (kindergarten) for 5-year olds. Secondly, Law and Justice enacted what they called a reform of the school system, modifying the one that was introduced in late 1990s. The 1990s reform had consisted in introducing a new type of schools: 3-year gymnasiums (gimnazjum) between the former primary and secondary school, while shortening the primary school from 8 to 6 grades, general secondary schools (liceum ogólnokształcące) from 4 to 3, and technical secondary schools (technika zawodowe) from 5 to 4 grades; at the same time extending compulsory education by one year (from 8 to 9), by adding the gymnasium as an obligatory school as well. Within this system, gymnasia operating in rural areas gained special importance – with additional investment they were supposed to mitigate the gap of educational opportunities between rural and urban areas. Results achieved in the recent years by Polish pupils in the PISA studies coordinated by OECD (Programme for International Student Assessment) prove that, carefully speaking, the system had reached a very decent efficiency level. Without any rational justification and against the opinions of experts, local authorities, parents and the largest professional teachers' association, PiS decided to modify this system to a very large extent. In reality, this means going back to the system before the transformation: gymnasia have been removed, the old primary school has been brought back with 8 years of compulsory education and additional optional general high school of 4 years, technical high school of 5 years and the reactivated vocational school that takes 3 years and prepares for professional work. Let us notice the undeniable result–unfortunately, so rarely mentioned in the public discourse–of PiS's education policy, policy that defines the life chances of children and adolescents: instead of 10 years of compulsory education (1 year in pre-school for 5-year olds + 9 years of school starting at 6 years of age), we now have 8 (starting at 7 years of age). What is the meaning and significance of these changes for social workers and social services? Will these modifications affect the challenges they will have to face in the short and long term?

As to the Family 500+ programme, we can already see that social transfers (financial aids) on their own are not enough to eradicate poverty; first of all, because it is not the main objective of the programme, so poverty eradication will not be a factor taken into account to correct the programme in the future; and secondly, because the phenomenon of poverty is much more complex than just lack of money. What is more, in some types of families, unconditional generous benefits cause negative side effects, such as weaker motivation to undertake own efforts to get out of poverty for good. Moreover, considering its enormous costs, we should expect that the programme's eligibility criteria will rather become restricted than expanded; while the lack of indexation mechanism in the programme will cause a gradual reduction of the actual value (purchasing power) of the benefits. Therefore, it is to be expected that Family 500+ will reduce the frequency of applications for material aid reviewed by social workers, although it also makes them play the ungrateful role of controllers in the cases when it is suspected that parents spend their children's allowances in a way that does not comply with the law.

The changes in the education system will have much more impact. Przemysław Czapliński – one of the most meticulous observers of the social and cultural changes happening in Poland – has described this very accurately. He points out that:

> shorter education starting one year later gives advantage to children from families with high cultural capital. (...) Education starting at the age of 6 and lasting for 9 years was favourable for children from households with lower cultural capital. It evened out opportunities and acted in an egalitarian way. The current reform acts against these families. Children from these families will have it very difficult to close the gap between the culture they receive at home and the competences needed to study. As a result, the lower class will become more and more numerous and will have less and less chances for social ascension, while children from the middle class will reproduce the economic status of their parents. This, in turn, can give rise to social anger (Czapliński, 2017, p. 8).

If we consider the Family 500+ programme in addition to that, it is hard to deny Czapliński's thesis that PiS's government "is populist and at the same time anti-people: it preaches egalitarianism, but at the same time its policy is more and more elitist; they preach progress, but create conditions that perpetuate the existing limitations for social mobility" (Czapliński, 2017, p. 8). There is no need to describe and additionally justify herein the manifold impact that such reinforcement of social inequality and petrification of poverty will have on the conditions of social work and social services.

The Family 500+ programme is already in operation, the school system reform was implemented on 1 September 2017, while on 28 October 2017, new legal regulations came into force, aimed at moulding the 3rd sector to the illiberal democracy state management structure, to provide the central authorities with greater control over NGOs.

The third sector in Poland is not as strong as in stable Western democracies – chances for its real development did not emerge until the early 1990s – but its importance is invaluable: it is often referred to as the best developed pillar of civil society, and it is a provider – in some cases the basic provider – of numerous social services. At least until now, the 3rd sector in Poland – in line with its *raison d'etre* and the scope of its capabilities – has tried to solve those problems and to satisfy those needs that, for a variety of reasons, were not successfully (or not at all) addressed by the public sector. The Polish third sector still seems to have a very valuable characteristic: the fact of not being ideological, in spite of the differences naturally occurring between the worldviews of different entities (people and organizations) operating within it. This situation is undoubtedly the result of legal regulations prepared at the beginning of the last decade, that pragmatically regulated the relations between public authorities and non-governmental organizations, as well as the principles of granting them public funds. These regulations included the Civic Initiative Fund (Fundusz Inicjatyw Obywatelskich, FIO) financed from the state budget and providing the largest source of funding for the 3rd sector; as well as the public benefit consulting and advisory councils at the local, regional and central level, formed by representatives of public authorities and NGOs. These regulations had been created through a long process of dialogue between both sectors, and thanks to that, at least at the formal level, they created a possibility to reconcile, in the spirit of cooperation, the managing role of the state with the bottom-up, civic character of non-governmental organizations, taking into account the freedom of their creation and operation.

The changes enacted by the current government have been prepared without any dialogue with NGOs. They consist, basically, in creating a central state agency with an extensive staff of officials that will decide on granting a fundamental part of the governmental funding (the current FIO) according to any criteria they choose to apply. Therefore, the government would like to gain control over the 3rd sector via the new institution, by redirecting the flow of funds to those organizations whose activities correspond to the policy of the government (that is, the party–PiS), and taking funds away from those who do not please the government (PiS) for any reason. The destructive effects of these rules for many individual NGOs, as well as for the entire sector in general, are obvious. In response, the NGO sector addressed the MPs, asking them to vote against this governmental proposal in its entirety, an effort which unfortunately proved futile.

On the basis of documented practices until mid-2017 (OFOP, 2017) it became clear which organizations have a high chance of receiving support from PiS's government, and which do not: the first group includes patriotic, national and catholic organizations (especially in a fundamentalist version), promoting the conservative family model; while the second group includes organizations helping refugees/immigrants, sexual and national minorities, and fighting for women's rights (among others, combating domestic violence).

Such weakening of the 3rd sector will limit the possibilities for development of social work and the operation of social services within it. It is a pity all the more, because – as empirical studies show – the institutional environment of this sector facilitates a professional provision of social services, while the public sector more often than not transforms social workers into clerks (Rymsza, 2011).

Problems with the Legitimization of Social Work and Social Services

Social work is a construct that combines three elements into an integral whole: knowledge, skills, and a very clearly defined set of values. However, social work is also a kind of public practice that is usually financed from public funds and, at least for that reason, is managed by public bodies and is subject to public control. Therefore, an obvious question we have to ask is the following: What happens to social work when the environment in which it is carried out – the public institutions that finance, manage and control it, but also so-called public opinion – are guided by values different than the ones inherent to social work itself? In other words, how does a weakened legitimization influence social work? Not so long ago I would treat such questions only as an interesting intellectual challenge; nowadays – when illiberal democracy is being implemented in Poland – they acquire a very real character. It is definitely too soon to try and answer them, even in a preliminary way. Herein, I would only like to point out (some of) the values shifting currently – in a more or less overt way – that are important for the degree of social work legitimization:

- until recently, social equality and social justice – understood, most of all, as equal chances – seemed to be an obvious factor that indicated the direction of social policy and the activities of public authorities; currently, a different approach prevails, consisting in deliberate structural favouritism for certain social categories, while handicapping others; which manifests very clearly in the changes introduced to the education system;
- the anti-immigrant and national-patriotic discourses, together with the figure of Pole-Catholic linking them, and the slogan: "Poland for Poles" (expressed loudly by extreme nationalist organizations, and silently accepted by PiS "circles"), accompanied by a critique of political correctness and usage of hate speech, have contributed to the appearance and escalation of incidents in public spaces (including acts of aggression) that discriminate against and exclude not only people who differ by their skin not being white or religion not being Catholic, but every kind of "other", such as LGBT communities or – which would be unthinkable until recently – the disabled. This permissiveness (the incidents are not condemned by representatives of the governing party, they are also not actively combated by the pertinent enforcement agencies) signals that in fact the belonging of vulnerable groups in the political community is being questioned;
- the civic becomes less important than the national; civil society implies equality, voluntary participation, embracing diversity – including disabilities; while the national discourse demands homogeneity and subjugation;
- there is a conservative turn in the approach to the family: in the traditional, catholic understanding, family is more important than its members – their

wellbeing, interests and needs – and is considered worthy of deciding their members' destiny and of receiving greater protection/care than individuals; the superiority of family over its members means that its influence may be in certain instances negative, which affects the weakest family members: women and children.

Undoubtedly, the above-mentioned shift in values must affect social workers and social services, redefining what "society expects from them". Therefore, it is to be expected that in order to adapt to these new demands, in practice, the deontological standards of social work will suffer a regression, and the intensity of ethical dilemmas in the conscience of social workers and other helping professions will increase.

Final Considerations

At this moment, it is impossible to predict how long Poland will remain an illiberal democracy. Perhaps, although it is by no means certain, PiS could lose power in the next elections, and the new government might bring back liberal democracy institutions and the rule of law. But what if PiS remains in power?

I have mentioned before that until now, social work/social services and their institutional and legal framework have not been a main focus of the government of Law and Justice. Declarations contained, among others, in the Strategy for Responsible Development – the programme document of the government – are different: they promise future reforms, but, interestingly, they are not revolutionary, but rather refer to ideas that have been known for many years, but for certain reasons have not been implemented so far. Therefore, clearly no intentional threats towards social work and social services are expressed by the PiS's government, at least not like we saw from real socialist ideology in the past. The obvious, existing threats that may affect the coherence and deontology of social practice are indirect, and result from the character of state under the rule of PiS. Perhaps, apart from threats, there are some new opportunities as well? In order to be intellectually just, one cannot omit such possibility. One way or the other, if nothing changes in the political sphere, the upcoming years will bring a lot of data and opportunity to identify, describe and explain specific sources and nature of such threats, together with their possible opportunities and impacts for social work and services. The hereby paper is an attempt to identify the first manifestations of such impact.

References

CBOS (2017), Stosunek Polaków do przyjmowania uchodźców [Attitude of Poles towards Accepting Immigrants]. Research Report No 1/2017. Retrieved from: www.cbos.pl/SPISKOM.POL/2017/K_001_17.PDF.

Czapliński, P. (2017, April, 22-23). Dryfujemy [Drifting], Gazeta Wyborcza.

GUS (2017) Zasięg ubóstwa ekonomicznego w Polsce w 2016 r. [Scope of Economic Poverty in Poland in 2016] Retrieved from: www.stat.gov.pl/obszary-tematyczne/warunki-zycia/ubostwo-pomoc-spoleczna/zasieg-ubostwa-ekonomicznego-w-polsce-w-2016-r-,14,4.html.

Markowski, R. (2017a). Transformation Experiences in Central and Eastern Europe. The Case of Poland in Comparative Perspective, Friedrich-Ebert-Stiftung, International Policy Analysis, Retrieved from: http://library.fes.de/pdf-files/id-moe/13169.pdf.

Markowski, R. (2017b). Supply Side Revolution? On the Development of a Clientelistic Authoritarianism in Poland, Report prepared for a workshop on "Authoritarian Backsliding? Erosion of Democracy in Unlikely Places", Duke University, April 21-22, 2017

OFOP (2017). Zestawienie udokumentowanych przypadków naruszenia zasad współpracy ministerstw z organizacjami pozarządowymi. [Collation of Documented Incidents of Breaching the Principles of Cooperation between Ministries and NGOs] Report 2/2017, www.repozytorium.ofop.eu/wp-content/uploads/2017/04/Raport_Repozytorium_2_2017.pdf (access: 10.07.2017)

Rymsza, M. (Ed.) (2011). Czy podejście aktywizujące ma szansę? Pracownicy socjalni i praca socjalni 20 lat po reformie systemu pomocy społecznej. [Does the Enabling Approach Stand a Chance? Social Workers and Social Work 20 years after the Reform of the Social Assistance System] Warsaw: Institute of Public Affairs.

Social Policy and Social Work under Pressure in Russia

Olga Borodkina

Over the past few years, Russia has often been at the center of major international discussions (Ukraine, Syria, and others). Definitely, international policy has an impact on the welfare of Russian citizens. Partly, Russian authorities are trying to hide internal social problems behind international problems. The arguments of Russian politicians, on both the left the right generally coincide with regards to social policy. Political discrepancies mainly concern issues of economic development and international activity, but with regard to social policy, most advocate populist slogans about social justice.

The problem is that social justice is a very broad concept, and many different definitions are held by those using this notion (Barry, 1998). Political actors present many varieties: sometimes justice means equality, sometimes law, and sometimes retribution. Social work is an institution for the implementation of social policy, and from this point of view social justice issues are also at the center of political discussion about social work. It is, therefore, important to look at the current status of both social policy and social work in Russia.

In this chapter, the general trends of the development of social policy, the weaknesses of the social support system in Russia, and the development of the non-state sector of social services will be discussed. The final part of the chapter will be devoted to the social situation of people with disabilities in Russia. This topic was chosen because disabled people are, on the one hand, one of the traditional – as well as one of the largest – target groups in social work and, on the another hand, one of the greatest examples of the application of new political approaches in Russian social work. In addition, the social situation of people with disabilities is an example of a key social problem in Russian society.

Russian Social Policy: Past and Present

Russian social policy in the period after the collapse of the Soviet Union has gone through several stages of reform, each characterized by internal contradictions. The paternalistic nature of Soviet social policy is, to a large extent, the dominant characteristic of the present stage of social policy. In addition, the result of the continuation of Soviet policy is that social policy does not fulfill the function of social protection, on the contrary, has increased social and economic disparities (Grigoryeva, 2010, p. 9). In the opinion of Russian sociologist Shkaratan (1998), Soviet social policy was directed to protect the interests of the ruling class, and not to harmonize interests of different social group. In this respect, as the Russian sociologist Grigoryeva (2010) points out, Russian social policy showed much greater continuity with the Soviet social policy than with the economic policy of the same period. The statistics indicate a significant stratification of Russian society by income level (see Table 1.), and in this sense social policy has not fulfilled the promise of social justice.

Table 1 Percentage of Population by Income (in Rubles)

	2012	2013	2014	2015	2016
7,000	12.6	9.8	8.1	6.2	6.0
7,001 - 9,000	7.9	6.8	6.1	5.1	5.0
9,000 -12,000	12.0	10.8	10.0	8.9	8.8
12,001 - 15,000,0	10.8	10.3	9.8	9.2	9.1
15,001 – 20,000	14.6	14.5	14.4	14.0	14.0
20,001- 25,000	10.7	11.2	11.4	11.6	11.6
25,001 – 30,000	7.8	8.4	8.8	9.2	9.2
30,001 – 35,000	5.6	6.3	6.7	7.2	7.3
35,001 – 40,000	4.1	4.7	5.1	5.6	5.7
40,001 - 50,000	5.4	6.3	7.0	7.9	7.9
50,001 - 60,000	8.5	3.8	4.2	4.9	5.0
60,001 - 70,000	0	7.1	2.7	3.1	3.2
Over 70,000	0	0	5.7	7.1	7.2

Source: Federal State Statistics

In accordance with the liberal model Russia adopted in the early 1990s, the importance of the state in social policy has been constantly decreasing. At the same time, this model assumed an increase in the importance of social policy institutions that could provide a more equitable distribution of benefits from the development of a market economy. The expectations of the population were connected with a strong state, but in the Western model, strong state means strong legal state. In the Russian case, social policy only nominally fulfills these functions, primarily because the principles of the rule of law are frequently violated. Adopted laws do not have binding force for all and are not implemented at all levels. As a result, insecurity, both social and economic, has become one of the most common characteristics of Russian life.

Some researchers of social policy believe that social protection should be only one and, sometimes, not the most important direction of social policy. In more balanced models, social protection can be secondary to education policy, employment policy, wages, etc. However, in the Russian situation, where significant parts of the population live in poverty (see Table 1.) and experience a very low quality of life (and this includes the working poor) the importance of social protection as a means to prevent various forms of exclusion is growing (Shkaratan, 2004; Grigoryeva, 2010). At the same time, the population itself has developed various strategies for survival, including through its own resources and mutual assistance.

In recent years, there has been a shift towards the liberalization of social policy. However, considering the negative social consequences of radical economic reforms in the 1990s, the government often covers up its neoliberal tendencies with traditional welfare rhetoric, and this inconsistency leads to rather low efficiency in the social support system and insufficient development of the non-state sector of social services. These issues will be the focus of the following parts of the chapter.

System of Social Support in Russia: Efficiency Issues

The issues of reforming the system of social support and social work in Russia are related to its insufficient effectiveness. Experts describe the existing system of social support for the population in Russia as complex, not transparent and badly managed: there are many programs, and they are administered by different departments that do not coordinate among themselves. It is extremely difficult to estimate the amount of expenditures for certain programs, however currently, according to experts, there are 800 forms of social support at the federal level and an average of 100 in each region. Moreover, 65% of the Russian population are covered by various measures of social support, which costs 3.2% of GDP. Often federal and regional benefits overlap, there is not a unitary register of recipients, and very rarely the regional authorities attempt to consolidate information about recipients from different databases (Nazarov & Posharatz, 2017).

Despite substantial funding and a high number of recipients, the impact of Russia's social support programs is not significant, and they have not led to a reduction in poverty in the country (see Table 2.).

One of the reasons for this situation, according to statistics, is that the main beneficiaries of social support are citizens who are not poor in terms of income. The current system of social support is not primarily aimed at helping citizens who are in need, but to provide benefits to citizens who have served the state in order to ensure the attractiveness of civil service or jobs with health risks.

Table 2 Rate of Total Population With Income Below International Poverty Level

Year	<$1.90 per day	<$3.90 per day	<$5 per day	<$10 per day	<Russian subsistence level
2010	0	0.5	1.2	8.6	12.5
2011	0	0.5	1.1	8.3	12.7
2012	0	0.4	1.0	7.7	10.7
2013	0	0.3	0.8	6.5	10.8
2014	0	0.3	0.8	6.7	11.2
2015	0	0.3	0.9	6.9	13.3
2016	0	0.4	1.0	7.7	13.4

Source: Federal State Statistics

At the federal level, 17% of the funds going to social payments are spent on social support to citizens receiving benefits due to their public status. At the regional level, payments for these special services constitute about 42% of all social payments. In sum one-fourth of the total budget of social payments is used for social support for special services (for example, for "veterans of labor," which is an honorary title in the Russian Federation given to people for long-term work: 20 years for women and 25 years for men). The Russian social support system consists of several main measures, which are presented in Figure 1.

To make the social support system more efficient, experts recommend that the system be reoriented to protect citizens from the main social risks that lead to a decrease in income level, as well as to target support to vulnerable groups in need.

These experts propose to exclude the allowances provided to citizens as a substitute for their "social package," as well as the allowances for special merits. At the federal level, this solution has been partially implemented since 2016, but at the regional level the situation remains the unchanged. Experts also recommend improving the effectiveness of the social support system by better exploiting its targeting potential. Only about 10% of the consolidated social support budget is currently spent on targeted measures (Nazarov, & Posharzt, 2017).

Figure 1 Social support measures in Russia

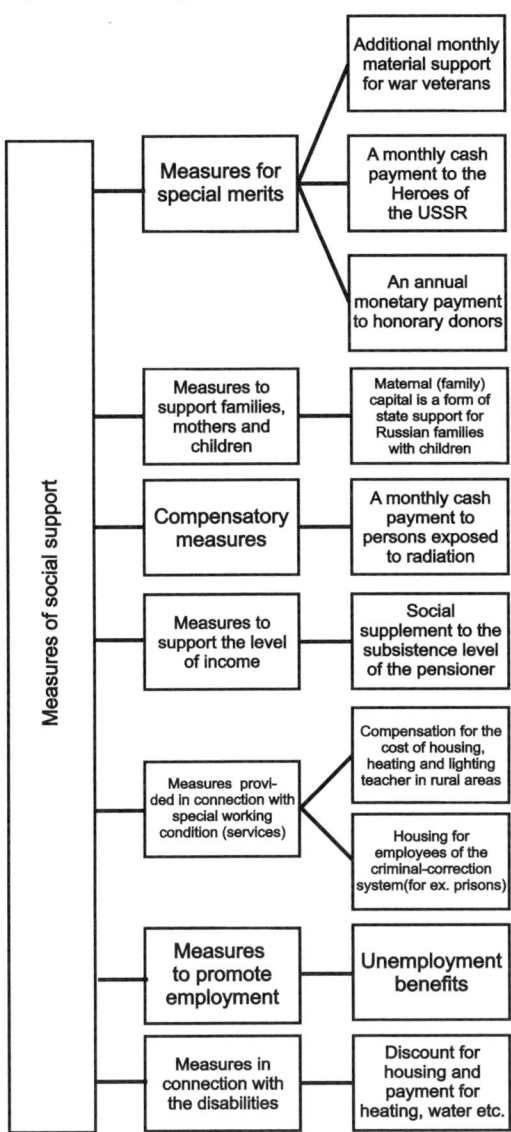

Source: System of social support (Nazarov & Posharatz 2017, p. 25)

It should be noted that not only experts but also the authorities are talking about the need to reform the social support system. President V.V. Putin in his March 2018 address to the Federal Assembly (Parliament) of the Russian Federation said the following: "We need to build the whole system of social assistance on the principles of justice and targeting, we talk a lot about it, but this must be done in the end. Citizens and families who really need it should receive it" (President of the Russian Federation's Address, 2018). This statement is a vivid example of populist rhetoric; justice is one of the Russian people's most popular values. It should be noted that Putin's speech took place before the March 18, 2018 presidential elections, and in recent months, measures aimed at achieving social justice have not been proposed.

At the same time, it is necessary to understand that such reforms would not be popular or supported by the population. To gain that support, these reforms must be accompanied by an increase in wages. At the present time, when there is a lot of working poor in Russia, deprivation of social bonuses is viewed as a social injustice. In this situation, the government prefers to engage in populism, while without any public discussion introducing measures that can affect the interests of millions of citizens.

The Russian social support system is controversial because it includes elements of neoliberalism and populism, which are both problematic approaches to social welfare. The populist agenda deals with the expectation of the majority of the population, and often the government will put off social policy reforms that are economically necessary but unpopular, or will conduct them in a hidden form without public discussion. A good example of this is retirement policy. In Russia, raising the retirement age has been discussed for many years, but the government has not yet been able to decide on this unpopular measure. Currently, men retire at age 60, women retire at age 55, and Russia is one of few countries where the retirement age remains so low. The experts argue that raising the retirement age is inevitable and the only way to provide pensions at a decent level. The government had not been able to decide on this unpopular measure before the March 2018 presidential elections, but after V.V. Putin was reelected as Russian President, a law was adopted in September 2018 on the gradual increase of the retirement age, despite the fact that public opinion was strongly against such measures. As a result, after a transition period, the retirement age will be increased by 5 years, and it will be respectively 65 for men and 60 years for women. At present, retirement is accompanied by a significant decline in ones standard of living. In 2017 the average pension of retirees registered in the Pension Fund of the Russian Federation was 17,425.60 RUB (about 240 EUR), and in 2018 it was 13,323.10 RUB (about 180 EUR) (Population: Older generation, 2017). The neoliberal agenda is focused primarily on the economically active part of the population and market driven-solutions and has not been accompanied by developing social support systems for all citizens. In other words, while trying to maintain political support, Russian authorities have not yet developed a coherent, economically-justified concept of social support.

NGOs in Russia as a Reflection of the Contradictions of Russian Social Policy

The development of the non-state (or non-governmental) sector of social work has long been practiced in the most countries. In Russia, this process is also taking place, and it reflects the main contradiction of Russia's social policy, namely, the attempt to liberalize social work under strong state control.

The right-liberal ideas related to the development of the non-state sector of social services received their legal basis with the adoption of the law "On the fundamentals of social services in the Russian Federation" (December 28, 2013), which replaced the two previous laws: "On social services for senior citizens and people with disabilities" (1995) and "On the fundamentals of social services in the Russian Federation" (1995). The new law guarantees non-governmental organizations equal rights with state and municipal organizations to compete over state contracts for the provision of social services. As part of the public contracts, socially-oriented NGOs are able to get state subsidies and grants.

Back in 2008, the Government of the Russian Federation approved the document "The Concept of long-term social and economic development of the Russian Federation for the period up to 2020," in which the development of non-governmental non-profit organizations in the sphere of social services was considered a top priority. The implementation of this policy included the following actions:

> transformation of the majority of state and municipal institutions of the social protection system that provide services to the elderly and disabled into non-profit organizations and creation of a mechanism for attracting them on a competitive basis to fulfill the state order for the provision of social services; ensuring equal conditions for taxation of providers of social services of various organizational and legal forms; reducing administrative barriers in the sphere of activity of non-governmental non-profit organizations; creation of a transparent and competitive system of state support for non-state non-profit organizations that provide social services to the population; implementation by government and local governments of programs to support the development of non-governmental non-profit organizations; reducing administrative barriers in the sphere of non-profit organizations; introducing tax preferences for non-state non-profit organizations (The Concept of long-term social and economic development of the Russian Federation for the period up to 2020...2008, p. 70).

Unfortunately, it is currently impossible to report on the successful achievement of these tasks. The contradictory attitude of the state towards NGOs led to the creation of additional barriers to the development of the non-state sector of social services. On the one hand, the state declares support for activities of socially-oriented NGOs, on the other hand, a number of laws and legal norms have been adopted that make the process of creating and developing NGOs very difficult. The procedures for registration, regular reporting, and liquidation of NGOs are handed over to the control of the Ministry of Justice and are quite complicated. The most controversial and discussed law in connection with NGOs for several years now remains the so-called "law on foreign agents." According Russian law:

> a non-profit organization performing the functions of a foreign agent is understood as a Russian non-profit organization that receives money and other property from foreign states, their state bodies, international and foreign organizations, foreign citizens, stateless persons or persons authorized by them and (or) from Russian legal entities... receiving money and other property from these sources (except for open joint-stock companies with state participation and their subsidiaries) (hereinafter referred to as foreign sources), and which participates, including in the interests of foreign sources, in political activities carried out on the territory of the Russian Federation (Federal Law 121-FL 2012).

In other words, NGOs that have in any form funding from abroad (in the form of grants, sponsors, etc.) and engage in political activities must be registered by the Ministry of Justice as foreign agents. Registration by itself does not mean the cessation of the activity of the organization, but it puts these organizations in a discriminated position (more reports, control, difficulties to obtain funding from the state, etc.). The most significant problem is that Russian authorities interpret "political activities" very widely, and not only human rights organizations, but also social service and research organizations having any foreign funding have become "foreign agents." Many previous social work organizations providing services to such groups as drug users, people living with HIV, homeless people, and migrants were forced to stop their activities. The "law on foreign agents" significantly slows down citizen initiatives to establish social agencies and creates obstacles to the introduction of the best social work practices.

As a result of existing legal practices, the process of developing the non-governmental sector of social work becomes increasingly bureaucratic. There are two explanatory trends. Firstly, in some Russian regions, municipal social organizations just changed their legal status and became autonomous non-governmental organizations fully controlled by the regional authorities. The second trend is connected with the establishment of non-governmental organizations affiliated with state authorities, which are aimed primarily at obtaining funding from the state, and the quality of social services is not the key concern.

Russian authorities, while declaring the development of socially-oriented non-governmental organizations, pursue policies that restrict citizens' initiatives in this sphere. This is primarily due to the intention of the authorities to control the financing of social services and to limit democratic trends that are manifested in the free development of the social sector.

Taking an integrative approach to disability policy in Russia

According to official data, on January 1, 2017, there were 12,314,000 people with disabilities registered in Russia, including 5,264,000 males and 7,050,000 females. The group breakdown was in the following proportions: 628,000 children and young people under age 18, and 3,651,000 people of working age (including 552,000 aged 18-30; 3,098,000 males aged 31-59 and women aged 31-54), and 8,035,000 people over working age (The situation of persons with disabilities, 2017). These figures show that persons with disabilities make up a significant part of the Russian population.

Contemporary Russian social policy focuses on the social integration of people with disabilities. Monitoring of the population's living conditions is conducted annually, and the research questions concern various areas, such as leisure, education, and employment. Integration is possible if certain conditions are met: firstly, an accessible environment is created; secondly, disabled people are quite active themselves; and thirdly, they have good social relationships. If these three conditions are satisfied, they provide a base for a good quality of life for disabled persons.

In the recent years, there have been many discussions in Russia about social integration and inclusion of people with disabilities. Most regions adopted special programs to establish accessible environments, which is a necessary condition for an active life. However, when looking at more recent data, one can discern that, unfortunately, the situation related to active life has not changed significantly and even worsened. According to the findings, in 2016 only 5.9% of disabled people over 15 years old were able to conduct an active lifestyle on par with others. Moreover, there was no significant difference between people with disabilities living in cities and those residing in the countryside: 5.7% living in urban areas were able to lead an active lifestyle, while for residents of rural areas the figure was 6.5%. Only 11.2% of people with disabilities of working age (55 years for women and 60 years for men) reported engaging in social activities; the figure was slightly higher for young people (respondents aged 15 to 29) at 16.6% (The situation of persons with disabilities, 2017).

The research also found a lack of social activities among people who are disabled. In 2016, only 6.5 % of persons with disabilities aged 15 years and older visited cinemas, 6.8 % visited theaters, 12.8% attended concerts, 6.2% attended art exhibitions, 11.9% went restaurants, cafés, or bars, and 4.6% attended a sport event as a spectator (The situation of persons with disabilities, 2017). These figures, indicating limited recreation activities for disabled persons, raise serious concerns.

These conclusions are supported by the results of a local study, which was conducted in St. Petersburg in 2011-2012 (Borodkina, 2012). St. Petersburg, the second largest city in Russia, certainly offers more opportunities for people who are disabled than smaller towns, but the data shows the situation is still not quite satisfactory. Because of insufficient accessibility of the environment, people who are disabled are not able to visit public places. Figure 2. shows the list of public places in St. Petersburg which, according to the respondents' responses, they either did not attend at all or attended no more than once a month.

Figure 2. Visiting of public places

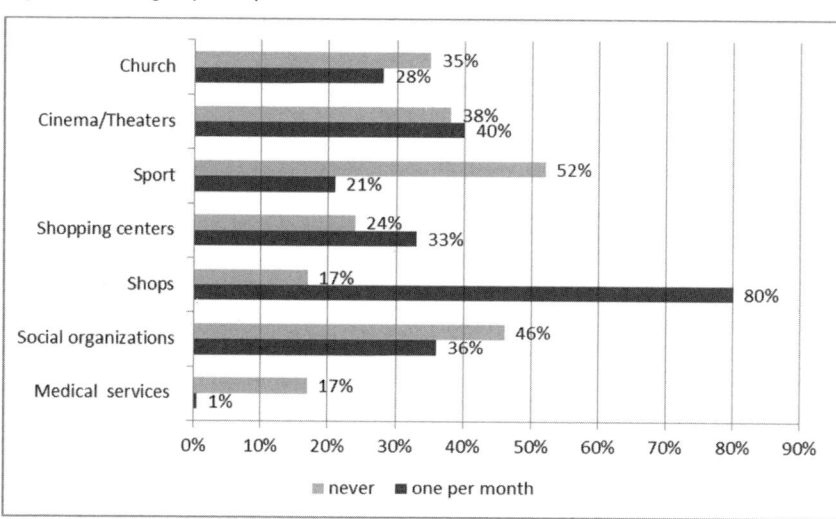

There is little room for doubt that this is largely due to the accessibility of the environment, but this factor is not the only one; the data shows that, for example, in St.Petersburg accessibility of many public places is quite high.

Figure 3 Accessibility of public places/organizations

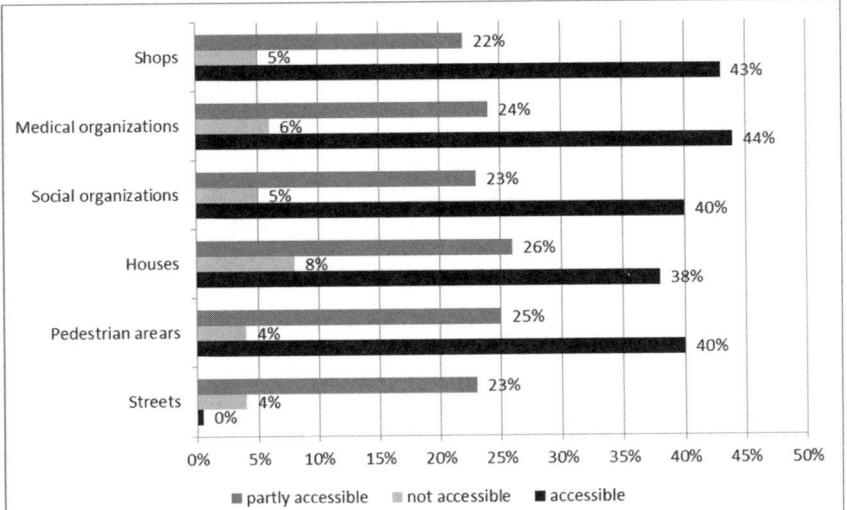

The analysis of research data suggests that the level of accessibility of public places is higher than the frequency at which disabled people visit them. The interviews revealed that many respondents demonstrated a passive attitude, a lack of willingness to be included in social activities, and a lack of motivation to lead an active social life (Borodkina, 2012, pp. 90-93). Thus, empowering disabled people as well as developing accessible environments remain important objectives of disability policy in Russia (Borodkina, Torronen. & Samoylova, 2013).

In contemporary society, Internet technology plays a special role in all spheres of human interaction, including education, employment, and everyday life. Access to the Internet is seen as a necessary part of modern life. It is particularly important for disabled people: for them the Internet is not only a means of communication, but also a key tool of integration and inclusion. The Internet creates a range of new opportunities for disabled people. However, according to a mass survey, in 2011 only 14.9% of disabled people were able to enjoy access to the Internet. This indicator was higher among those disabled people living in the cities (16.0%) in comparison with that of disabled people living in rural areas (11.8%) (The situation of persons with disabilities, 2017). At present, many social services for disabled people can be provided through the Internet. Limited access to the Internet for most of the individuals with disabilities represents, in Sen's terminology, capability deprivation.

An active life largely depends on the financial status of persons with disabilities. The material well-being of disabled people is an important dimension of capability because economic resources contribute to the creation of new opportunities. In Sen's framework, poverty and disability are linked very closely (Sen, 1999). Data from many countries confirm this thesis. According to a survey of the World Bank devoted to disability and poverty, disabled people are estimated to make up 15 to 20 per cent of the poor in developing countries (World Health Organization, 2011).

The results of the surveys demonstrated decreased incomes among the households with the disabled people. According to the data, in 2015 an average income per member of a household consisting only of disabled people was 23,590.6 RUB per month (346.76 EUR), and in 2016 the figure was 23,403 RUB per month (314.60 EUR taking into account growth rate) (The situation of persons with disabilities, 2017).

It is important to note the significant differences in the structure of income between disabled and able-bodied citizens in Russia. In 2016, social benefits made up an overwhelming portion of the income of persons with disabilities (87% of total income), of which pensions contribute 68.8% and benefits, compensation, and other social benefits provide 18.2%. Employment income constitutes 10.7% of the total income. This data shows there are limited opportunities to improve the financial situation for disabled people because the government regulates social benefits, indexation rarely takes place, and when it does, it is often being below the rate of inflation.

An important indicator of the well-being of persons with disabilities is living conditions (housing). According to the St. Petersburg study, a large portion of disabled people are not satisfied with their housing conditions, and 45.3% of respondents were living with their parents or other relatives. Many respondents stated that they could not live independently, not only because of the health conditions, but also due to economic reasons, meaning that they did not have enough financial resources for independent living. In addition, respondents estimated the possibilities of improving their living conditions as very low. The opportunities to improve ones living conditions and quality of life, in general, undeniably depend on income, which is determined by one's level of education.

Education is a key determinant of well-being. "Education forms people's existing capabilities into developed internal capabilities of many kinds" (Nussbaum, 2011, p. 132). As revealed in the 2011 study on living conditions, disabled people aged 15 and over had the following levels of education: 25.1% of the total number of respondents had secondary professional education, 23.9% achieved higher professional education, 18.3% finished secondary school, 17.5% had primary professional education, 9.6% did not go beyond primary school, 3.4% had no formal education, 1.5% had incomplete higher professional education, and only 0.9% had post-graduate professional education. The rather high percentage of people with secondary and higher vocational education is related to the fact that the sample included elderly people who acquired a disability after retirement. With regard to persons with disabilities of working age, their opportunities for secondary and higher vocational education are limited.

Over the past few years there have been positive shifts in public consciousness regarding people with disabilities. One important indicator is attitudes about inclusive school education. According to a telephone survey of residents of St. Petersburg conducted by the Centre of Sociological Internet-Research at St. Petersburg University, the majority of respondents (50.8%, n = 788) have a positive attitude toward the fact that children with disabilities are taught in the same school with their children, while 37.1% adhere to a neutral position on this issue, only 0.3% are against co-education, and 5.8% think that such children should study separately. Also, 57.9% of respondents believed that co-education of students in high schools, colleges, and universities may have a positive impact on both disabled and able-bodied students who, through this interaction, will develop more humane values. In contrast, 28% of respondents believe that the joint training will not have any effect, only 3.8% expressed an opinion that it will negatively affect the learning process, and 3.6% believed disabled student can be subjected to ridicule and even abused by other students (Borodkina, 2015, p. 105). Despite the increasing public support for co-education, there are still significant barriers. Most colleges and universities are not equipped with technical facilities for disabled student, distance learning programs are not sufficiently developed, and tutors are lacking.

Generally, the data demonstrate increasing tolerance of and support for people with disabilities in Russia. This is largely the result of the transition from the medical to the social model of disability, initiated under pressure from the disabled community and human rights organizations.

Major changes in disability policy became possible for several reasons. First, non-governmental organizations (NGOs) working on disability issues have a long tradition. In Soviet times, public activities were strictly regulated and controlled by the state. The situation changed significantly in the 1990s, when NGOs became the new social service providers as well as key actors in political movements. This was facilitated by new political freedoms, as well as financial and organizational support at the international level. When the ideology of independent living was introduced to Russia, NGOs received not only financial support, but also modern methods of social assistance for disabled people, including peer support, self-help, and natural networks. Since the 1990s, NGOs for disabled people have taken on various social roles: reducing social inequality; diversifying social services; mediating the interaction of individuals, social groups, private and public institutions; increasing opportunities for employment, mobility, and civic participation of disable people; and the development of political culture (Romanov, 2005). As a result, they have had an important influence on the government around disability issues. Authorities now support social programs which aim to integrate disabled people in social life and improve social services for disabled people, and, as a result, to enhance the quality of life of this group (e.g., special transport services, lifts, ramps, etc.).

The state and political structures supported the creation of an accessible environment, i.e., an environment that takes into account the special needs of disabled people. However, at the same time, there are significant barriers to disabled people exercising their rights to education, work, and leisure activities. Substantial improvements in the quality of life of disabled persons are possible only with comprehensive disability policy, grounded in a capabilities perspective. Under the capabilities approach, policy-makers should respect human dignity and freedoms and takes into consideration individual abilities of each person. Society should be committed to equal opportunities for disabled people in education, recruitment, employment, and leisure. In today's Russia, these aims have not been achieved, as they require social structural changes, including a new view of social work practice. The empowerment of social work is still a pressing issue in Russia (Borodkina, Toronnen, & Samoylova, 2013).

In Russia, in a relatively short period, disability policy was drastically reformed, and the medical model was nearly dispensed with. Thus, disability is understood more as a social and political issue rather than as a medical one; meaning that disability is not just a condition of a person, but also the result of his or her relations with the social environment. The social model is closely linked to political movements aimed at active participation of persons with disabilities in economic and political life, both at national and at international levels (Oliver, 1996; Campbell & Oliver, 1996). In Russian disability policy the positive changes have taken place were possible to the combination of efforts by the disabled community and state support. Under the pressure of civil society, the state adopted social programs aimed at creating an accessible environment and developing inclusive education, sports, and leisure activities. However, considerable efforts are still required in order to ensure that the rights of disabled people are fully respected and that they have an equal set of capacities.

Conclusion

Russian social policy is in the process of reforming, and this process is characterized by contradictions. The declared goal of making social assistance systems fair and targeted have not yet been realized, and only a few steps are being taken in this direction.

As the state tries to reduce social tension, in enacts many neoliberal reforms aimed at increasing the personal responsibility of citizens that are masked in a populist form. The reform of social work service delivery is connected with the transfer of some social services to NGOs working on a contract basis. However very contradictory laws concerning non-profit organizations have been adopted, which do not allow for the full development of the non-state sector. In addition, it is obvious that state control over civil society leads to a weakening of civil initiatives and does not allow the development of modern forms of social work that include active interaction with individuals, families, groups and society as a whole.

At the same time, it is necessary to note positive changes in social policy and social work. A vivid example is the transformation of disability policy due to the transition from the medical model to the social model of disability. This has led to improvements in the quality of life of disabled people during the last ten to fifteen years. The improvements are the result of special governmental programs, the activism of disabled people, and changes in public opinion in relation to disabled people. The next step is to provide greater choices and freedoms for individuals with disabilities.

References

Barry, B. (1989). Theories of justice: A treatise on social justice. Berkeley, CA: University of California Press.

Borodkina, O. (2012). Social Integration of Disabled People in Russia. In: GesellschaftlicherWandel - wohin?. Wien: Peter Lang Verlag, 81-96.

Borodkina, O. (2015). Problems and perspectives in the professional education of young people with disabilities in Russia. Journal of Sociology and Social Anthropology, 5 (82), 96-109 (In Russian).

Borodkina, O., Törrönen, M., & Samoylova V. (2013). Empowerment as a current trend of social work in Russia. In Empowering social work: Reseach & Practice. Kotka: KopijyvaOy, pp. 22-35.

Campbell, J., & Oliver, M. (1996). Disability politics: Understanding our past, changing our future. London: Routledge.

Concept of long-term social and economic development of the Russian Federation for the period up to 2020 (2008). Retrieved from http://www.consultant.ru/document/cons_doc_LAW_82134/28c7f9e359e8af09d7244d8033c66928fa27 e527/ (In Russian)

Grigoryeva, I. (2010). Russian social policy in recent years: between the path already traversed and the still uncertain future. Journal of Social Policy Studies, 5(1), 7-24 (In Russian).

Federal Law 442-FL "On the Fundamentals of Social Services for Citizens in the Russian Federation" (December 28, 2013). Retrieved from http://www.consultant.ru/document/cons_doc_LAW_156558/ (In Russian)

Federal Law 121-FL "On Amending Certain Legislative Acts of the Russian Federation Regarding Regulation of Activities of Non-Profit Organizations Performing Foreign Agent Functions" (July 20, 2012). Retrieved from http://base.garant.ru/70204242/#ixzz5BRaaHq58 (In Russia)

Nazarov, V., & Posharatz, A. (Eds.) (2017). Development of effective social support of population in Russia: address, need, universality. Moscow: Scientific Research Financial Institute, World Bank. (In Russian)

Nussbaum, M. (2011). Creating capabilities: The human development approach. Cambridge, MA: Harvard University Press.

Oliver, M. (1996). Understanding disability: From theory to practice. Hampshire: Palgrave Macmillan.

Population. Standard of living. Poverty level. Federal State Statistic Service (2017). Retrieved from http://www.gks.ru/wps/wcm/connect/rosstat_main/rosstat/ru/statistics/population/poverty/#

Population. Older Generation. Federal State Statistic Service (2017). Retrieved from http://www.gks.ru/wps/wcm/connect/rosstat_main/rosstat/ru/statistics/population/generation/

President of the Russian Federation Address to the Federal Assembly of the Russia Federation (2018). Retrieved from http://www.consultant.ru/document/cons_doc_LAW_291976/ (In Russian)

Romanov, P. (2005). The role of public organization of disabled people in the policy of independent life. Human, community, management, 3, 83-97 (in Russian).

Sen, A. (1999). Development asfFreedom. New York: Oxford University Press.

Shkaratan, O. (1998). Social policy in the context of the post-Soviet economy (federal and regional environment). World of Russia, 1-2, 5-30 (in Russian).

Shkaratan, O. (2004). Social stratification in modern Russia: The drama of a split society. World of Russia,1, 3-48 (in Russian).

The situation of persons with disabilities. (2017). Federal State Statistic Service. Retrieved from http://www.gks.ru/wps/wcm/connect/rosstat_main/rosstat/ru/statistics/population/disabilities/

World Health Organization (2011). World report on disability. Geneva: WHO.

Anti-feminist and Familyist Positions in Gender and Sexual Politics: Right-wing Populist Challenges for Social Work

Christiane Leidinger & Heike Radvan

Alongside migration as a central complex of thought, family, gender, and sexual politics provide pivotal, strategic domains within the extreme right wing and in right-wing populism. In contrast to this, the actual significance of gender-based subject matter within public and scientific discourse is belittled, barely mentioned, or not even mentioned at all (Vorländer et al., 2016). At the same time one can find instructive insights on the anti-feminism and anti-"genderism" of the New Right within recent collections of essays (e.g., Häusler, 2016; Grigat, 2017) and segments of monographs (e.g. Salzborn, 2017, pp. 177-182). To a certain extent this development is partly due to research by gender studies scholars as well as decades of critique by feminists and advocates of the androcentric nature of social science contributions on (extreme) right wing groups (e.g. Birsl, 1994; Antifaschistisches Frauennetzwerk, 2005; Amadeu Antonio Stiftung/Fachstelle, 2013; Kemper, 2014; Hark & Villa, 2015; Hechler & Stuve, 2015; Lehnert & Radvan, 2016; Sauer, 2017).

The (extreme) right wing has created a devalued image of feminism, and with this of feminists, who are presented as the ultimate image of an enemy. However, attacks on women's movements and accordingly on women's- and gender-equality policy are by no means new, but have been part of the behavioral repertoire of the extreme right for over a century. By 2006, "organized crusade like attacks" (Lang, 2017, p. 63) against gender and feminism began to surface in articles printed in conservative editorials. An article by Volker Zastrow published that year in the conservative German newspaper FAZ is an example of this. Zastrow (2006) polemicized against gender mainstreaming as a type of "political gender reassignment" (as cited in Lang, 2017, p. 62). These discourses do not acknowledge gender equity as a relevant goal for state and society. Political tools such as quota systems within professional life are vilified and depicted as favoritism toward women. Initially these particular voices belonged to a specific group of journalists, who were white, heterosexual members of the (upper) middle class. Nevertheless, the number and range of social positions of those who openly stir up hatred against feminist and women-centered political perspectives as well as the scope of what is utterable within public discourse, not only in regard to feminism and equality of women, has become perceptibly greater.

These developments and the consequent anti-feminist atmosphere in society as a whole have effects on social work (Staub-Bernasconi, 2007). A human rights profession in both practice and scholarship must adhere to the equality of all humans and be premised upon the restraint of any kind of discrimination (Staub-Bernasconi, 2016, 2019). Right-wing populists and the extreme right alike assume that humans have different values based on affiliation. Social Work must recognize these issues, scrutinize them, and intervene when necessary to ensure that all members of society are equally supported and that society is organized among (more) democratic lines.

To achieve these developments we look to the third (or political) mandate of social work. Besides laying down the scientific foundation for social work as a profession, it moreover comprises its ethical guidelines. In other words it contains the goal of adhering to human rights and social justice and the responsibility of the DBSH (German professional body of Social work) to take any type of discrimination seriously. According to a 2004 resolution of the International Federation of Social Workers (IFSW) and the International Schools of Social Work (IASSW), it is the "duty" of a professional to counteract discrimination (DBSH, 2014, p. 30). The DBSH states within its "professional ethical guidelines" that it is social worker's "duty" to "refrain from any type of discrimination and not to tolerate, but to prevent third parties from discriminating others" (DBSH, 2014, p. 33).

The text at hand explores the problems that right wing populism causes for social work. These issues do not only emerge within the various practical fields of social work, but also within universities and schools where future social workers are trained. Topics such as violence against women, reproductive rights, and sex education are of particular interest to us as they offer a broad intersection with social work as a profession. Our initial focus lies on the array of right-wing populist thought concerning the above named issues. The question of how far right-wing populist, extreme-right and ultra-conservative Christian-fundamentalist groups differ on subjects such as gender- family- and sexual politics remains unanswered due to the current state of research.

Right-wing Populist Organizations and Gender-Related Topics

A diverse number of groups are situated on the spectrum of right wing populist parties and initiatives (Notz, 2015; Schmincke, 2015; Siri, 2015) and have fluent boundaries with the extreme right wing. These include the parliamentary party of the AfD (Alternative for Germany), a German right wing populist party with thematic and personnel intersections with the extreme right founded in 2013, along with various affiliated groups (Kemper, 2014; Kemper, 2016); the party of evangelical Christians; coalitions such as Pegida (Patriotic Europeans against the Islamisation of the West/Occident); a German nationalist, anti- Islam, far-right political movement with varying local spin-offs; supporters of men's rights, masculists (Claus, 2014); so called pro-lifers; alignments such as "Besorgte Eltern," an alliance of parents opposing sexually diverse sex education in schools (Billmann, 2015); "Demo für Alle," a group of protestors who are close to "Besorgte Eltern" content-wise and specifically against legalized same sex marriage; "Initiative Familienschutz," a right-wing populist initiative against the legal equation of gay rights aligned with evangelical parishes; representatives of conversion therapy (Wolf, 2013); and conservative ecologists, just to name a few.

Right wing populists take on pivotal gender-related topics such as sexual education at school (an approach to sex education which conveys its diversity), women's reproductive rights, reproductive medicine including so called embryo protection (Kemper, 2014; Jentsch, 2016), motherhood as an occupation (Sauer, 2017) and vocation, demotion of same sex domestic partnerships, especially regarding the legalization of same-sex marriage (Kemper, 2014a), rights of fathers, divorce law, single parents, (AfD, 2017), ethnicization of (sexualized) violence against women, gender mainstreaming, (quota, gender pay gap, anti- discrimination), gender studies, and gender neutral language. We would like to point out that we do not make a claim of completeness within our enumeration, e.g., intersections such as racism and ableism have not been taken into account. Furthermore, the order of the topics is not of significance.

Familyism as an Analytical Tool

We suggest making use of familyism as an analytical tool to uncover right wing populist statements on topics like gender and intersectionality (Appelt, 1997; Leitner, 2013; Notz, 2015). The concept is inherently useful as it unveils the extent to which familyist mindsets and conduct are compatible with the so-called center of the political spectrum of society. For this reason they are perceived as not so problematic or anti-democratic. The potential of certain right wing populist topics to connect with right-wing and extreme right-wing audiences has been emphasized within research literature to date for good reason (e.g., Siri, 2016). Taking into account the above named findings and the current state of research on right wing females and social work, this paper explains the problems of right wing populism's compatibility with, and deliberate use by, the center of the political spectrum of society.

The sociological term "familyism" essentially refers to an ideology promoting the bourgeois nuclear family as the ideal form of household within a social structure (Notz, 2015, p. 17). Familyism is not restricted to extreme right-wing agents. Instead, it has developed over time and was even inscribed in the German constitution of 1949, which "incorporate[ed] the notion of marriage and family as the principle building stone of society [..] solidifying a conservative family ideology" (Notz, 2015, p.10). White (here: German-white) heterosexual families are given a pivotal position as "an instance which secures the existence of the individual as well supporting as society as a whole" (Notz, 2015, p. 17). The system in which these families operate forms the local community, which in turn is framed by the nation state and its coherent citizenship and ultimately benefits white, heterosexual men both on an individual and communal level. (Appelt, 1997; Leitner, 2013; Notz, 2015).

"In actual fact familyist systems exclude all persons who are not part of a family (e.g. singles, people living in care institutions or asylums, in communes or other self-paced networks)" (Notz, 2015 p. 17). Within this framework of thought people without a family do not exist. One assumes that "sooner or later these individuals will establish a family or find their way back to it" (Notz, 2015, p. 17). Even though the prevalent way of life is not formed any longer by heteronormative, monogamous nuclear families with married parents, the image of a complete intact family remains familyism's guiding principle (Notz, 2015). Deviances from this principle are mainly bemoaned in reference to childlessness (Notz, 2015, p. 197).

Familyism is closely connected to evaluations and appeals regarding demographic policies. Accordingly, people who decide not to have children are believed to be "conscientious demographic objectors" (Püttmann, 2012, as cited in Notz, 2015, p. 202). Familyism's compatibility with extreme right wing audiences who invoke catastrophic demographic and political developments is manifested herein (Siri, 2016). Within right wing familyist diction, the demand for reproduction is solely directed at German-white (Caucasian), middle class families. It is therefore in alignment with nationalist demographic policies and charged with classist notions (Kemper, 2016; Notz, 2015). This is illustrated within a headline of AfD's manifesto from 2016: "More children rather than mass migration" and the following statement: "Every fifth woman today remains childless, furthermore in the year of 2012 every third female university graduate remained childless" (AfD, 2016, p. 41).

Thus, the term familyism includes key dimensions of gender-based and (partly intersectional) racialized aspects, which are represented within right-wing populist and extreme right-wing views. Accordingly, single parents or similar constellations with children or affiliated persons who must be cared for or require assistance represent ways of life which deviate from heteronormative families and are excluded. They are consequently not supported, or even negated and openly rejected as a form of family. These constellations are depicted as minorities and depending on the degree of liberalism tolerated, respected or discriminated against.

This naturalized idea of a family is based on heterosexuality and is accompanied by a sexist-hierarchical concept of binary and diametrically opposed gender (roles) regarding men and women. Gender hierarchy within the division of family chores and gainful employment is a capitalistic-economic expression of this notion. (Leitner, 2013; Notz, 2015). This imbalance is particularly noticeable within reproductive labor: unpaid and privately afforded care work – in other words domestic, parenting, and child rearing work – are mostly carried out by women. In the case of middle-, or upper-class families these services are often purchased from migrants who in most cases are underpaid and not well secured (financially and socially, as well as contractually) (e.g. Notz, 2015, p. 183). Within research, this is referred to as "global care chains" (Hochschild 2000).

In 2016, the AfD referred to single parents as allegedly incomplete families. Within a draft of their manifesto, they proposed to cut financial support for single parents. Instead, they proposed to re-introduce a type of principle of liability following a divorce (AfD, 2016a, Ch. 5). According to the German juridical term "Schuldprinzip," the prerequisite for a divorce was that one of the parties was liable, or responsible for the failure of the marriage. Until this principle was abandoned in 1977, the spouse who had acted in an extramarital manner was at fault, and the "culprit" was left with a juridical-materialistic disadvantage. Within their 2017 national election program, the AfD referred to the family law reform of 1977 (Annulment of the liability principle in the case of divorce) in the following manner: "A jurisdiction of this kind is not suited to encourage conjugal solidarity and impairs the stability of existing marriages" (AfD, 2017, p. 38). This comment on the 1977 juridical reform suggests that the AfD desires a comeback of the liability principle. In any case, they are aiming for the stabilization and preservation of marital union regardless whether both partners wish to be in a relationship or not.

When it comes to one-parent-families, the AfD postulates that single parents do not represent the "ideal case," but that one must differentiate between those who choose this way of life on their own accord and those who are in this situation through no fault of their own. It is suggested that state support should be granted accordingly: "To choose the life of a single parent is a private matter, however the community is made liable for the resulting indigence." (AfD, 2017, p. 38). In addition the AfD gives credit to care work performed in families, accordingly "the welfare system should offer better support for relatives of people in need of care" as this type of "family occupation" is equivalent to a professional career and should be acknowledged as such (AfD, 2017, p. 39).

History shows that familyism has not remained unopposed: Notz (2015) points to (early) socialist, anarchist, Marxist, neo- ethical, and various feminist critiques of familyism (pp. 56-70, 108-147). The potential overlap between the so-called center of the political spectrum of society and the extreme right is what we currently categorize as especially critical. This overlap can be found in the following familyist concepts: (1) the naturalized heterosexual idea of family, (2) a rigid binary understanding of gender/sex, (3) sexist gender images, (4) the attribution of reproductive work to women, (5) racist notions on nation, and (6) the problematisation of low birth rates (Notz, 2015, pp. 168-174). Familyism may offer a key reason for European right-wing populists' and extreme right-wing organizations' and parties' focus on gender. According to Birgit Sauer (2017) "gender relations can offer a key to understanding current strategy" (p. 4). They not only reveal "the anti-pluralist, anti-liberal and anti-democratic project called right wing populism" (p. 4) but render it editable, being "an intensification of the gender inequality and sexism within capitalistic society and liberal democracies which has existed all along" (p. 4). Against this backdrop it is understandable that right wing organizations and parties have begun to attend to minor and marginalized areas of politics (Sauer, 2017, p. 3) and have declared feminism as the enemy. Additionally, gender plays a major role in mobilizing right wing populists (Sauer, 2017). The orientation towards "feminism" and "gender studies" seems understandable within this context. According to their alignment, these groups stand for emancipatory change in familyist societies: gender politics, in any case, is depicted as "something that opposes the unity of family" within right wing politics (Siri, 2016, p. 74). Henceforth, we have chosen three quintessential social work topics, which are being monopolized by right wing populists.

The Basic Structure of Reasoning: Externalization

As we will display within the following segments of our work, the three thematic areas we have chosen to focus on – violence against women, women's reproductive rights, and sex education – feature overlaps with familyism. Conjointly, both argumentations display a similar structure: The (extreme) right wing resorts to the strategy of externalization. This is, amongst other things, related to the functional aspect of familyist arguments. Using case examples taken from field work we will demonstrate that a human rights orientated social work is near impossible to realize if the above mentioned strategy remains undetected and, therefore, not questioned, but simply acquired.

Externalization I: Violence Against Women

The debates ensuing the (sexually motivated) attacks on women on New Year's Eve 2015-2016, not only in Cologne, were marked by racialized assertions. Particularly Muslim migrants and refugees were generally accused of having a backward, sexist image of women and of being homophobic and violent (Madjlessi-Roudi, 2016). Such an instrumentalisation of women's rights is often accompanied by the idea of one's own country's progressiveness, setting it in stark contrast to other – mostly Muslim – societies and thereby devaluing them. This is what is coined "femonationalism" within critical, political, and scientific discussions (Farris, 2011). Farris (2011) developed this expression in conformity with the term "homonationalism,"coined by Puar (2017), describing the instrumentalisation of gays and lesbians by rights wingers. Spivak (1998) and Ahmed (1992) in particular mapped out the function-generated argumentation for colonialism: "white men are saving brown women from brown men" (Spivak, 1988, p. 297).

This instrumentalisation of women's rights and hierarchical construction of differences involved in this process is highly adaptable for use by the so-called center of the political spectrum of society and its predominant debates. This adaptability is displayed, for example, when Heinz Buschkowsky (former SPD borough mayor of Berlin- Neukölln) claims on a public radio station that "people with a migrant background have a totally different image of women than what is common to us" (Leidinger, 2016).

Such statements, while though not new (e.g. Jäger, 2000), became more frequent after Cologne. They classify as racialized othering and constitute a familyist construct: the white German society is claimed to be woman-friendly and is elevated in a femo-nationalist manner. Accordingly, violence against women which takes place in white-German families belonging to the majority of society – which represents a common social space – is not addressed. Violence against women seems non-existent in these families according to femo-nationalist reasoning, which deems sexism merely as an issue related to the "others."

The line of argumentation making use of externalization of violence against (white German) women can be found in statements of AfD politicians (Lang,

2017, p. 71) and within racially-motivated protests on the streets: In the autumn of 2015, 700 people attended a demonstration themed "70 young men are just too many" against the accommodation of refugees in a small locality in Saxony. One can find slogans such as "Wake up for our children," "families," and "homeland" on placards brought to the demonstration, an associative chain which, in the light of the mantra of the demonstration, ostracizes and "others" the refugees while implying that children must be protected from these 70 young men (AAS/Fachstelle, 2016, p. 2). Thus, it is apparent that racism and externalization are highly compatible with the nucleus of German society.

The exploitation of sexual abuse of children or sexual violence in general is another topic that is used to externalize violence against women within extreme right-wing discourses. Neo-Nazis have demonstrably used this subject since 1997, but increasingly since the 2001 "Nationalists against child molesters" initiative. The perpetrators are always the "others," the "foreigners," or to be more precise foreign young men. The victims on the other hand are portrayed as white young girls.

In the beginning, especially within the debate surrounding sexual perpetrators, this was directed at men who did not belong to the victim's direct social or respectively local sphere, so in other words were labeled as outsiders. In the course of the controversy surrounding refugees this process of labeling has referred to "foreign" perpetrators. In any case it concerns perpetrators who are alien to the artificially constructed "Volksgemeinschaft" (AAS, 2016; Junge Freiheit, 2014, p. 9). The modifications of the (extreme) right's strategic instrumentalisation of this subject matter is illustrated in other respects regarding "normalization," infiltration, and compatibility:

> Thus over time the titles of their campaign sites differ, evolving from titles such as 'death penalty for child molesters' to 'no mercy for child molesters' to 'Germany against child molesters'. Especially the new sites seem harmless upon first glance (…). The fact that Neo-Nazis are the key players on these sites can only be recognized by closer examination" (AAS n.d., p. 19-22).

This is where the externalization of perpetration and its associated "ethnicisation of sexism" manifest themselves (AAS, 2016, p. 6).

An editorial published within an issue of the "magazine of the German society of philologists" in 2015 in Sachsen-Anhalt poses a further example for the compatibility of such positions with civil society. It states: "young, strong, mostly Muslim men come, among them many who do not always have honest intentions." These "mostly uneducated men" have a desire for sexuality" and "[e]manating from talks with acquaintances in many different places," one hears of occurrences of "sexual harassment in daily life, especially in public transport and supermarkets" (Deutscher Philologenverband, 2015, as cited in AAS 2016, p. 2). On the one hand the "theory of drives," specifically the idea of a "boiler" surfaces here, which has been discarded and criticized both by science and feminist groups for quite some time (e.g. Schweikert, 2000, p. 76). On the other hand this displays the racist-occidental tradition of a stereotype depicting a sexualized image of the black man. This tradition has played an important role within German colonial history, demonizing black soldiers as brute savages (e.g. Wigger, 2007,196f., p. 202) and thus evoking the "myth of a black rapist" (Davis,1982, pp.165-191).

A Glance into Social Work

Public awareness for the existence, forms, and scale of domestic violence against girls and women in Germany is a pivotal achievement of the women's and lesbian movements, which have fought for this awareness since the 1970s. The field of work dealing with anti-violence, e.g., support for victims of abuse, is a relatively new area within social work and is equally an outcome of the feminist movement: women's shelters, women's hotlines, and institutions offering counseling were only founded within the last four decades. Today this field of work is part of the infrastructure forming social work. Its objective is to protect girls, women, and lesbians from discrimination, to support them to stand up for their right to a life without violence, and ultimately to engage in public advocacy regarding violence against women (by men) to achieve this goal. Overcoming taboos at the time, the women's rights movement elucidated the scale to which these crimes rather took place within families (by partners and close relatives) and to a lesser extent by "strange/foreign perpetrators" from the exterior. The problematized strategy of externalization of violence against women can also be found within the professional sphere of practice in social work. The following case study illuminates this.

A white-German mother who has an Arabic/German family background consults a counseling center due to the fact that her child has problems in school: the child is behaving aggressively toward his fellow students. The mother is separated from the child's father, with whom she shares custody. Alternating weekly, the child lives with his mother and the father and his new partner. In the course of the consultation, the counselor accuses the father of physically abusing his new partner in the presence of the child based on ethnicized ascription. In the counselor's opinion, this is what has led to the child's problems in school. Other reasons such as the experience of discrimination and racism in school are not considered. Consequently, the mother breaks off the consultation. This example constitutes a normalized, racist image of violent Muslim men, superimposing violent behavior, while by way of contrast, potential violence within white-German families disappears from view.

Externalisation II and III: Sexual Politics – Sexual Education and Autonomy

The strategy of externalization shows itself within two areas of sexual policies: the right-wing populist struggle against the autonomy of women and its attack on sexual education, and particularly against a sexual education which encompasses the diversity of sexuality.

The goal of these approaches is to establish a way of dealing with sexuality and different ways of life that is preferably anxiety-free and to reframe sex education within an extra-curricular setting. The prevention of violence and facilitation of empowerment are key elements in this context. In opposition to this, right-wing populists have constructed the myth of "premature sexualisation" of children and youths through sex education (e.g. AfD, 2017, p. 40). By using "an argumentative reference to children and even more so to child's welfare" children are symbolically super elevated while referring to their "innocence and dependence" (Schmincke, 2015, p. 93). Schmincke (2015) reveals the familyist agenda thusly:

> children embody the core definition of a conjugal relationship between binary sexes which form a community based on procreation and lineage. Hence, children are instrumentalised by those who wish to justify heterosexual exclusivity and fend off, as well discredit sexual diversity (p.100).

Sexual education in schools that renders homosexual ways of life visible is defamed as "premature sexualisation," from which the need to protect families and children is derived.

In their 2017 electoral program, the AfD stated:

> the AfD opposes any attempt to rid the established, traditional image of a family through state funded reeducation programs in schools and elementary schools. Our children may not be used as a pawn in the hands of a loud minority group. The ideological experiment of premature sexualisation must be ended immediately (AfD, 2017, p. 40).

The semantics of a "re-education/ sexualisation of *our* children" makes use of a figure of speech which clearly stresses the immediate danger to local families and communities (Siri, 2015, p. 251; Schmincke, 2015, p. 100). Upon first glance this focus on the local community being threatened may seem contradictory to the strategy of externalization, but after closer examination one can see that it too presents a construction of a threat to "the family" which stems from the outside. Hereby the threat is not merely embodied through violence, but rather in form of sexuality, especially homosexuality and sex education (Schmincke, 2015, p. 99). The right-wing-coined and discrediting term "homo lobby" is often used in connection to this form of externalization, providing an equivalent to the term "gender lobby" (e.g. Stein, 2014).

The connectivity of this standpoint to so-called "premature sexualisation" is demonstrated within the following example: an interview given by Professor Karla Etschenberg within the right wing weekly magazine "Junge Freiheit" in 2014. Etschenberg was the vice president of the German association of social scientific sexual research at the time and currently still holds this post. Within the interview she stated the following:

> sex educational initiatives rather interpret the acceptance of sexual diversity as a necessity to confront children with the diversity of sexual practices for them to have an open relationship towards sexual diversity. And this is where I say: this is sexualisation! (…) now, all at once, gender ideology is appearing which is questioning the principle of biological binary sexuality and aiming to fundamentally modify society, gender relations and sexual behavior….re-education is more likely a policy used by totalitarian states (Etschenberg, 2014, p. 3).

A Glance into Social Work

As a result of right wing populist assumptions on premature sexualization, experts conducting sex education in schools based on the premise of sexual diversity are being confronted with accusations and attacks on their work and the materials they use (such as methods and manuals). Accordingly, these educational opportunities are offered less frequently. As a result, sexual education; the prevention of violence, teen pregnancy, and of sexually transmitted diseases such as HIV; and anti-discrimination work promoting sexual and gender diversity is rendered impossible. The AfD grounds its attack on (sexual diversity by denying the existence of anti-gay and lesbian sentiment, with statements such as: "Nowadays there is no considerable discrimination against homosexuals anymore" (AfD, 2016, as cited in Lang, 2017, p. 65).

The fight against reproductive rights of women and consequentially against women's autonomy in general represents another scope of (extreme) right wing sexual policies. The relationship between Christian fundamentalist forces and Protestant, Evangelical and Catholic positions, has yet to be systematically researched (for an exception, see Billmann, 2015, on the resistance against the education scheme in Baden Wuerttemberg in 2015). Nonetheless, scientific articles list various examples of personnel overlaps, including the example of Beatrix von Storch, an incumbent member of the AfD within the European parliament, who attended the "march for life" in 2013 and 2014, an amalgamation of radical opponents of abortion (Notz, 2015, p. 208). "The protection of unborn life" is constituted within the AfD's 2017 national electoral manifesto

(AfD, 2017, p. 39). This entails the idea of compulsory consultation for women who wish to have an abortion and stresses the necessity to tighten the law (§219StGB)to guarantee the protection of unborn life.

> "Counseling on pregnancy options must de facto serve the protection of life (...) where necessary statutory corrections must be undertaken to ensure an effective protection of life." The fundamental right of sexual self-determination for women is questioned in AfD rhetoric: "We reject any aspiration which interprets and pronounces the killing of unborn life as a human right" (AfD, 2017, p. 39).

The right-wing populist reaction to women's reproductive rights is racist and familyist. Accordingly, the electoral program of the AfD in 2017 postulates the need to "incorporate the increase of births within the domestic population (...) and the preservation of the constitutive people (...) as a national objective within the German constitution" (AfD, 2017, p. 37). The hard-earned right of self-determination of women, which was fought for by generations of feminists, is here depicted as an externalized threat for German-white families and the nation.

In rural areas, especially those predominantly characterized by the catholic and evangelical church (hence presumably first and foremost within western Germany) it is difficult to find supportive advice that enables a reasoned and unbiased decision as well as doctors in close proximity who will conduct the actual procedure (Bruhn, 2017). By normalizing the protection of life and simultaneously pitting it against women's right to self-determination, the pressure is rising on facilities which offer counseling in these areas representing a vital part of the infrastructure of social work, as well as on involuntarily pregnant women (and possibly their partners).

Conclusion

When analyzing the dangers of right-wing populism, one should endeavor to do this from a gender reflecting perspective. This is especially relevant when in reference to social work. Otherwise, an integral component of (extreme) right lines of argument is overlooked. Familyism is the analytical instrument we propose to use for this matter as it lends itself to making all gender related topics visible and examinable. Right wing populism must be recognized as a hazard particularly for democratic culture, and for social work as a human rights profession, because it challenges the notion of the equality of all humans. Even if this is not as blatantly recognizable as within the decidedly extreme-right scene, it is crucial for social workers to perceive the linguistic constructs which introduce this inequality and intervene on an elementary level. This applies for clients as well as colleagues (Radvan & Leidinger, 2017). A common development and discussion of democratic mission statements for institutions within the field of social work and early childhood education can hereby be of help (Radvan, Leidinger, 2017).

As we demonstrated within the article, a structure of reasoning in the line of externalization is what forms the base of the right wing populist's method of reinterpreting topics such as violence against women, sex education, and a women's right to self- determination both in content and language. By constructing a threat from the outside, externalization serves as a tool to enhance one group while denouncing the other. In this sense sexism, and with this violence against women, is solely an issue concerning "other" societies, as is discrimination of LGBTQ people. Strategies of externalization–and this forms our fundamental argument–must be recognized, particularly in the case of gender related topics. Once recognized, we can avoid adhering to them and can intervene directly. This is of particular importance in the light of hazardous familyist statements by political leaders and their specific ability to relate to the center of the political spectrum of society. If antifeminism is not realized as a threat to democracy, we face fundamental issues and a degradation of professional standards. The (extreme) strategy of externalization is, above all, highly attractive due its nature of appreciating the white-German middleclass majority of society.

Against this backdrop, it is vital to undergo critical analysis of these strategies within the training, methods, and practices of social work. The latter must hereby realize that feminism does not involve the idea of an enemy, but moreover offers an emancipatory impulse and serves as a generator of ideas. Critical feminist alignments embody theories and praxis, which boast potential to further develop the understanding of social work as a profession and critically expand its areas of action. For this purpose social workers can be trained to be more sensitive to perceiving strategies of inequality, which can empower them to intervene and support victims of discrimination. By doing this they ultimately ensure the progression of society and democracy.

References

AfD (2016). *AfD*-Grundsatzprogramm. Retrieved from https://www.alternative-fuer.de/wp-content/uploads/sites/7/2016/05/2016-06-27_afd-grundsatzprogramm_web-version.pdf

AfD (2016a). Freie Bürger sein, keine Untertanen. Das Parteiprogramm der Alternative für Deutschland (Entwurf Grundsatzprogramm). Retrieved from https://

www.correctiv.org/media/public/a6/8e/a68ed5e4-32a8-4184-8ade-5c19c37ff524/2016_02_23-grundsatzprogrammentwurf.pdf

AfD (2017). AfD-Bundestagswahlprogramm. Retrieved from: https://www.afd.de/wp-content/uploads/sites/111/2017/06/2017-06-01_AfD-Bundestagswahlprogramm_Onlinefassung.pdf

Ahmed, L. (1992). Women and gender in Islam. Historical roots of a modern debate. New Haven/London: Yale University Press.

Amadeu Antonio Stiftung/Fachstelle Gender und Rechtsextremismus (2013). Instrumentalisierung des Themas sexueller Missbrauch durch Neonazis. Analysen und Handlungsempfehlungen. Berlin: Selbstverlag.

Amadeu Antonio Stiftung (AAS)/Fachstelle Gender und Rechtsextremismus (2016). Das Bild des "übergriffigen Fremden". Warum ist es ein Mythos? Wenn mit Lügen über sexualisierte Gewalt Hass geschürt wird. Berlin: Selbstverlag.

Amadeu Antonio Stiftung & Radvan, H. (Ed.). (2013). Gender und Rechtsextremismusprävention. Berlin: Metropol.

Antifaschistisches Frauennetzwerk, Forschungsnetzwerk Frauen und Rechtsextremismus (2005). Braune Schwestern? Feministische Analysen zu Frauen in der extremen Rechten. Münster: Unrast.

Appelt, E. (1997). Familismus. Eine verdeckte Struktur im Gesellschaftsvertrag. In E. Kreisky & B. Sauer, B. (Ed.), Das geheime Glossar der Politikwissenschaft. Frankfurt: Campus, pp. 114–136.

Billmann, L. (Ed.). (2015). Unheilige Allianz. Das Geflecht von christlichen Fundamentalisten und politischen Rechten am Beispiel des Widerstands gegen den Bildungsplan in Baden-Würtemberg. Berlin: Rosa-Luxemburg-Stiftung. Retrieved from https://www.rosalux.de/fileadmin/rls_uploads/pdfs/Materialien/Materialien8_Unheilige_Allianz.pdf.

Birsl, U. (1994). Rechtsextremismus: weiblich – männlich? Eine Fallstudie zu geschlechtsspezifischen Lebensverläufen, Handlungsspielräumen und Orientierungsweisen. Opladen: Leske+Budrich.

Bruhn, E. (2017, March 6). Die ungewollte Patientin. taz. Retrieved from https://www.taz.de/!5386152/.

Claus, R. (2014). Maskulismus. Antifeminismus zwischen vermeintlicher Salonfähigkeit und unverhohlenem Frauenhass. Berlin: Friedrich-Ebert-Stiftung. Retrieved from https://www.library.fes.de/pdf-files/dialog/10861.pdf

Davis, A. (1982). Rassismus und Sexismus. Schwarze Frauen und Klassenkampf in den USA. Berlin: Elefanten Press.

DBSH (2014). Forum sozial. Die berufliche soziale Arbeit 4, "Berufsethik des DBSH. Ethik und Werte", Berlin: Selbstverlag.

Farris, S. R. (2011). Die politische Ökonomie des Femonationalismus. Feministische Studien 2, pp. 321–334.

Grigat, S. (Ed.). (2017). AfD & FPÖ. Antisemitismus, völkischer Nationalismus und Geschlechterbilder. Baden-Baden: Nomos.

Hark, S., & Villa, P. (Ed.). (2015). Anti-Genderismus. Sexualität und Geschlecht als Schauplätze aktueller politischer Auseinandersetzungen. Bielefeld: transcript.

Häusler, A. (Ed). (2016). Die Alternative für Deutschland. Programmatik, Entwicklung und politische Verortung. Wiesbaden: VS.
Hochschild, Arlie Russell (2000). Global Care Chains and Emotional Surplus Value. In Tony Giddens and Will Hutton (Ed.), On the Edge: Globalization and the New Millennium (130-146). London: Sage Publishers.
Jäger, M. (2000): Fatale Effekte. Die Kritik am Patriarchat im Einwanderungsdiskurs. Münster: Unrast.
Jentsch, U. (2016). Die "Lebensschutz"-Bewegung und die AfD. Nur ein Teil der Bewegung ergreift Partei. In: A. Häusler (Ed.) (2016): Die Alternative für Deutschland. Programmatik, Entwicklung und politische Verortung. Wiesbaden: VS, pp. 99–106.
Junge Freiheit (2014). Junge Freiheit. Wochenzeitung für Debatte, 47.
Kemper, A. (2014b). Keimzelle der Nation? Teil 2. Wie sich in Europa Parteien und Bewegungen für konservative Familienwerte, gegen Toleranz und Vielfalt und gegen eine progressive Geschlechterpolitik radikalisieren. Berlin: Friedrich-Ebert-Stiftung Retrieved from https://www.library.fes.de/pdf-files/dialog/11163.pdf.
Kemper, A. (2014a). Keimzelle der Nation? Familien- und geschlechterpolitische Positionen der AfD – eine Expertise. Friedrich Ebert Stiftung, retrieved from www.library.fes.de/pdf-files/dialog/10641.pdf
Kemper, A. (2016). Antiemanzipatorische Netzwerke und die Geschlechter- und Familienpolitik der Alternative für Deutschland. In: A. Häusler (Ed.), Die Alternative für Deutschland. Programmatik, Entwicklung und politische Verortung. Wiesbaden: VS, pp. 81–97.
Lang, J. (2017). Feindbild Feminismus. Familien- und Geschlechterpolitik in der AfD. In: S. Grigat (Ed.), AfD & FPÖ. Antisemitismus, völkischer Nationalismus und Geschlechterbilder. Baden-Baden: Nomos, pp. 61–78.
Lang, J. (2015). Familie und Vaterland in der Krise. Der extrem rechte Diskurs um Gender. In: Hark, S., & Villa, P.-I. (Ed.), Anti-Genderismus. Sexualität und Geschlecht als Schauplätze aktueller politischer Auseinandersetzungen. Bielefeld: transcript, pp. 167–181.
Lehnert, E., & Radvan, H. (2016). Rechtsextreme Frauen-Analysen und Handlungsempfehlungen für Soziale Arbeit und Pädagogik. Opladen/Berlin/Toronto: Barbara Budrich.
Leidinger, C. (2016, May 9). "Die Nacht den Frauen". Wider den Gedächtnisverlust in der Post-Köln-Debatte. Retrieved from Online: StreitWert-Blog des Gunda-Werner-Instituts: Neue Männer, altes Feindbild. Feminismus in der Einwanderungsgesellschaft. Retrieved from https://www.streit-wert.boellblog.org/2016/05/09/die-nacht-den-frauen-wider-den-gedaechtnisverlust-in-der-post-koeln-debatte/.
Leidinger, C., & Radvan, H. (2018). Antifeminismus und Familismus von rechts. In: A. Häusler, Alexander (Ed.), Völkischer Populismus. Der Rechtsruck in Deutschland und die AfD. Eine Flugschrift. Hamburg: VSA (im Erscheinen).

Leitner, S. (2013). Varianten von Familialismus. Eine historisch vergleichende Analyse der Kinderbetreuungs- und Altenpflegepolitiken in kontinentaleuropäischen Wohlfahrtsstaaten. Berlin: Duncker & Humblot.

Madjlessi-Roudi, S. (2016). Unsäglicher Rassismus. Wie die Köln-Debatte den politischen Diskurs im Land verändert hat. In: F. Burschel (Ed.), Durchmarsch von rechts. Völkischer Aufbruch: Rassismus, Rechtspopulismus, rechter Terror. Rosa-Luxemburg-Stiftung, Manuskripte 17. Berlin: Selbstverlag, pp. 107–118.

Notz, G. (2015). Kritik des Familismus. Theorie und soziale Realität eines ideologischen Gemäldes. Stuttgart: Schmetterling.

Puar, J. K. (2007). Terrorist Assemblages. Homonationalism in Queer Times. Durham: Duke University Press.

Radvan, H. (2013). Geschlechterreflektierende Rechtsextremismusprävention. Eine Leerstelle in Theorie und Praxis. In: Amadeu Antonio Stiftung & H. Radvan (Ed.), Gender und Rechtsextremismusprävention. Berlin: Metropol, pp. 9–36.

Radvan, H., & Lehnert, E. (2015). Rechtsextremismus als Herausforderung für frühkindliche Pädagogik. In: A. Hechler, O. Stuve (Ed.), Geschlechterreflektierte Pädagogik gegen Rechts. Opladen, Berlin und Toronto: Barbara Budrich, pp. 177–192.

Radvan, H., & Leidinger, C. (2017). Demokratische Leitbilder als Prävention in der Sozialen Arbeit. Diskriminierende, antidemokratische und rechtsextreme Positionen als Herausforderung in Kindertagesstätten. Demokratie gegen Menschenfeindlichkeit 2/2017, pp. 73-86.

Salzborn, S. (2017). Angriff der Antidemokraten. Die völkische Rebellion der Neuen Rechten. Weinheim/Basel: Beltz Juventa.

Sauer, B. (2017). Gesellschaftstheoretische Überlegungen zum europäischen Rechtspopulismus. Zum Erklärungspotential der Kategorie Geschlecht. PVS 1, pp. 1–20.

Schmincke, I. (2015). Das Kind als Chiffre politischer Auseinandersetzungen am Beispiel neuer konservativer Protestbewegungen in Frankreich und Deutschland. In: S. Hark, P. I. Villa, P.-I. (Ed.), Anti-Genderismus. Sexualität und Geschlecht als Schauplätze aktueller politischer Auseinandersetzungen. Bielefeld: transcript, pp. 93–107.

Schweikert, B. (2000). Gewalt ist kein Schicksal. Ausgangsbedingungen, Praxis und Möglichkeiten einer rechtlichen Intervention bei häuslicher Gewalt gegen Frauen unter besonderer Berücksichtigung von polizei- und zivilrechtlichen Befugnissen. Baden-Baden: Nomos.

Siri, J. (2016). Geschlechterpolitische Positionen der Partei Alternative für Deutschland. In: A. Häusler (Ed.), Die Alternative für Deutschland. Programmatik, Entwicklung und politische Verortung. Wiesbaden: VS, pp. 69–80.

Siri, J. (2015). Paradoxien konservativen Protests. Das Beispiel der Bewegungen gegen Gleichstellung in der BRD. In S. Hark, P. I. Villa (Ed.), Anti-Genderismus. Sexualität und Geschlecht als Schauplätze aktueller politischer Auseinandersetzungen. Bielefeld: transcript, pp. 239–255.

Spivak, G. C. (1988). "Can the subaltern speak?" In C. Nelson, & L. Grossberg (Ed.), Marxism and the interpretation of culture. Urbana/Chicago: University of Illinois Press, pp. 271–313.

Staub-Bernasconi, S. (2019). Soziale Arbeit und Menschenrechte: Vom beruflichen Doppelmandat zum professionellen Tripelmandat. Leverkusen und Toronto: Barbara Budrich.

Staub-Bernasconi, S. (2016). Legalität und Legitimität in der Sozialen Arbeit : Menschenrechte im Verhältnis zur nationalen Gesetzgebung. Leverkusen und Toronto: Barbara Budrich.

Staub-Bernasconi, S. (2007): Vom beruflichen Doppel- zum professionellen Tripelmandat: Wissenschaft und Menschenrechte als Begründungsbasis der Profession Soziale Arbeit. Sozialarbeit in Österreich H. 2, pp. 8–17.

Vorländer, H. et al. (2016). PEGIDA. Entwicklung, Zusammensetzung und Deutung einer Empörungsbewegung. Wiesbaden: VS.

Wigger, I. (2007). Die „Schwarze Schmach am Rhein". Rassistische Diskriminierung zwischen Geschlecht, Klasse, Nation und Rasse. Münster: Westfälisches Dampfboot.

Wolf, G. (2013). Konversionsbehandlungen. Stand November 2013. Retrieved from https://www.vlsp.de/files/pdf/konversionsbehandlungen_0.pdf.

Right-wing Populism in Germany: Challenges for Social Work

Kurt Möller

Is right-wing populism a subject in social work and, if so, how should it be dealt with? The following contribution addresses these two linked questions by, first of all, explaining briefly what is generally meant by "right-wing populism," what especially characterizes right-wing populist attitudes, and why these attitudes present a set of problems that can on no account be ignored by social work. The next step will be to identify which factors are conducive to the adoption and consolidation of right-wing populist attitudes, based on empirical findings. The third and final step, which will be gone into more extensively, will be to examine the question of which social work methods appear to be most promising.

Right-wing Populism and Right-wing Populist Attitudes: Clarification of Terms

Although the term "right-wing populism" is frequently used in day-to-day speech, in the scientific sphere, it is controversial and subject to many interpretations. While some researchers would rather avoid the term, seeing the phenomena described by it as coming under the aegis of investigations into right-wing extremism (e.g., Salzborn, 2015), others (e.g., Birsl, 2016) prefer to speak about the "radical right-wing" to differentiate it from the extreme right) thereby making it possible to emphasize the contents rather than the style of this political direction. Still others are willing to use the term but define it quite differently. Without going into the specialist discourse (for this, see e.g., Betz, 2002; Decker, 2018; Mudde, 2007; Priester, 2012) and without engaging in terminological sophistry, we will take the following theses, necessarily shortened, as our starting point.

Right-wing populism is a phenomenon that is located within a basic current of ideas denoted "the extreme right" and, as such, occupies an outsider position in the political spectrum, even though some of its orientations display a certain attractiveness, which extends into the so-called "political center" (Arzheimer,

2008). At the margins of this movement, elements can be seen that unmistakably represent right-wing extremist and thus antidemocratic parties, such as the so-called *Nationaldemokratische Partei Deutschlands* (NPD); however, there are other positions that see themselves as nominally committed to democracy or even present themselves as guardians of democratic principles that they see as having been violated by the party system. Within the political spectrum in Germany, such self-positioning is especially to be seen in the *Alternative für Deutschland* (AfD), founded in 2013 and holding a political mandate in 14 federal state parliaments. The AfD obtained 12.6% of votes in the most recent central governmental elections in September 2017, and thus advanced to become the third strongest political power in the country.

The central core of right-wing populism can neither be discerned in a particular ideology, nor in a strategy for the acquisition and preservation of power, nor in any mere style of discourse (cf. Priester, 2012). More than just a populist-contoured mixture of nativism and authoritarianism (cf. Mudde, 2007) or a product of "ordinary nationalism" divorced from ethnic-cultural affiliations and taking for granted that it validates national state interests (Pogge ,2002), right-wing populism is a monocultural and anti-pluralistic mood that expresses handed-down modes of thought and mentalities about traditional social relationships of inequality.

To extend the analyses of political science and sociology that largely lean on organizational aspects, it is necessary to focus on individuals and groups that have these points of view, i.e., on orientations and activities that are the focus of day-to-day social work. There may be an illiberal "indigenous nationalism" which propagates homogeneity coupled with a belief in social hierarchies and traditional moral codes seen as worthy of protection, and these may indeed be the essential foundations of a point of view that dresses itself in right-wing populistic clothing and positions itself as representing the supposed "will of the people" i.e., "us down here" as opposed to the supposedly self-serving political (and partly also economic) "establishment" of "them up there" as well as in opposition to "them out there" (Lewandowsky, 2017). However, the central core has more to do with the politics of identification (Betz, 2002). This arises out of a feeling of being threatened and–via processes of identification and by turning away from democratic principles–an attempt to recreate the experience of a local, regional, and/or national "heartland" (Taggart, 2004) that is seen as in danger of dissolution; in other words, it is an attempt to create a backwards-looking, sealed-off utopia as a remedy to the heterogenization of the modern world with its accompanying uncertainties, but without following any new quintessential values.

In these attempts, the central aspect is that materials that convey right-wing populist ideas are less concerned with inner consistency, systematic development of argumentation, or convincing systems in the form of theory-supported ideologies based on rational logic, but rather consist of mental representations that may have cognitive elements but are overwhelmingly grounded in affect. As "unformed" or "fluid"–though not random–and simultaneously relatively enduring manifestations of states of feeling, they are stored as "first-order" ideologies and form something like "residues" (Pareto, 1916) of a pre-reflexive, atmospheric "state of mind" (Geiger, 1932, p. 77). They consist of representations of reality (or at any rate, that which their proponents consider to be reality) that rest on a strongly emotional and affective ensemble of images, metaphors, symbolic references, and habitual personifications that is intuitively and associatively accessible (Moscovici, 1988). Finally, their efficacy results from the fact that they possess a certain accessibility and apparent relevance for processing socio-political experiences without demanding further reflection because they are taken for granted and are based on subjective perceptions, superficial phenotyping, habit, and direct and partly physical impressions.

Not only the overlaps between right-wing-populist notions and the extreme right-wing spectrum, but also the democracy-hostile, authoritarian, and racially-oriented nationalistic temper of right-wing populism, with its rejection of people with different origins or a history of migration and its acceptance of anti-Semitic and anti-Muslim and other misanthropic viewpoints that demonstrably increase propensities for and approbation of political violence (Zick, Küpper, & Krause, 2016), make it essential for social work to tackle right-wing political tendencies proactively. This becomes all the more important as a not inconsiderable portion of the rejecting attitudes expressed here affect social groups that are the recipients of social services: homeless and long-term unemployed people, migrants, refugees, etc. Additionally and perversely, a form of communication which draws on the rhetoric of victimization is used towards such groups and also towards the apportionment of responsibility for the atrocities of national socialism, in which the roles of the evildoers and their victims are exchanged, i.e., those who were politically responsible and those who suffered are transposed.

Anyone wishing to confront the resulting professional challenges, and not merely address the symptoms, must certainly acquire knowledge about what constitutes the attractiveness of right-wing populist attitudes and how they gain a hold in people's biographies.

Right-wing Populist Attitudes–Conducive Factors

Empirical investigations from which reasons for the adoption of right-wing populist attitudes can be elicited are few and far between. Nonetheless, a few quantitative and qualitative findings are listed here.

The claim made by right-wing populists, that they, and they alone, speak for "the people" (*das Volk*) and, in so doing, assume grounded knowledge about who does and does not belong to the people is made concrete in their rejecting attitudes towards Muslims, asylum-seekers, Sinti and Roma, as well as generally any so-called "strangers" has been quantitatively and empirically detailed in research. A further feature is their authoritarian, law-and-order position and mistrust of the (representative) democratic practices of the party-political system and people with a political mandate (e.g. Zick, Krause, & Küpper, 2016). With this in view, findings currently identify right-wing populist potential in 40% of the German population. An unequivocally right-wing orientation is to be found in around every fifth person (Zick, Krause, & Küpper, 2016, p. 117).

Any analysis of so-called "new-right-wing" attitudes requires scientific investigations to be extended to include the anti-pluralistic, right-wing political spectrum. By this is meant a conglomeration of attitudes that includes the "anti-establishment" position of the extreme right, alleges a dictatorship of opinion in public discourse, insinuates that there is an Islamic conspiracy to infiltrate German society, and demands a "national change of heart" concerning the EU. Tendencies to hold such attitudes can be found in nearly 28% of the German population, while 83% of people eligible to vote and who intend to vote AfD show these new-right ideas (Küpper, Häusler, & Zick, 2016, p. 160); similarly, people with extreme right-wing and right-wing populist positions are also more likely to profess agreement with them (e.g., Vehrkamp & Wratil, 2017).

Research into attitudes such as these cannot investigate behavior directly; nevertheless, it can make statements about propensities to act. Of particular interest are attitudes towards the use of violence. Here we can indeed see that people with extreme right-wing attitudes tend toward the use of violence much more than people who do not possess these attitudes. This applies to the perceived acceptability of violence as well as willingness to use violence oneself (Zick, Krause, & Küpper, 2016). Research into the motives for turning to extreme right-wing attitudes and behavior has, on the one hand, been carried out in the context of social psychological research into prejudice, and on the other—expanding into the area of current socio-economic developments—in the context of tendencies towards extremism in conforming to the demands of the market (Groß & Hoevermann, 2014; Hoevermann & Groß, 2016).

Leaning from Fiske's work (2004), Zick (2018) recognizes five main motivations for turning to prejudice and right-wing-populist attitudes. In his view, this serves: first, to construct identity and a feeling of belongingness within a group perceived of as "us"; second, to function as a means of making the world more understandable; third, to create the illusion of control and influence; fourth, to establish orientation through categorizing groups of people and information according to their trustworthiness or untrustworthiness; and, fifth, to acquire or improve self-esteem through the construct of group affiliation. In addition, a highly volatile socio-economic influence can be discerned: a growing trend to think in business terms that propagates a flexible, competitively oriented, assertive self and self-optimization. In its most extreme form, conformity to the demands of the market advocates "business-oriented self-optimization norms" in the sense of a neoliberal "business-oriented universality," "keenly competitive ideologies" and "marginalizing, economically-based evaluations of people," "according to pure cost-benefit calculations" (Gross & Hoevermann, 2014, pp.103-105). AfD sympathizers and people especially affected by (economic) crises agree with such positions in above average numbers and almost equally strongly.

The findings of qualitative and reconstructive studies that investigate the biographical processes involved in the construction of extreme right-wing orientations and activities as well as in the adoption of sweeping, rejecting generalizations in this context, e.g. rejection of people on grounds of their origins or migration, for anti-Semitic or anti-Muslim reasons, for reasons of variation from a heteronormative lifestyle, and that examine factors that promote and stabilize such attitudes can be summarized as follows, albeit in a very much shortened form (for a longer exposition, see e.g., Moeller, 2016).

The background to the construction of rejecting attitudes consists, on the one hand, of repeated experiences by the holders of these attitudes that convince them that they, as an individual person or as a member of "their" group, have been denied life opportunities that they see legitimate, or have been granted only limited access to them. On the other hand, there is involvement in particular cliques or scenes that seem to offer the chance to compensate these perceived disadvantages. The separate elements are as follows:

1. A perception of inadequate opportunities to satisfy one's basic needs by means of socially accepted, democratic actions, but especially, the experience of lack of personal control and efficacy in the attempt to master one's own life and destiny,
2. Problems with integration, which on the one hand, and for whatever reason, lie in a partial or complete inability to use socially accepted paths to integration and, on the other, a perceived chance to obtain and maintain feelings of belongingness, confirmation of one's own worth, participation and identification only through paths that lie outside socially accepted ways, i.e. in the extreme right-wing or violence-oriented scene,
3. Deficits in the experience of sense and meaning in socially recognized and propagated areas of life such as work, education, personal relationships, etc. with, at the same time, a perception of apparently attractive compensations within the extreme right-wing scene,
4. Limitations in sensual experience and sensory feelings leading to a broad reduction in the ability to have "peak-experiences" that, in turn, provokes action, violence and demonstrations of superiority, as well as excessive consumption of alcohol,

5. Exposure to representations that help to structure experience but that provide a view of reality that is warped, biased or simplistic and, at the same time, subjectively offer substance for socio-political interpretations, not least and especially because, without requiring much reflection, they appear to be intuitive and developed through association,
6. A comparatively low level of personal and social competences, the low quality of which is centrally responsible for perceived deficits in the areas of control, integration, a sense of meaningfulness and sensual experience, and to which the problematic mental representations propagated by the right and lacking in reflection and empathy can be ascribed.

Right-wing Populist Attitudes–Promising Social Work Approaches

Social work is only rarely directly concerned with populist right-wing leaders and organizations. Irrespective of the principal responsibility of social work to become involved in politics, dealing with them–in contrast to political stakeholders–takes only second place after the practical requirement to counter or prevent right-wing populist attitudes in the day-to-day life of service users and their social environments in which such ideas can be found or are at risk of developing. In this sense, and without doubt, social work is just as much an authority and has just as much responsibility as any stakeholder in extra-curricular political education. But more than that, social work is a profession that more than any other combines two aspects: it empowers its recipients to organize their social life and supports them in doing so by demonstrating and making available chances to discover and realise politically relevant needs and interests. Insofar as social matters are never apolitical, social work can also not be conceived of as apolitical. And inasmuch as social work is ultimately engaged in the organization of social matters, it fulfills an educational function (in the truest sense of the word), i.e., it has political educational effects.

Against this background, the following ten basic points concerning promising social work approaches for tackling the causes and expression of right-wing populism can be mentioned (without any claim to completeness):

1. In contrast to classical political education, that generally takes place within traditional teaching or seminar contexts, and thus suffers from short-term learning effects and is perceived as irrelevant to the everyday lives of its recipients, social work in principle has wide-ranging possibilities to tackle *political themes in their everyday context*. For this reason, it has comparatively good opportunities to direct its responsibility to provide political education towards the day-to-day experiences of the people with whom it is

concerned, rather than being exhaustively limited to the transfer of cognitive knowledge. This is especially the case in situations in which there is generally longer-term client contact, that is, in institutions serving children and young people. Such institutions serve attendees and residents whose political socialization and political opinions, due to their age, are still comparatively fluid; this means that the tasks in the primary and secondary prevention of socio-political positions hostile to democracy (here is meant right-wing-populist notions and activities) could become (more) central, albeit without losing sight of the influence of parents and other adult socialization agents on the young people's growing self-image and worldview and bearing in mind any possible need to counter their impacts professionally.

2. Approaches to prevention and intervention face different challenges according to the point in time in which they are initiated–namely, whether they are *proactive or reactive*. In addition to any indicated, tertiary prevention, in the first place, it is also necessary to proactively offer activities at any time, even when there is no concrete or immediate occasion to do so; this applies to groups of recipients that are already directly involved in the scene but also to influence the problematic contexts in which they move by addressing both the people and structural conditions. In the second, professional action in situ is frequently reactive in the form of interventions as a response to particular situations. This is the case when, for example, statements are made by clients that, in the opinion of the professional, cannot remain uncommented because they violate principles of democratic modes of behavior, or when types of behavior are demonstrated that require immediate intervention because they directly constitute an unacceptable attack on respectful coexistence or could even result in concrete injury to others. Nevertheless, an immediate reaction on the part of professionals is not always indicated. This can be true, for example, in cases in which there is not enough time to respond appropriately or when the situation is so strongly influenced by group dynamics or so emotionally charged that professional intervention is either doomed to failure or could even be expected to result in counterproductive effects. In such situations, it may be more appropriate to react after the situation has ended, in order to take advantage of the lapse in time and discuss the event more calmly. A further problem that cannot be overseen is that in social work, the basic conceptions and best-practice approaches for proactive activities are considerably better developed than those for dealing with situational and post-situational (re)actions; this means that professionals in such situations have to more or less rely on their own personal (and therefore not always expert) feelings about what the best spontaneous reaction might be. To avoid the vagaries of chance, but at the same time take into account the variability and complexity of such challenges, a standardized handbook as the basis for interventions would be too inflexible. A better solution is for professionals to provide an open space–preferably in the form of cooperation

between scientists and practitioners–in which it can be considered which concrete, behavior-modifying, general strategies for appropriate action in such situations could be or be developed as a professional habitus that is prepared for recurring educational situations and–due to its being internalized–can be actualized without time-consuming reflection (Moeller, 2017).

3. If we accept, as postulated above, that right-wing populist attitudes are not simply to be construed as "wrong thinking" or as mistakes resulting from inadequate knowledge, but instead are grounded in the person's experiences, then it follows that any successful strategy for dealing with them cannot simply consist of countering them with didactic arguments. Instead, without changes in the person's experiential base, any attempts to change perceived meanings will fall on deaf ears as long as these meanings continue to appear subjectively functional. After all, the fact that such meanings are perceived as functional by their bearers is what gives them their durability (if not functional in the sense of organizing their lives, at least in the sense of dealing with their life situations and providing a basis for the evaluation of facts and groups of people). With its mandate to work on and with social affairs, social work as a profession is uniquely placed to influence the day-to-day experiences of its service users and to connect them with new experiences. Repelling the development of perceived attractiveness in (extreme) right-wing positions generally works quite well in the context of planned encounters. Thus, encounters with refugees, Muslims, Roma and Sinti or other groups that are generally rejected by the right-wing of the political spectrum can help to put preconceived images and prejudices into a different perspective. Of course, the conditions that have been identified as being necessary for the success of such encounters (for discussion of contact hypothesis, see Pettigrew & Tropp, 2006) and for reducing prejudice remain valid: the encounter must be wanted from both sides, both sides must meet as equals, have shared intentions, as far as possible, work cooperatively and productively towards a shared aim, and the encounter must be supported by relevant authority figures. Experience has shown that the pursuit of shared sporting, cultural or media interests is often helpful in this respect.

4. The direction taken by the attempt to provide new experiences is not only intended to address symptoms, but to actually have an effect on the causes. In so doing, this approach has the objective of developing and providing a functional equivalent for those experiences that are conducive to the development of right-wing populism or which make young people susceptible to offers made by the extreme right-wing. Additionally, *orientation help* should be offered to enable the processing of experiences. This help should be clearly superior to right-wing populist assumptions by being more functional in providing guidance for the organization of one's life. To put it briefly, the aim is to provide alternative experiences and alternative interpretations. The following points follow from this basis. They form

a strategy for dealing with right-wing populistic attitudes, known by the acronym KISS (control german: Kontrolle], integration, sensory experiences and sensemaking), that can only be briefly sketched and concretized here (for a more detailed description, see Moeller, 2016, p. 779).

5. The deficits in the opportunities to control one's life perceived by the subjects–whether as individuals or as members of "their" group–in comparison with their *expectations of control* should be taken seriously. Consequently, opportunities to provide individuals with more control over the organization of their lives and more self-determination concerning the conditions of dependencies should opened up by means of improved orientation and enhanced experiences of self-efficacy; these should contribute to the development of self-assurance in influencing and planning one's own life in relevant ways. This means, for example, being concerned with making experiences available in the three important areas of life–education, work and public life–that make such experiences (of self-efficacy) possible. This leads to further questions, such as: What qualities must work have, in order to be seen as not merely a means of earning a livelihood, but as interesting and important (also for others)? In the educational system and especially in the school system, with its competitiveness and selection functions, how can an alternative, cooperative context that is oriented towards understanding be established in political education, pedagogical activities and school social work so that students can obtain sustainable individual experiences of self-efficacy as well as collective experiences of success? In what way is a more positive view of the democratic regulation of public matters to be encouraged, given the perceived failures in the channels of political participation that are open to them that cause them to eye the realities of democracy with mistrust and to seek their salvation in right-wing-populist promises? What changes in infrastructure must be undertaken on the part of social work or at least demanded by others so as to develop strategies for political involvement and make such experiences possible?

6. The efforts at *integration* made by social work–which, indeed, has always been one of its key responsibilities–should be oriented towards prevention and dealing with right-wing-populist attitudes so that they, first, open up or optimize possibilities for orientation and intervention in relevant life-contexts by means of systemic integration. Second, procedures that maintain integrity should be (further) developed that enable the articulation of interests and balance of conflicts as well as allow access to the formation of collective identity by means of social integration. And, third, affective relationships between subjects should be created or, where they already exist, strengthened by means of collective-societal integration. In this endeavor, the facilitation of feelings of belonging, participation, recognition, and identity-formation is central. Here, conformity to the demands of the market in the organization of one's life will be counter-productive. In concrete terms, this means encouraging affiliations to the structures of social

subsystems (such as work, accommodation, consumption) by opening up opportunities to establish autonomous positioning within them, by creating or maintaining access to intermediary entities such as clubs, associations, unions, etc., and by stabilizing socially accepted, affective, and habitual bonds to primary groups. On the level of participation, it follows that, for example, chances to gain access to material goods and rights should be assured, participation in public discourse and decision-making processes and political action should be extended, and emotional relationships within community milieus should be developed. In cases where the aim is to gain recognition, respect for systemic role positions should be safeguarded and chances to maintain social and personal value should be fostered. Moreover, possibilities for identification with systemically given roles (e.g., as employee, as school student, and as a publicly respected person) should be strengthened, opportunities for social identification via improved options to develop a collective sense of self that is compatible with democracy should be realized, and community identities within face-to-face relationships that enable the development of personal and social identities should be opened up. The current state of knowledge in research into alienation makes it clear that people who experience integration within socially accepted and democratically structured contexts do not need to seek belongingness in extremist groups or their environments.

7. Political education on this topic should not, as has been the case almost without exception, continue to neglect the aspect of *sensory experiences,* which make right-wing populist attitudes appear so attractive to many. Right-wing populism ignites feelings of self-worth through promoting feelings of superiority over all those who are shut out from and eliminated from the "heartland"; it provides the feeling of fighting for a "good cause" and feelings of being fortified and militant against alleged injustice and the elites responsible for them; via rallies, demonstrations, and fora (including violent ones) it offers collectively experienced assertiveness and feelings of success and much more. To combat this, it is necessary to develop sensitivity for differentiated sensory impressions in the affected people, to facilitate the experience of positive physical and psychological states and processes that are not connected to extreme right-wing contexts, and make chances accessible to them that enable them to seek and organize the relevant conditions for such experiences.

8. *The experience of sense and ascription of sense* generally fulfill the purpose of establishing a meaning of order, of reducing complexity, of processing contingencies, of understanding the world and finding one's place in it, of maintaining identity and maybe even distancing oneself from the world. For social work, this leads to the emergence of a number of questions: By way of which day-to-day experiences can this search for sense be served in ways that fit into democratic contexts? What roles can social work and education, sporting, cultural, media, and civic activities play, here?

9. KISS experiences have to counter *representations that structure experience*. Such representations, which are permeated by right-wing populist notions, are not only discursively present in individuals' environments, but have also been constructed biographically as a repository of attitudes and mentalities, as well as graphic notions, symbols, codes and habits that have grown over a long process of searching for meaning, perceptions, explanations, evaluations, and categorizations of experience and that enable these experiences to be communicated. As a result, any new, democratically-framed KISS experiences must offer alternative mental representations of the world that are more commensurate with reality, so that existing hostile attitudes are questioned and new attitudes can be constructed. Certainly, this means starting at the affective-emotional foundation of extreme right-wing attitudes and being able to develop functional equivalents for them. The provision of information that is limited to the level of cognition can do little to counter strong emotions such as fear, aversion, anger and hate, nor indeed, the negative connotations attached to images propagated by right-wing populist agitators. Experience shows that deeply rooted, negatively tinged mental images of "Moslems," "Jews," or "refugees" cannot be dissipated by mere instruction and certainly not by critical moralizing. As such images grow out of concrete engagement with the topic, its images and the groups of people whose characteristics and modes of behavior are represented in them, they have to be replaced by images that are also concrete and more commensurate with reality. In order to motivate people with a right-wing populist orientation to even consider a thorough examination of their beliefs in any kind of educational or social work setting, it is necessary to not only have a basically accepting attitude towards them that is able to discriminate between clients as human beings and their attitudes, but also to have special qualities in the relationship with them. Positive professional relationships between educators and clients only rarely arise in an ad hoc manner. Generally, they rest on long-term experiences of dealing with each other in which mutual acceptance, and trust can grow. Qualities such as these on the part of clients are normally essential prerequisites for any kind of serious, critical discussion about their sociopolitical attitudes. For this reason, the establishment of new, desirable attitudes, perceptions and meanings concerning sensitive topics is almost never the result of short-term pedagogical interventions. The more comprehensively and sustainably interventions seek to replace deeply rooted representations which rest on ideologies of the intrinsic social worthlessness of groups of people, and thus the more they have to combat resistance, the more stable a "bridge" between people is needed; precisely, this is a factor that has to be established through continued work on relationship-building in the context of social work.
10. Focusing on the level of *social and personal competences* among people who have developed or are at risk of developing a right-wing-populist orientation, less trust should be placed in pertinent training formats than to

investigate the possibility that such competences could arise "of their own accord" out of satisfactory KISS experiences together with the development of the ability to reflect on their meanings in day-to-day life (for practice-based experiences with the KISS strategy, see Projektgruppe "Rückgrat!", 2017).

Conclusion

Right-wing populism as a stream within the extreme right wing does not confront social work in an organized form, but rather in the shape of orientations and activities. The challenge that this danger to democracy presents to the profession especially rests in the fact that it cannot be countered by arguments alone. This is because the genesis and development of such attitudes is based on certain experiences and, as such, "the whole person" is involved. Counter strategies with any chance of success cannot, therefore, concentrate on the cognitive transfer of knowledge and trust in the "power of superior arguments." Instead, they must find functional equivalents for those experiences that were instrumental in the adoption of extreme right-wing attitudes and, furthermore, use emotionally effective materials to counter representations containing affective and symbolic right-wing-populist metaphors and social images. To do this, the KISS approach is to be recommended.

References

Arzheimer, K. (2008). Die Wähler der extremen Rechten 1980–2002. Wiesbaden: VS.
Betz, H. (2002). Rechtspopulismus in Westeuropa: Aktuelle Entwicklungen und politische Bedeutung. Österreichische Zeitschrift für Politikwissenschaft, 31, 251-264.
Birsl, U. (2016). Rechtsextremismusforschung reloaded – neue Erkenntnisse, neue Forschungsfelder und alte Forschungsdesiderate. Neue politische Literatur, 16, 251-276.
Fiske, S. T. (2004). Social beings: Core motives in social psychology. Hoboken, NJ: Wiley
Decker, F. (2018). Rechtspopulismus in Europa. Ein Überblick. In K. Möller, & F. Neuscheler, (Eds.), "Wer will die hier schon haben?" Ablehnungshaltungen und Diskriminierung in Deutschland. Stuttgart: Kohlhammer.

Geiger, T. (1932). Die soziale Schichtung des deutschen Volkes. Soziographischer Versuch auf statistischer Grundlage. Stuttgart: Ferdinand Enke.

Groß, E., & Hövermann, A. (2014). Marktförmiger Extremismus – ein Phänomen der Mitte? In A. Zick, & A. Klein (Eds.), Fragile Mitte – Feindselige Zustände. Bonn: Dietz.

Hövermann, A., & Groß, E. (2016). Menschenfeindlicher und rechtsextremer – Die Veränderung der Einstellungen unter AfD-Sympathisanten zwischen 2014 und 2016. In A. Zick, B. Küpper, & D. Krause (Eds.), Gespaltene Mitte – Feindselige Zustände (pp. 167-183). Bonn: Dietz.

Küpper, B., Häusler, A., & Zick, A. (2016). Die Neue Rechte und die Verbreitung neurechter Einstellungen in der Bevölkerung. In A. Zick, B. Küpper, & D. Krause (Eds.), Gespaltene Mitte – Feindselige Zustände (pp. 143-166). Bonn: Dietz.

Lewandowsky, M. (2017). Was ist und wie wirkt Rechtspopulismus? Der Bürger im Staat, 67(1), 4-11.

Möller, K., Grote, J., Nolde, K., & Schuhmacher, N. (2016). "Die kann ich nicht ab!" Ablehnung, Diskriminierung und Gewalt bei Jugendlichen in der (Post)Migrationsgesellschaft. Wiesbaden : VS Verlag.

Möller, K. (2017). 'Rückgrat!' – Eine Wissenschaft-Praxis-Kooperation gegen Rechtsextremismus und gruppierungsbezogene Ablehnungen. Abschlussbericht. Esslingen: Hochschule Esslingen, University of Applied Sciences.

Moscovici, S. (1988). Notes towards a description of social representation. European Journal of Social Psychology, 3, 211–250.

Mudde, C. (2007). Populist radical right parties in Europe. Cambridge: Cambridge University Press.

Pareto, V. (1916). Trattato di sociologia generale. Firenze: G. Barbera.

Pettigrew, T. F., & Tropp, L. R. (2006). A meta-analytic test of intergroup contact theory. Journal of Personality and Social Psychology, 90, 751–783.

Pogge, T. (2002). World poverty and human rights. Cosmopolitans responsibilities and reforms. Cambridge: Polity Press.

Priester, K. (2012). Rechter und linker Populismus: Annäherung an ein Chamäleon. Frankfurt a.M.: Campus.

Projektgruppe „Rückgrat!" (2017). Mit Rückgrat gegen PAKOs! Eine Step by Step-Anleitung für die Jugendarbeit zur Gestaltung und Selbstevaluation von Angeboten gegen Pauschalisierende Ablehnungskonstruktionen. Hamburg: Drucktechnik Altona.

Salzborn, S. (2015). Rechtsextremismus. Baden-Baden: Nomos.

Taggart, P. (2004). Populism and representative politics in contemporary Europe. Journal of Political Ideologies, 9, 269-288.

Vehrkamp, R., & Wratil, C. (2017). Die Stunde der Populisten? Populistische Einstellungen bei Wählern und Nichtwählern vor der Bundestagswahl 2017. Gütersloh: Bertelsmann Stiftung.

Zick, A. (2018). Menschenfeindliche Vorurteile. In: K. Möller, K. & F. Neuscheler (Eds.), "Wer will die hier schon haben?" Ablehnungshaltungen und Diskriminierung in Deutschland. Stuttgart: Kohlhammer.

Zick, A., Krause, D., & Küpper, B. (2016). Rechtspopulistische und rechtsextreme Einstellungen in Deutschland. In A. Zick, B. Küpper, & D. Krause (Eds.), Gespaltene Mitte – Feindselige Zustände (pp. 111-142). Bonn: Dietz.

Zick, A., Küpper, B., & Krause, D. (2016). Gespaltene Mitte – Feindselige Zustände. *Rechtsextreme Einstellungen in Deutschland*. Bonn: Dietz.

Social Work under Trump: Experiences from the USA

Michael Reisch

The election of Donald Trump in November 2016 shocked many social workers in the U.S., most of whom anticipated and ardently supported the candidacy of Hillary Rodham Clinton. In the words of Charles Howard (2017), President of the Maryland chapter of the National Association of Social Workers (NASW), "We didn't see the storm coming and now we must rush to prepare for the next four years" (p. 2). In the aftermath of the election, social workers in the U.S. felt compelled to address many questions about their political views and the future of the social work profession under the Trump administration. These questions included: "What are the implications for social work practice and education? What can social workers do to connect with those who believe they have been forgotten and voted for Trump? What can social workers do to help heal the deep divisions that the election exposed? How can individual social workers respond to ethical dilemmas under this administration?" (Reardon, 2017, p.10).

Psychologically and practically unprepared for this electoral outcome, both individual social workers and professional organizations have struggled over the past eighteen months to respond effectively to the impact of the Trump presidency on the nation's politics, policies, and social relations, all of which have had significant consequences for social work practice and the well-being of clients and constituents. For the most part, however, social workers in the U.S. have failed to grasp the underlying causes of the Trump phenomenon or to recognize the contributions of the profession to its emergence. As a result, social workers have been to slow to adapt to or counteract its effects. This essay briefly traces the origins of Trump's political ascendancy, its effects to date on social policy and social work practice in the U.S., and the likelihood that the profession will be able to resist or reverse these consequences.

Background: The Emergence of Right-Wing Populism in the U.S.

In retrospect, the rise of right-wing populism should not have surprised social workers in the U.S. as the indicators have existed for decades, dating back to right-wing resistance to New Deal legislation during the 1930s and, more recently, to the backlash against the modern civil rights movement, second wave feminism, and widespread cultural changes during the 1960s (Reisch & Andrews 2002). Since the mid-1970s, the sources of Americans' well-being during the post-war "boom years" (1945-1975), including U.S. dominance of the world economy, strong unions, relatively progressive taxation, and a modest expansion of social welfare provision have been eroded by economic globalization, social policy retrenchment, and their accompanying neoliberal rationale. For over 40 years, as inequality has steadily increased, during times of both prosperity and recession, under both Republican and Democratic administrations, the insecurity it produced merged with long-standing cultural animus about race and gender that simmered beneath the surface.

As economic insecurity among the working and middle classes increased, opportunistic politicians, abetted by media and corporate allies, directed the ensuing anger away from its structural causes in the private sector towards government, so-called "cultural elites," the goals they supported, and particularly state-sponsored policies that attempted to address long-standing racial and gender inequalities. The employment of so-called "wedge issues" (e.g., welfare, abortion, Affirmative Action, LGBTQ rights), combined with "demographic panic" over the changing "face" of America, focused the resentment and fears of white Americans that the "American dream" had become a nightmare away from concerns about socio-economic inequality and towards issues of race, gender, religion, sexual orientation, and citizenship status. Conservative politicians not only encouraged this misdirection, they compounded it by focusing on matters of fiscal costs and the effects of taxation on their constituents (i.e., austerity) instead of the social costs that dramatic economic, social, and environmental changes had produced.

The election of an African American President in 2008 brought these populist forces to a head. Mistrust of government, encouraged for decades by an increasingly conservative Republican party, now acquired an explicitly racial dimension. The relatively moderate response of the Obama administration to the 2008 economic crisis, the failure to punish Wall Street for the crisis it precipitated, and the passage of the 2010 Affordable Care Act (dubbed "Obamacare" by its critics) spurred the emergence of the so-called Tea Party. This unusual coalition combined traditional conservative positions on taxation and government spending with religious (largely evangelical) opposition to abortion and gay rights. With ample, if often hidden corporate support, the growing power of the Tea Party, especially in primary elections, led to the election of more right-wing Republicans in Congress and state legislatures. These officials often had little experience or knowledge of policy issues and strong animosity to government itself. Their election pushed traditional Republicans even further to the right as a matter of political self-preservation. This, in turn, contributed to the increased polarization of American politics, best illustrated by the refusal of Congressional Republicans to support any of the Obama administration's proposals, from major legislation to judicial appointments.

The 2016 election campaign added two volatile elements to this combustible political situation. First, the Presidential candidacy of Hillary Rodham Clinton inspired not only misogynistic rhetoric, it also led to a revival of often absurdist conspiratorial suspicions about the Clintons that had existed since the early 1990s. Second, and of greater importance, the rise of Donald Trump, whose campaign rhetoric broke virtually all American political traditions, unleashed long-suppressed racist, xenophobic, homophobic, and anti-Semitic sentiments, and legitimized beliefs and behaviors that many observers believed had been driven to the margins of American cultural and civic life.

The Impact of the Trump Administration

The policies and politics of the Trump Administration and the behavior of the President himself have exacerbated these neo-populist trends. Even prior to his inauguration, the U.S. experienced a marked increase in physical, verbal, and Internet attacks on women, immigrants, racial minorities, and members of the LGBTQ community. Neo-Nazi demonstrations, such as the one in Charlottesville, Virginia during the summer of 2017, and the emergence of nearly 1,000 hate groups since Trump's election heightened the anxieties of many Americans. Trump's refusal to criticize these groups or to repudiate their support raised additional concerns, as did the specific policy proposals issued by the new President and their accompanying rationales.

Among the latter were anti-Muslim restrictions on immigration under the guise of protecting "national security," the rollback of protections for women and transgendered persons (criticized as "special rights"), and virulent verbal attacks on the media ("fake news"), law enforcement agencies, legislative bodies, and the intelligence community. These policies and the rhetoric justifying them have increased social conflict and political polarization to a level not seen in the U.S. since the Civil War. They have produced conditions that could precipitate both a constitutional crisis and irreparable schisms in American society.

The effects of the Trump presidency appeared within weeks of the November 2016 election. Responses to Trump's surprising victory ranged from inspiration among his supporters to devastation among his opponents (Cox & Wood, November 12, 2016). Shortly after the election, the Southern Poverty Law Center's Teaching Tolerance project distributed a survey to over 10,000 school personnel in the U.S. Most respondents (90%) reported that their school climate experienced negative effects, such as increased verbal harassment, the use of racial and ethnic slurs, and the display of Nazi symbols and Confederate flags. They also reported heightened anxiety among students from marginalized populations, particularly immigrants, African Americans, Muslims, and LGBTQ students. Perhaps of greatest concern, is that most of those surveyed believed this current climate would have long-lasting effects (Southern Poverty Law Center, November 28, 2016). Events since the election have done little to assuage these fears.

The Initial Response of the U.S. Social Work Profession

Given the severity of the current political and social crisis, the response of the social work profession in the U.S. has been well-intentioned, if often rather tepid. In hindsight, this should not be surprising. Since the 1970s, the market-oriented values produced by globalization have transformed the environment of social work practice and compelled the profession to revise or diverge from its fundamental tenets (Soss, Fording, & Schram 2011). The resultant "marketization" of social welfare heightened the contradiction between the profession's social justice rhetoric and day-to-day practice and research and altered the mission and character of many social service organizations, particularly in the non-governmental sector (Reisch, 2009). In addition, the shift from universal to identity-oriented conceptions of practice, which began in the 1970s, made it even more difficult to narrow the gap between the profession's stated values and the nature of its contemporary practice.

Ironically, despite its attempts to accommodate neoliberal imperatives, the social work profession in the U.S. has considerably less influence in policy-making circles today than it did in the past. A major reasons for this diminished influenced is the depoliticisation of its basic theoretical assumptions, practice, and research. At the organizational level, the withdrawal from politics, in the broadest sense, normalized neoliberalism's underlying assumptions and produced a shift in the focus of practice from resistance to accommodation and resiliency (Jani et al., 2011). Consequently, although the profession's *Code of Ethics* and educational accreditation standards emphasize social justice, the practice of most social workers stresses adaptation to the neoliberal reality and rationalizes this capitulation through the application of a veneer of cultural sensitivity (Council on Social Work Education, 2015; NASW, 2010, 2017). The increasingly apolitical nature of social work practice and the retreat from a universal framework as the basis for policy advocacy have also made it more difficult for social workers to respond to the emergence of right-wing populism or to articulate a viable alternative to the individualistically-oriented philosophy that currently dominates U.S. society and politics.

Prior to the November 2016 election, however, the organized social work profession took several cautious steps to promote its proper representation in the next administration's policymaking decisions, regardless of who became President. In September 2016, before the election's outcome could be known, social work leaders sent 50 policy recommendations to all the major presidential and congressional candidates developed at the Social Work Grand Challenges' first policy conference in St. Louis. This initiative, created by the American Academy of Social Welfare and Social Work (AASWSW, n.d.), represented an attempt to harness the research capacity of the profession to the service of wide-ranging policy changes in areas ranging from socio-economic inequality to family violence.

In addition, shortly before Trump's inauguration, NASW released a lengthy document, *Advancing the American Agenda: How the Social Work Profession Will Help* (NASW, 2017), apparently intended for both the transition team of the new President and the organization's membership. The document's title was a not so subtle attempt to reinterpret the slogan of the Trump campaign, "Make America Great Again," in a manner that reflected social work's underlying values. If this was not sufficiently clear, the document's authors stressed that

> our profession wanted to make sure the advancement of America's economy and society works for everyone, not just the top one percent. *Advancing the American Agenda* is about choosing investments that not only make us stronger today, but also reflect the kind of country we aspire to be and the kind of country we want to build for future generations (Wheeler ,2017, p. 3).

The well-referenced statement emphasized four core themes: Ensuring Child and Family Well-Being; Fortifying the Social Fabric; Building a Just Society; and Strengthening the Social Work Profession.

In retrospect, this initial formal response of the organized social work profession to Trump's election reflected cautious, if somewhat naïve optimism. The introduction of the November 2016 document acknowledged that the recent election had "exposed and exacerbated class, race, sex, gender, and ideological divisions in the United States" (p. 3). Nevertheless, it went on to state, "We hope that the Trump administration reflects mutual respect, civility, and compassion that can transcend these differences. We are willing to work with the incoming administration on shared values to protect vital resources that advance the American Agenda…" (p. 3).

Similar to the AASWSW recommendations, this document contained a long list of policy proposals and, in several places, cited the role that social work played during the Progressive Era, the Great Depression, and the War on Poverty "to change the face of the nation." It concluded with this offer:

> Despite our differing of [sic] opinions during the election cycle, we are willing to work with the new administration and 115th Congress to develop and implement policies and initiatives that provide positive sustainable solutions to the challenges that we face as a nation (p. 28).

Much to the profession's regret, however, it soon became clear that the Trump administration did not share NASW's values or policy goals; nor was it willing to compromise with its opponents.

The Policies and Politics of the Trump Administration

Despite his populist rhetoric during the 2016 campaign, the policies of the Trump administration have produced few benefits for the disgruntled voters who supported him. This became obvious during the first 100 days of his presidency (Center for American Progress, 2017). Instead, they have reflected a combination of traditional right-wing fiscal conservatism (tax cuts that favor the wealthy and corporations, fiscal austerity for the remainder of the population), the cultural priorities of Christian (largely evangelical) conservatives around such issues as abortion and LGBTQ rights, and the policy goals of nativists and white supremacists. The Trump administration's policy priorities appear in its frequent attempts to restrict immigration from Muslim countries, reduce or eliminate social welfare programs, rollback of environmental and labor regulations (Howard, 2017), and attack women's rights in the areas of reproductive health and protections against sexual assault and harassment (Enda, 2017). Although the Trump Administration and its Congressional allies have succeeded in implementing a number of these policy initiatives, unified resistance from Democrats in Congress and popular outcries have, thus far, blocked others from taking effect.

Three policy initiatives in 2017 represent the clearest expressions of Trump's overall policy agenda: his budget proposals for FY 2018 and FY 2019; partially successful efforts to repeal or undermine the 2010 Affordable Care Act; and changes in the U.S. tax code. As of this writing, however, a number of the Draconian measures Trump initiated have gone into effect. For example, while proposing large increases in military spending and reductions in the tax rates for corporations and the top 1% of Americans, Trump's FY 2018 budget called for deep cuts in many programs that assist the most vulnerable populations in the U.S. These cuts included:

- The elimination of the Meals on Wheels Program (a part of the Older Americans Act that provides supplemental nutrition to millions of elderly); the Emergency Food and Shelter Board Program that serves hungry, homeless, and at-risk for homelessness persons; the Low Income Energy Assistance Program that affects nearly 7 million households; and the funds in the Community Development Block Grants that rehabilitate housing and neighborhood infrastructure and provide senior and youth service programs;
- The elimination of the Legal Services Corporation that provides legal representation to low-income persons who lack such representation in civil cases;
- A 35-50% reduction in funding for federal-financed job training programs;
- Dramatic cuts in family planning programs, before and after-school programs, and funds that support public housing subsidies;
- A nearly one-third cut in funding for the Environmental Protection Agency; and
- A shift in public education funds to charter and private schools.

Trump's proposed FY 2019 budget is potentially even more damaging. Less than two months after signing massive tax cuts that largely benefit the wealthiest Americans, the budget he proposed makes broad cuts in basic assistance to millions of low and moderate-income individuals and families. "Taken together, the cuts are far deeper than any ever enacted and would deepen poverty and hardship and swell the ranks of the uninsured" (Center on Budget and Policy Priorities, 2018, p. 1). Its highlights include:

- Cutting Medicaid and subsidies for private insurance coverage by $763 billion over the next decade, with cuts reaching $172 billion annually by 2028;
- Supporting a Senate bill that would repeal the ACA and further cut funding for health coverage programs beyond what the bill proposes;
- Eliminating the ACA's expansion of Medicaid to low income adults and its subsidies that help low and moderate income people obtain marketplace coverage;
- Cutting the Supplemental Nutritional Assistance Program (SNAP, formerly food stamps) by nearly 30 percent over the next ten years;
- Cutting Department of Housing and Urban Development (HUD) programs by $6.8 billion (14.2 percent) below the 2017 level, not counting losses due to inflation;
- Reducing funds for programs, such as Social Security Disability Insurance (SSDI) and Supplemental Security Income (SSI), which help support low-income individuals with disabilities and low-income seniors by $72 billion;

- Reducing the Temporary Assistance for Needy Families (TANF) block grant and eliminating the related TANF Contingency Fund, a cut of $21 billion in funding over the next decade;
- Eliminating the Supplemental Educational Opportunity Grant (SEOG), which would reduce Pell Grants for needy students, make deep cuts in work-study programs, and make changes that would raise the cost of student loan borrowing.

Few of these policy changes will produce any benefits for the 30-40% of the electorate that still supports Trump. In fact, according to the Center on Budget and Policy Priorities (2018)

> President Trump's new budget would severely damage ... many of the very people he has said would be his priority, people who have been left behind by today's economy or live in distressed urban or rural communities. Coming on the heels of a costly tax cut that's heavily tilted to the nation's wealthiest households and corporations, the budget highlights the vast gulf between President Trump's promises and his actual policies (p. 7).

Proposed cuts in Medicaid (the federal-state program that provides health care for low-income Americans) and changes to the Affordable Care Act will leave millions of Americans without health insurance coverage and exacerbate growing public health problems such as the opioid abuse epidemic that has plagued the regions of the country where Trump had the most support. Reductions in immigration, the elimination of environmental regulations, the promotion of fossil fuel production, and the imposition of tariffs on steel and aluminum imports will not generate jobs for those displaced by structural economic forces. The tax cuts passed in December 2017 will produce only small, short-term benefits for most Americans and will saddle them with greater debt in the future. Taken together, the tax legislation, the recent budget deal approved by Congress, and – if enacted – Trump's FY 2019 budget would dramatically increase the federal deficit and the nation's debt. In addition to saddling future generations with the costs of this borrowing, they also diminish the resources available for fixing the nation's decaying physical infrastructure and, of greatest concern to social workers, provide right-wing legislators with a rationale for further cuts in social protections, under the guise of "reforming entitlements."

To mask these effects, the Trump Administration has doubled down on its anti-immigration, anti-LGBTQ, anti-Muslim, and racist rhetoric in a conscious effort to distract its political base from objective economic and environmental conditions. It has lashed out at the media, law enforcement agencies, the judiciary, and the intelligence community for criticizing, resisting, and blocking its initiatives, or contradicting the rationales for its policy proposals. The President has also repeatedly attacked Special Counsel, Robert Mueller and Congress for their investigations of Russian meddling in the 2016 election and the related actions of Trump associates and family members. By doing so, Trump and his allies have created an incendiary situation in American society that affects not only political life but threatens to destroy what elements of community still hold the nation's social fabric together.

The Response of the Social Work Profession

For the most part, the social work profession in the U.S. has adopted a reactive, defensive stance to these developments. For example, shortly after the release of the President's proposed FY 2019 budget, the Council on Social Work Education (CSWE, 2018) expressed its concern in an email message to its members "that the budget request would eliminate programs that help students pursue social work careers" and would also lead to "reductions and changes to critical safety-net programs that support communities, families, individuals, and children" (p. 1). This response reflected a continuing pattern in how the profession reacted to the policy initiatives the Trump administration has attempted to implement through its executive actions, judicial appointments, budget proposals, and legislation. Social workers have largely focused on shielding vulnerable client groups, preventing the elimination of long-established social policies, and, as the CSWE statement attests, protecting the status of the profession itself. Given the hostile political environment in Washington and many state legislatures, and the persistence of gridlock in Congress, this self-protective stance is somewhat understandable.

On some occasions, however, the profession has taken a more forthright position in response to particularly egregious policies proposed or adopted by the Trump administration and its Congressional allies. For example, in November 2017, the National Association of Social Workers (NASW) opposed the Tax Cuts and Job Act (that eventually passed by a narrow margin) on the grounds that it "would produce a windfall for the 'super rich' while decimating safety-net programs that serve low-income elderly, children and families" (NASW, November 28, 2017). The following month, it opposed the confirmation of a Trump nominee to a lifetime appointment on the U.S. Court of Appeals for the Fifth Circuit, on the grounds that he had "held radical positions that have impinged on the rights of vulnerable and marginalized Americans throughout his career" (NASW, December 6, 2017). Four weeks later, NASW criticized the Trump Administration for its attempt to bar employees at the Centers of Disease Control and Prevention (CDC) from using seven specific words and phrases (vulnerable, entitlement, diversity, transgender, fetus, evidence-based, and science-based). It based this criticism on its assertion that these terms "help to describe populations and quality control standards that are essential for managing threats to the nation's public health and well-being" (NASW, January 4, 2018).

The Trump Administration's failure to address or respond adequately to emerging or persistent social problems has spurred some of NASW's actions, although some of the organization's responses appeared to give the President more credit than he deserved. In late October 2017, for example, NASW supported Trump's declaration that the nation's opioid epidemic was a public health "crisis," although the President failed to follow the recommendation of his own commission that it be declared a public health "emergency," a declaration that would have carried much more fiscal and political weight (NASW, October 31, 2017). Ten days later, following mass shootings in a Texas church and at a concert in Las Vegas, Nevada, NASW called for the passage of sensible gun control laws and the declaration of a public health emergency (NASW, November 10, 2017) despite the intransigence of the Republican Congressional leadership and most state legislatures to the adoption of even modest gun control measures. (A similar pattern of protest and lack of policy response occurred most recently after a mass shooting at a high school in Florida.) Also in November 2017, as part of a broad-based Coalition to End Violence against Women and Girls Globally, NASW backed the introduction of the International Violence against Women Act in the U.S. Senate, a bill that would make ending such violence "a top diplomatic, development, and foreign assistance priority" (NASW, November 15, 2017). Congress, however, has yet to take action on that bill.

The Effects on the Social Work Profession and its Clients

The *Code of Ethics* of the U.S. National Association of Social Workers (NASW) states:

> social workers should engage in social and political actions that seeks to ensure that all people have equal access to the resources, employment, services, and opportunities they require to meet their basic human needs and to develop fully. Social workers should be aware of the impact of the political arena on practice and should advocate for changes in policy and legislation to improve social conditions to meet basic human needs and promote social justice (NASW, 2017).

The consequences of Donald Trump's election have underscored the importance of assessing the implications of this historic mission in today's turbulent environment.

To address the effect of these issues, NASW's Office of Ethical and Professional Review hosted a roundtable discussion in April 2017 to examine effects of the current environment on social work ethics and political opinion. Participants discussed the following questions:

- How do social workers navigate differences in their political opinions with colleagues, clients, and employees?
- How do social workers participate in political action while adhering to the *Code of Ethics*?
- How will the current administration's proposed policies affect the grain of social work values?
- How do social workers adhere to the core principles of respect, dignity, and worth of all people including those with opposing views in this current political climate?
- Is supporting President's Trump administration policies against social work ethics or not?
- Finally, if social workers promote policies that are discriminatory and critical to the most vulnerable people in society, are they violating the Code of Ethics? (Pace, June 2017).

Immigration policy is one issue around which social workers' actions have gone beyond verbal protest and self-examination. A year prior to the 2016 election, NASW issued a remarkably policy statement on this issue:

Often, social workers' capacity to assist clients is constrained by immigration especially policies that limit family visitation and family reunification. Immigration policies intervene in social work practice when family offenses become grounds for deportation and thereby impede willingness to report (as quoted in Haidar, 2017).

Given this policy position, Trump's decision to discontinue the Deferred Action for Childhood Arrivals or DACA program that the Obama Administration established through executive order unless Congress takes action by March 5, 2018 (which has not occurred as of this writing) produced considerable consternation among social workers. Many social workers work closely with this population of young adults (the so-called "Dreamers"), who are fighting to prevent deportation to countries they barely remember.

Social workers in California, where about one-fourth of the Dreamers reside, have been particularly active on two aspects of this issue. They supported passage of the California Values Act that prevented federal immigration authorities from using the state's law enforcement resources to harass, arrest, or cooperate in any way with federal immigration officials. In addition, they advocated for legislation that would protect the state's "sanctuary cities," including Los Angeles, San Diego, and San Francisco. Reflecting the growing political resistance in California to virtually all of the Trump Administration's policies, the state's social workers have also supported a variety of related progressive legislation.

One bill would bar the state government from "doing business with contractors building [Trump's proposed] wall." Another would train public defenders who assist immigrants in criminal court cases, while a third would "prohibit local or state authorities from disclosing information to the federal government about religious affiliation, national origin or ethnicity to create, implement or enforce" a national database (Laurio, 2017, p. 8.). In addition to its lobbying efforts in defense of immigrants, the California chapter of NASW has engaged in a variety of public education campaigns and encouraged its members to write op-ed essays and blogs and to organize community forums.

California social workers have also been active in fighting federal cutbacks to Medicare, Medicaid, and Social Security, and promoting state initiatives to establish a single-payer health care system. Social workers in Texas, New York, and Florida, which all have large numbers of immigrants and recipients of government health care benefits, have also become increasingly involved in efforts to protect Medicaid benefits and the Children's Health Insurance Program, which have been threatened during the past year by a combination of Presidential executive orders and Congressional action and inaction. The hurricanes that devastated parts of Florida, Texas, and virtually all of Puerto Rico have made the needs of these populations increasingly dire.

Since the fall 2016 election, there have been some other encouraging signs of increased social work activism at the state level, particularly among young social workers and social work students and faculty. A survey conducted by social work professors Mimi Abramovitz and Terry Mizrahi found that nearly all NASW chapters are regularly engaged in policy advocacy and that "these chapters brought about 12,000 social work students and professionals to their state capitals to educate elected officials about substantive policy issues..." (Pace, 2018, p. 1). The researchers expressed hope that such collective actions can become "a starting point for national initiatives, such as voter mobilization" (p. 4).

On a smaller scale, in response to the overt resurgence of white supremacy produced by the Trump administration, a committee of the Maryland chapter of NASW, titled Social Workers Unraveling Racism (SWUR), hosted a forum for practitioners, faculty, and students entitled "Resurgence of White Supremacy: A Dialogue Regarding the Implications on Social Work Practice." The forum addressed the question "What does the dialogue around race and racism sound like in this current volatile political climate?"

In addition, growing interest in events sponsored by the Congressional Research Institute for Social Work and Policy (CRISP), including the Social Work Student Advocacy Day on the Hill, the Annual Social Work Day on the Hill, and a summer "campaign school" provide further encouraging signs. Increased enrollment in the Campaign School organized by the Nancy A. Humphrey Institute for Political Social Work at the University of Connecticut is another positive indicator. Social workers have also become more involved in voter engagement, education, and mobilization, including a national campaign led by Mizrahi, Tanya Rhodes Smith of the Institute for Political Social Work, and other social work faculty and students. This effort expands on the Voting Is Social Work Initiative that began in 2017. The midterm elections in November 2018 will reveal the effectiveness of these efforts.

Conclusion: Social Work's Options for the Future

Although there has been a modest increase in activism among social workers since the election of President Trump, the dominance of clinical practitioners within the profession and social workers' ongoing concerns about licensing laws and professional titles continue to create obstacles to the mass mobilization of social workers (Dale, 2018; Pace, 2018b; Wehrmann, 2018). Nevertheless, suggestions as to how social workers could resist the politics and policies of the Trump administration appeared even before his inauguration. Social work authors of an op-ed in the *Huffington Post* (Hayes, Karpman, & Miller, 2016) called on the profession to live up to its ethical commitment to counter discrimination against oppressed and vulnerable populations and to promote social justice through "social action aimed at changing the political structure" (p. 2).

Their specific recommendations included supporting schools, churches, and cities to become "trauma-informed sanctuaries for immigrant families," joining and/or contributing to a local or national advocacy group, participating in direct action, and using contemporary events as "teachable moments" with students, colleagues, neighbors, and family members. They conclude on a cautious but optimistic note, "We have the capacity to contribute to dialogue versus despair and hope rather than fear and anger. [But] it will not be easy. It's going to be a long journey, and for some of us, this work will require being and feeling uncomfortable and even unsafe" (p. 5).

Several months after Trump assumed the presidency, an article in *Social Work Today* made similar assertions (Reardon, 2017). The author cited a number of practitioners and prominent scholars, all of whom acknowledged the challenges that the profession will face under the Trump administration while simultaneously recognizing the potential for social workers to act on behalf of vulnerable populations. The solutions they proposed, however, reflected longstanding debates within the profession. Some practitioners interviewed focused on how social workers could help clients who experience "a great deal of negative emotions" and "feel depressed and betrayed" caused by "posttraumatic election disorder" (p. 10). Others adopted a macro perspective and expressed concerns about the "effects [of policy changes] on the vulnerable populations with whom social workers engage every day" and the "threat to democracy if people are afraid to speak out" (p. 10).

On a more sanguine note, some social workers commented on the opportunities that existed for the profession "to raise its profile, [its dedication] to social justice and demonstrate its ability to heal the deep divisions that the election exposed" (p. 11). Specific proposals ranged from the necessity for political action and advocacy, to the initiation of dialogue within agencies, communities, schools of social work, and the profession itself, the expanded use of all forms of media, including social media, to educate the public and policymakers, and increased participation in electoral politics, including running for office.

The social workers quoted in the article also acknowledged the practical and ethical obstacles that social workers would have to overcome to pursue these activities. One person interviewed stated that, at the most basic level, the profession "needs to recognize that there is a disconnect between [its proclaimed] identity as a fighter against injustice and discrimination and how the profession is often practiced on a day-to-day basis." Social workers need to stop deceiving themselves that "they can practice in hermetically sealed environments" and recognize that the "election [was] a ... consequence of not doing enough [to advocate for vulnerable populations" (Reardon, 2017, p. 10).

The election of Donald Trump re-opened the century old "case vs. cause" conflict within the social work profession. Should social workers continue to assist individuals and families whose problems the policies and politics of the Trump Administration have exacerbated, or rekindle its historical commitment to social reform and political action? Looked at through this lens, the election of Donald Trump provided the social work profession with an unprecedented opportunity to reexamine its basic mission, values, and goals, to forge new alliances, and to take united action on behalf of socially-excluded and vulnerable populations (Reardon, 2017). The policies and politics of the Trump presidency have touched on virtually every issue that affects the profession, its clients, and its constituents: poverty and inequality, reproductive rights, treatment of sexual and gender minorities, gun violence, immigration, the environment, health care, peace, and the future of the nation's social welfare system.

But how exactly could the social work profession respond in these challenging times? Bryan Stevenson, the President of the Equal Justice Initiative, offers several valuable suggestions. First, it is important to recognize that self-interest and collective interest are not necessarily incompatible; in fact, in this era they are inextricably connected. As Walt Whitman wrote, "Whoever degrades another degrades me."

Despite media efforts to drown out reasoned discourse, most Americans subscribe to these beliefs. According to the Pew Research Center, approximately 90% of Americans believe social welfare programs such as Social Security and Medicare are good for the country and, by a 2:1 margin, they think that maintaining these programs is more important than cutting the federal deficit. Although negative attitudes about racial and religious minorities, particularly Muslims, and low-income persons persist, Pew found that around 60% of Americans think the latter group should not lose their Medicaid benefits. To engage in policy advocacy today that would support these vulnerable populations, however, social workers will have to keep in mind its two basic rules: (1) Nothing happens overnight; and (2) You cannot change Rule #1.

One thing that social workers can do immediately is protest against any attempts to "dehumanize others," whether this demonization occurs through blatantly racist, sexist, or homophobic statements based on outright lies or distortions, or on more subtle forms of denigration that attribute people's problems to their personal failings, rather than those of society. This will also require social workers to stop ignoring, excusing, or unintentionally abetting the behavior of those who engage in this behavior, even family, friends, and colleagues.

In addition, in an increasingly present-oriented, a-historical climate, social workers have to remind themselves what the profession accomplished when it translated its core value of social justice into specific policies and programs. Understanding the contemporary significance of this history is important because, as James Baldwin wrote, "History does not refer merely, or even principally to the past...We carry it within us, are unconsciously controlled by it in many ways. It is literally present in all that we do." To heed this wisdom, U.S. social workers will have to listen carefully to, and struggle with, the interpretation of history and contemporary realities as expressed by the "Black Lives Matter" movement, LGBTQ activists, and advocates for immigrants' rights.

In whatever method or field of practice, social workers will need to get closer to the issues, and be more critical of the fatuous statements made by political candidates, those who already hold office, and media figures who amplify their distorted statements. This requires heightened understanding of the connection between individual and structural issues and the ability to deconstruct what passes for "truth" in this era of "alternative facts."

In addition, social workers need to recognize that as much as individual efforts matter they are insufficient without concrete expressions of collective responsibility, especially in the face of widespread institutional indifference, intolerance, and outright hostility. At the same time, at the personal level, social workers have to make concerted efforts to resist succumbing to feelings of hopelessness and powerlessness. This includes avoiding the natural temptation to adopt a defensive posture in today's difficult climate. It involves imagining what a just society looks like and proposing innovative solutions to today's problems rather than focusing merely on how to ameliorate the effects of unjust policies or rehashing old ideas.

Finally, social workers in the U.S. need to get uncomfortable, take more risks, and encourage others to do likewise. This involves posing new questions, refusing to accept the "givens" imposed by others, not preaching solely to the choir, and meeting people face-to-face rather than through virtual internet posts. There are numerous political strategies the profession could adopt: popular education, cultural activities, policy advocacy, expanded civic literacy and civic engagement programs, and more effective use of social media. As Plato said over 2,000 years ago, "One of the penalties for refusing to participate in politics is that you end up being governed by your inferiors."

A core issue in the U.S. today is how can American social workers apply long-standing ideas about social justice effectively in a fractious, multicultural society in which the nation's political leadership exacerbates social tensions rather than attempts to heal them? Unfortunately, to do this, social workers will have to become more comfortable with several difficult truths.

First, social justice is a complex, dynamic, conflict-laden, and subjective concept that appears differently in different contexts. No society, therefore, achieves social justice for all time. Second, current cultural and political divisions in the U.S. are not new phenomena. Distorted interpretations of social justice have rationalized a range of inhumane consequences throughout U.S. history: genocide of indigenous peoples, slavery, nativism, and racism, to cite just a few. The motives and sentiments that produce these injustices persist today. In an essay published in *Ebony* magazine in 1963, "The White Man's Guilt," James Baldwin wrote prophetically about today's social climate, "I imagine one of the reasons people cling to their hates so stubbornly is because they sense, once hate is gone, they will be forced to deal with pain."

The events of the past two years underscore another painful reality: the U.S. has not eliminated these injustices, despite the modest successes of 20th century social movements. Institutional and cultural barriers still systematically deny individuals and entire communities full access to various rights, opportunities, and resources that are normally available to members of the dominant social group, and which are fundamental to social integration and human well-being. Policies already adopted by the Trump administration and others under consideration exacerbate these existing injustices.

Finally, social workers need to recognize that each generation must re-fight even small victories and that past social progress was not a gift from benevolent elites, but the product of sustained collective struggle. If the profession can extract one lesson from the nation's tumultuous history and apply it to contemporary politics it is that nothing is inevitable. The struggle to become a more socially just society in the future will require both collective action and the synthesis of a class-based, structural analysis with one that acknowledges the particular needs of oppressed populations. This approach is more critical than ever in the precarious "neo-populist" environment that produced the Trump administration and its consequences.

References

AASWSW (n.d.). 12 Challenges. Retrieved from http://aaswsw.org/grand-challenges-initiative/12-challenges/.

Center for American Progress (2017, April 26). 100 ways, in 100 days, that Trump has hurt Americans. Washington, DC: Author. Retrieved from https://www.americanprogress.org/issues/general/news/2017/04/26/431299/100-ways-trump-hurt-americans/.

Council on Social Work Education (2018, February). Statement on the Administration's FY 2019 Budget Request. Retrieved from president@cswe.org.

Cox, E., & Wood, P. (2016, November 12). Trump victory sparks activism. *The Baltimore Sun*. Retrieved from http://www.baltimoresun.com/news/maryland/politics/bs-md-trump-advocacy-20161112-story.html.

Dale, M. (2018). NASW-Kansas advocating to preserve licensed social work jobs. *NASW News*, 63(2), 4.

Enda. J. (2017, July). Donald Trump is the best – and worst – thing that's happened to modern American feminism. Slate. Retrieved from http://www.cnn.com/interactive/2017/politics/state/womens-movement-donald-trump/.

Frazell, S., & Johnson-Lewis, B. (2017, Fall). Resurgence of white supremacy: A dialogue regarding the implications on social work practice. Maryland Social Worker.

Haidar, A. (2018). Social workers and the protection of immigrant and refugee rights. Advocates' Forum. Chicago: University of Chicago School of Social Service Administration. Retrieved from www.ssa.uchicago.edu.

Hayes, C. M., Karpman, H., & Miller, J. (2016, December 3). Social work at the crossroads: How to resist the politics of a Donald Trump presidency. Huffington Post. Retrieved from www.huffingtonpost.com/entry/social-work-at-the-crossroads-how-to-resist-the-politics_us_583f22ade4b0cf36455863a.

Howard, B.C. (2017, March). A running list of how Trump is changing the environment. National Geographic. Retrieved from https://news.nationalgeographic.com/2017/03/how-trump-is-changing-science-environment/.

Howard, C. (2017, Winter). Grand challenges: The winds of change. The Maryland Social Worker, 2.

Laurio, A. (2017, November). One year later: Trump policies negatively impact social work. NASW News, 62(11), 8-10. Washington, DC: National Association of Social Workers.

National Association of Social Workers (2017). Advancing the American agenda: How the social work profession will help. Washington, DC: Author.

National Association of Social Workers (2017, November 8). In aftermath of church mass shooting, NASW calls for sensible gun control laws, public health emergency declaration. Press Release. Washington, DC: Author.

National Association of Social Workers (2017, November 28). NASW is opposed to the Tax Cuts and Jobs Act and calls on Senate to reject bill. Press Release. Washington, DC: Author.

National Association of Social Workers (2017, December 6). NASW opposes confirmation of Don Willett to the U.S. Court of Appeals for the Fifth Circuit. Press Release. Washington, DC: Author.

National Association of Social Workers (2018, January 4). NASW says Trump Administration should refrain from word censorship. Press Release. Washington, DC: Author.

National Association of Social Workers (2017, October 2017). NASW supports President Trump's declaration of opioid epidemic as public health crisis. Press Release. Washington, DC: Author.

National Association of Social Workers (2017, April). NASW: Trump budget would hard well-being of all Americans. Social Work Blog. Washington, DC: Author. Retrieved from www.socialworkblog.org/featured-articles/2017/11/one-year-later-trump-policies-negatively-impact-social-work/.

National Association of Social Workers (2017, November 15). NASW welcomes introduction of International Violence against Women Act. Press Release. Washington, DC: Author.

Pace, P. R. (2017, March). Conservative viewpoints deserve social work recognition. NASW News, 62(3), 7.

Pace, P. R. (2017, June). Experts examine social work ethics and political opinion. NASW News, 62(6), 1.

Pace, P. R. (2016, November). Grand Challenges meeting focuses on policy. NASW News, 62 (11), 1

Pace, P.R. (2018a, February). New study shows strong chapter involvement in 'Advocacy Days'. NASW News, 63(2), 1, 4.

Pace, P.R. (2018b, February). Report on social work workforce reveals title issues. NASW News, 63(2), 1, 5.

Pace, P. R. (2017, June). Summit explores ways to maximize policy impact. NASW News, 62(6), 4.

Parrott, S., Dine, A. A., Rosenbaum, D., Rice, D., Floyd, I., & Romig, K. (2018). Trump budget deeply cuts health, housing, other assistance for low- and moderate-income families. Washington, DC: Center on Budget and Policy Priorities. Retrieved from https://www.cbpp.org/research/federal-budget/trump-budget-deeply-cuts-health-housing-other-assistance-for-low-and.

Reardon, C. (2017). Social work in a post-election nation: Facing challenges, encouraging hope. Social Work Today, 17(2), 10. Retrieved from http://www.socialworktoday.com/archive/032117p10.shtml.

Reisch, M., & Andrews, J. L. (2002). The road not taken: A history of radical social work in the United States. New York: Routledge.

Southern Poverty Law Center (2016). The Trump effect: The impact of the 2016 President election on our nation's schools. Retrieved from https://www.splcenter.org/20161128/trump-effect-impact-2016-presidential-election-our-nations-schools.

Wehrmann, K.C. (2018). Members needed to help shape policies. NASW News, 63(2), 3.

Wheeler, D. (2017, February). Social work leadership in times of historic change. NASW News, *62*(2), 3.

What Can Social Workers Do to Move Forward?

Social Work in Germany: Civic Education and the Concept of 'Bildung'

Julika Bürgin

In times of democratic crises civic education is called for. Who calls for it and why? Is education an appropriate answer to that crisis and its underlying social and political conditions? This article will discuss conceptions of civic education, focusing on social work. Most considerations derive from the German context.

(Trans-)forming Politics and Oneself

This article is about "Bildung", a concept specifically used in German-speaking countries. For Robert van Krieken (2013), Bildung is more extensive than education: "Bildung means something more than education, encompassing moral and political formation as well, and social pedagogy seems to lie somewhere between education and social work, so that in translation one would often alternate between those two concepts" (p. 14). It is here called education following the international discourse. However, the concepts are distinct: education represents strongly the logic of pedagogic intervention. It is close to the German concept of "Erziehung", whereas "Bildung" in a wide anthropological understanding refers to a process of better understanding the world, oneself, and each other in that world. By forming ("bilden") themselves, individuals and collectives also form the world. Education and Bildung overlap whenever education aims to promote Bildung (not always is education directed that way). But even then, efforts to develop a better understanding of the world may fail. Education has a strong impact on how individuals and groups make sense of the world, but it does not determine it. Moreover developing an understanding of the world and oneself does not happen exclusively in the education system. Hence, education and Bildung are specifically related without being identical.

Critical theory has worked out that education is a pre-condition for power structures as well as for emancipation. Human beings make society (under given conditions), and they can understand and transform society. Critical pedagogy pursues the normative objectives of education, above all a humane and just society, where no one is in wretched circumstances or deprived of rights, and everyone has a share and a voice and is allowed to be different without fear. Emancipation is seen as a process of individual and collective liberation. Democratization requires self-determination and co-determination. What is the role of education in this process?

Education is political when human beings become aware of their own interests and take action to assert them against illegitimate rule (Faulstich, 2016, p. 56). Different from school didactics, in this view civic education is not separated from civic or political action. In contrast education and action can be seen in close interrelation. Sturzenhecker (2007) considers civic education (politische Bildung) as political action. Political information and knowledge transfer should follow the contents and processes of political action and not be disconnected from them (p. 9). According to Sturzenhecker, action is political when actors publicly weigh in, claim, discuss, and democratically deal with their interests in a community (pedagogical institution, neighbourhood, commune, society). These processes (politics) have to integrate formal procedures and institutions of democracy and politics (polity), and they take place on subject areas with specific strategies (policy).

Civic education can thus be conceptualized as (trans-)forming politics, polity, and policies and (trans-)forming oneself by confronting politics. This connects to Kunstreich and Mays' (1999) argument that human beings form social relations and themselves by confronting these relations.

The present political conditions are discussed as post-democracy, authoritarian etatism, populism, or post-politics. The different analyses have in common the view that politics are becoming less efficacious in the face of global and local challenges. From the perspective of social work, dominant policy frameworks escalate social problems: neoliberal policy intensifies and stabilizes social disintegration, and right-wing authoritarian policy promises protection to some groups, while purposefully excluding others. Facing universal problems, there is a retreat to particularistic thinking. The exclusive and fatalistic swell is not unchallenged, but emancipatory social perspectives carry little hope to be realized in the foreseeable future. In politically explosive times concrete utopia is absent.

This does not denigrate or weaken the meaning of emancipatory democratic action. Pointing out the contemporary limits of (trans-)formive politics and policies, rather, reminds us of the lack of efficacious socially-just policy. That's why civic education is closely linked but not identical with political action. We have to educate ourselves to be able to realize what current political arrangements lack. A key element of civic education is working through social contradictions. Why is society unable to use resources and technological advances to allow everybody to have a decent life? The critical educationalist Heinz-Joachim Heydorn (2004) emphasized in the late 1970s that education

(Bildung) does not overcome social contradictions but makes the contradictions aware. This consciousness raises the question of adequate action. By educating themselves, individuals become able to assess and transform their practices. Based on this understanding: how can social work open spaces to understand and re-form the world, including politics?

Civic Education: Marginal in Social Work

Education in the sense of (trans-)forming the world and oneself is not situated in the center of German social work (Walther, 2014, p. 98). Even much less central is Civic Education (in German-speaking countries termed as "politische Bildung"). There are important exceptions, above all the small but profiled field of non-formal civic education with young persons and in youth organizations (for discussion see Schröder et al., 2014). Much more widespread is youth work (in youth organizations or in open youth centers) that is by law assigned to promote civic education: "Youth work (…) shall connect with the interests of young persons and be co-determined and co-created by them. Youth work shall enable self-determination, co-responsibility for society and encourage and guide social commitment" (Social Code Book VIII, Child and Youth Services Act, §11, 1, own translation).

Of course, youth work does not primarily take place in seminars and workshops. Rather the everyday practices and conflicts within an association, a club, etc. educate by (co)determining, (co-)creating and clarifying interests. Doing so, the practices themselves are (trans-)formed. Despite the legal directive, civic education does not run itself. First, a distinctive understanding of education is under pressure by the dominant paradigm of education that is striving for qualification and success. Second, the civic and political aspects of education have to be kept in mind. In both respects, youth work has lost impact. Scherr (2008) states that despite the legal specifications, civic education is no longer seen as a core mission, but as an additional service of youth work (p.167).

Beyond the field of youth work and education there is no specific discourse in social work about civic education. No book on civic education and social work, comprising theory and concepts in different areas of activities is published in Germany, even though relevant practices exist. Poorly regarded and with few supportive resources, they prove that social work can open multiple spaces to identify interests and to better understand oneself and the world. Social workers and educators can frame, initiate and guide these processes in community work, in refugee assistance or in gender sensitive youth social work, to give a few examples. Special attention to political and civic dimensions can be drawn. Practice can be reflected on, considering if and how new perceptions and (trans-)formations emerge.

So we have to recognize first the declining significance of youth work as civic education and second a lack of basic research and discourse about civic education in social work. Third, education policy and institutionalized civic education interfere in social work. Why is that important? Social work and the formal education system (schools and higher education) pursue distinct objectives. Social work strives for social justice, human rights, and social development. The lack of autonomy to act accordingly gives social work the status of a semi-profession rather than a profession, creating serious tension in practice. If we focus on schools, they habitually grip social workers to accomplish scholastic tasks, such as promoting social and democratic competencies. On closer inspection, hereby school flashes over on a conceptual level. Classroom democracy trainings separate democratic practice from its training. In the institutional setting imposed, school social workers have to abandon core elements of what they professionally perceive as civic education in practice.

Since civic education is of minor importance for social work, social work has a weak voice in the discourse on civic education (that is itself subordinated in the educational discourse). This is unfortunate for social work as well as for civic education. Social work has much to contribute: theories of appropriation, a more holistic approach towards civic education, expertise in fields of practice with disadvantaged individuals and groups as well as an anchor in areas of action that are distant from institutionalized education. Social work could conceptually enrich non-formal civic education, define its relationship to the formal education system, and (trans-)form the constitutive social texture.

Youth Work as Social and Democratic (Trans-)formation

Differently from politics seminars inside and outside schools, civic education in youth work does not follow a curriculum. Rather it is (or should be) embedded in social processes and conflicts that emerge from topics that interest the youth involved. Against any misconception it has to be emphasized that (civic) education does not happen by itself. The pedagogical approach demands advanced knowledge and skills. Sturzenhecker (2007) suggest the following criteria: youth have to be seen (and not be diagnosed); the topics of youth have to be taken up (and not the topics of pedagogues); their histories have to be listened to; their experiences with injustice have to be made subject of discussion; they have to be made visible with their claims and interests; they have to be allowed to engage in dialogue and response; and they should be offered opportunities to widen their perspectives by getting to know the perspectives of others. In order to argue about topics democratically youth have to be respected and recognized by the pedagogues, and institutions have to be democratically organized.

There is recent research on the question to what extent youth organizations and youth centers allow civic and democratic education. The findings are relevant not only for youth work, but for social work in general. Riekmann (2011) examined how youth organizations integrate democratic action and education, a topic which so far has been rarely researched. Her core result was that youth organizations not only see themselves as 'schools of democracy', and they do not only intend to prepare youth for 'real life'. Instead youth work is designed to realize democratic action in the lifeworld of youth by being democratic. Riekmann connects to Dewey: learning happens through experience. The reality in youth organization, however, often objects to its claim that it allows youth to learn about democracy. Riekmann observed familiarization, centralization, customer and market orientation as well as power structures. She suggests youth organizations must ascertain their objectives and form structures that permit youth to experience democratic processes.

Sturzenhecker and Schwerthelm explored how open youth work can support social commitment, including in public spaces (Schwerthelm, 2015; Sturzenhecker & Schwerthelm, 2015). Pilot projects were designed to develop approaches for subject-oriented civic and democratic education. These approaches were meant to register the concerns of disadvantaged youth and their reasons for social commitment in order to give opportunities for democratic participation. By doing so professional youth workers could encourage social commitment as well as civic self-education of youth. They were given opportunities to actively co-determine und co-construct the embryonic society of the youth center, partly reaching into the communal space. Revealed though were also deficient formal-democratic structures in the open youth institutions (Schwerthelm, 2015).

Civic Education as Reflection: More than Learning

Both of these studies call for practitioners to democratize structures of youth work in a way that allow youth to (trans-)form practices and themselves democratically. But another conclusion can be drawn: under the terms of dominant social relations, youth organizations and open youth work can neither be a power-free space nor a perfect democratic structure. This limits the potential of youth work to (trans-)form democratic structures. Democratic transformation is restricted by frameworks and by incorporated views on how to conduct everyday life under conditions that are hierarchical, even oppressive. This highlights the need for another aspect of formation, namely reflection. Democratic education in youth work also means to understand the limits of democratic determination. Exploring democracy's limits does not negate the objective of democratization. In fact it can be a precondition to do the next step of democratic action.

Hence, democratic (trans-)formation includes educating about the (trans-)formation and its contradictions, too. This is a challenge for civic education practitioners, whether they are professional pedagogues or reflective activists. They need not only pedagogical and methodical competencies; they also need knowledge about society, politics, policies, and topics about which youth care (in case of youth work), as well as reflective experiences with democratic action. In this light, the proposal that social workers be educators has to be thoroughly assessed. What quality and quantity of resources are provided to social workers to accomplish the objective? There may be a need for additional resources including funding, research, training, conceptual tools, supportive work conditions, and professional development. Moreover, practitioners and scholars have to act politically themselves to lay the foundations for the civic education models they demand.

Education about democratic (trans-)formation needs involvement in transformation and distanced reflection on transformation. We can learn from youth work that both dimensions of education can unfold from the topics raised by individuals and groups, given necessary resources. At that point it should be shown why we can not bypass the sophisticated concept of Bildung by instead applying instead the concept of learning. Human beings learn to solve problems: kids learn cheating and conformity to manage school requirements, teenagers learn to internalize social performance standards, young adults learn how racist mobilization can effectively keep away refugees from a community, etc. Learning is not bound to any quality. Learning can be counterfactual and regressive. Learning can narrow and lock ones understanding and appropriation of world, as we see in conspiracy theories. Bildung includes learning, of course, but it is not neutral regarding the content. Herein the concept of Bildung is close to transformative learning (Mezirow and Associates, 2000) or expansive learning (Holzkamp, 1995). History, social structure, and social relations can, and should, be understood. It is not enough to accept different points of view.

Walther (2014) identified three levels of understanding and appropriation (Aneignung): first, the fundamental viability and capacity to act and to confront oneself and the world; second, the active (re-)construction of experiences in the world; third, Bildung as reflexive transformation of self-world-relations or forming of identity (p. 101). However, applying action theory, Bildung remains subordinated to the individual's objective to expand agency (Verfügungserweiterung) (Holzkamp, 1985; Faulstich, 2016). Only with prospect of better directing ones life conditions is there reason to transform ones perception of the world.

Understanding the world should be considered a fundamental right of every individual. But it is also a social concern. Misunderstanding the world may result in harmful practices and policies. Throughout capitalist history social contradictions have been falsely interpreted as conflicts between population groups. At present we face new efforts to build "us" against "them". The core concept of populism is that of a homogeneous "people" distinct from an external enemy (Žižek, 2006; Demirović, 2016). Understanding the social world means to understand the complexity of social relations. It requires us to overcome simplifications, including the belief in purely cognitive solutions. Möller (2017) underscores that new interpretations emerge with new experiences (pp. 52-54).

Critique and Alternative Transformation

In the face of right-wing movements and authoritarian triumph in the global north, the political debate is very limited. Instead of demanding social and democratic progress, public discourse focuses on averting further restrictions and defending achievements. In Germany the dispute on authoritarianism is mainly projected outwardly and against an identified "other" within. At the same time social and democratic rights are cut back from the center, with little protest. At present refugees are the most vulnerable and targeted group. For many of them elementary rights like family reunification are withdrawn. Detention centers are designed to isolate them from society. The rule of law for many war refugees is reduced to the deportation order. These policies are implemented from established Christian Democrats in a grand coalition with Social Democrats. Both draw a line against populists. They even promote sanctions against refugees by saying they are directed against the rise of populism. With the use of anti-populist language, democratic rights of marginalized groups are undermined. Winkler (2014) sees a new form of politics emerging out of social relations that is highly authoritarian. It has little to do with democracy and justice but represents the demarcations that prevail in a capitalist society (p. 35).

In a representative survey of 2016 almost three quarters of Germans agreed to the statement that 'people like me cannot influence what the government is doing' (Decker u. a. 2016, p. 54). There is little ability left to imagine democratic progress. In a brochure of the federal agency for civic education, this resignation is turned into a program. The political scientist Hans Vorländer (2017) warns against applying high standards of critique (e.g. with the discourse on post-democracy) and expecting too much from democracy (p. 80). However it is precisely critique that gives democracy a chance to resurge. Inherent in the act of critique is the conviction that "democracy after demos" (Rancière, 2002, p. 111) is not inevitable. It is fatalistic to consider the democratic condition as fundamentally unchangeable, and it gives reason to search for solutions beyond democracy.

The crisis of democracy asks us to consider alternatives to given social relations. As a precondition all voices have to be listened to (Eis, 2016, p. 113). Against the handing over of politics to transnational governance-networks, ideas of radical democracy can be renewed, with all members of a community participating to define general interests and to make decisions (Demirović, 2016, p. 299). Furthermore economic and social justice should be moved to the center of democracy theory, identifying where inequality is produced and participation impeded (policy, education, media, urban planning, etc.). As a result, the interests of minority voices could be recognized and championed (Salomon, 2016).

The current order placed on the education system is to absorb the crisis of democracy (Eis, 2016). It is time to emancipate education from this directive. Instead, social work is asked to democratize its structures and open spaces to reflect on structures of social justice and democratic alternatives that are all-inclusive.

References

Balzter, N., Ristau, Y., & Schröder, A. (2014). Wie politische Bildung wirkt. Wirkungsstudie zur biographischen Nachhaltigkeit politischer Jugendbildung. Schwalbach/Ts.: Wochenschau.

Decker, O., Kiess, J., Eggers, E. & Brähler, E. (2016): Die »Mitte«-Studie 2016: Methode, Ergebnisse und Langzeitverlauf. In: E. Brähler, O. Decker & J. Kiess (Eds.): Die enthemmte Mitte. Autoritäre und rechtsextreme Einstellung in Deutschland: die Leipziger "Mitte"-Studie 2016. Gießen: Psychosozial-Verlag (pp. 67–94). Retrieved from: https://www.boell.de/sites/default/files/buch_mitte_studie_uni_leipzig_2016.pdf (24.09.18)

Demirović, A. (2016). Demokratie – zwischen autoritären Tendenzen und gesellschaftlicher Transformation. Zur Kritik der politischen Demokratie. In A. Demirović (Ed.). Transformation der Demokratie – demokratische Transformation (pp. 278-302). Münster: Westfälisches Dampfboot.

Eis, A. (2016). Partizipation und politisches Lernen in der postdemokratischen Aktivgesellschaft. In A. Demirović, (Ed.). Transformation der Demokratie – demokratische Transformation (pp. 104-122). Münster: Westfälisches Dampfboot.
Faulstich, P. (2016). Das Politische in der Bildung. In K. Hufer & D. Lange (Eds.), Handbuch Politische Erwachsenenbildung (pp. 52-61). Schwalbach/Ts: Wochenschau.
Heydorn, H. (2004). Überleben durch Bildung. Umriss einer Aussicht. In H. Heydorn (Ed.), Werke, Band 4 (pp. 254-273). Wetzlar: Büchse der Pandora.
Holzkamp, K. (1985). Grundlegung der Psychologie. Frankfurt am Main: Campus.
Holzkamp, K. (1995). Lernen. Subjektwissenschaftliche Grundlegung. Frankfurt am Main: Campus.
Kunstreich, T., & May, M. (1999). Soziale Arbeit als Bildung des Sozialen und Bildung am Sozialen. Widersprüche 73 (pp.35–52).
Mezirow, J. and Associates. (2000). Learning as Transformation. Critical perspectives on a theory in progress. San Francisco: Jossey Bass.
Möller, Kurt (2017). Rechtspopulismus jenseits von Argumenten begegnen. Sozialmagazin. Rechtspopulismus und Soziale Arbeit (pp. 47-54).
Rancière, J. (2002). Das Unvernehmen. Politik und Philosophie. Frankfurt am Main: Suhrkamp.
Riekmann, W. (2011). Strukturen bilden. Demokratie in der Jugendverbandsarbeit. In G. Flößer (Ed.), Jugendhilfeforschung (pp. 151-162). Wiesbaden: VS.
Salomon, D. (2016). Demokratisierung aller Lebensbereiche? Bilanz und Perspektiven Sozialer Demokratie. In A. Demirović (Ed.), Transformation der Demokratie – demokratische Transformation (pp. 249-164). Münster: Westfälisches Dampfboot.
Scherr, A. (2008) Gesellschaftspolitische Bildung – Kernaufgabe oder Zusatzleistung der Jugendarbeit? In: H. Otto, & T. Rauschenbach (Eds.), Die *andere Seite der Bildung. Zum Verhältnis von formellen und informellen Bildungsprozessen* (pp. 167-180). Wiesbaden: VS.
Schwerthelm, M. (2015). Förderung gesellschaftlichen Engagements Benachteiligter in der Offenen Kinder-und Jugendarbeit – Erfolge und Schwierigkeiten. Zur Evaluation des gleichnamigen Projekts der Bertelsmann Stiftung. Hamburg: Universität Hamburg. Retrieved from: https://www.ew.uni-hamburg.de/einrichtungen/ew2/sozialpaedagogik/files/schwerthelm-erfolge-gebe.pdf (24.09.2018).
Sturzenhecker, B.(2007). "Politikferne" Jugendliche in der Kinder- und Jugendarbeit. Aus Politik und Zeitgeschichte 32-33/2007 (pp. 9–14).
Sturzenhecker, B. (2015). Gesellschaftliches Engagement von Benachteiligten fördern, Band 1. Konzeptionelle Grundlagen für die Offene Kinder- und Jugendarbeit. Gütersloh: Verlag Bertelsmann-Stiftung.
Sturzenhecker, B., & Schwerthelm, M. (2015). Gesellschaftliches Engagement von Benachteiligten fördern, Band 2. Methodische Anregungen und Praxisbeispiele für die Offene Kinder- und Jugendarbeit. Gütersloh: Verlag Bertelsmann-Stiftung.

Van Krieken, R. (2013). Translating Heinz Sünker: reflecitions on the critical theoritisation of ‚Bildung' and social pedagogy. In: R. Braches-Chyrek, D. Nelles, G. Oelerich, A. Schaarschuch (Eds.): Bildung, Gesellschaftstheorie und Soziale Arbeit. Opladen/Berlin/Toronto: Barbara Budrich (pp. 13-19).

Vorländer, H. (2017). Demokratie – in der Krise und doch die beste Herrschaftsform? In: Bundeszentrale für Politische Bildung (Ed.): Informationen zur politischen Bildung, Heft 332 1/2017: Demokratie (pp. 72–81). Retrieved from: www.bpb.de/system/files/dokument_pdf/170510_BPB_667-17_IzpB%20332%20Demokratie_10_barrierefrei.pdf (22.6.2017).

Walther, A. (2014). Aneignung und Anerkennung. Subjektbezogene und soziale Dimensionen eines sozialpädagogischen Bildungsbegriffs. In: U. Deinet & C. Reutlinger (Eds.): Tätigkeit - Aneignung - Bildung. Positionierungen zwischen Virtualität und Gegenständlichkeit. Wiesbaden: Springer VS (pp. 97–112).

Winkler, M. (2014). Soziale Arbeit – dringende Erinnerung an ihr emanzipatorisches Potential. In M. Panitzsch-Wiebe, B. Becker, & T. Kunstreich (Eds.), Politik der Sozialen Arbeit – Politik des Sozialen. Opladen/Berlin/Toronto: Barbara Budrich (pp. 30–38).

Žižek, S. (2006?): Against the Populist Temptation. Retrieved from: http://www.lacan.com/zizpopulism.htm (15.09.2017)

Social Work in Post-Factual Times

Kerry Dunn

Social work has long recognized the role of collective meaning-making in group, community, and social change (Finn & Jacobson, 2003). Groups are stronger when multiple views are heard and knowledge is co-created (Bray & Lee, 2000). We get a better picture of the elephant as a whole when each person brings in the piece they see. But this assumes there is an elephant – something everyone in the room wants collectively to learn more about. The challenge has always been what to do when someone describes a snout or says elephants can fly. I do not refer here to resistance or psychosis, but to people with incongruent ideas about what is happening. I use this example to illustrate our post-fact existence in which people not only live in separate worlds of reality but also different sets of rules about how truth is achieved. The purpose of this chapter is to explore the characteristics of post-fact society and their implications for socially-just practice.

Social work is a profession as well as a social science. It is part of the collective effort to understand and solve social problems. We use evidence to guide practice, create and improve programs, and advocate for policies. We understand that information is never completely free from bias and is always incomplete. We have had to figure out how to reconcile empirical research with competing forms of understanding including practice wisdom and indigenous knowledge. Nonetheless, we have faith that through this process of conversation and contest, we can get closer to understanding social phenomena and their causes and to find solutions. While our role may seem less clear, or even phony, in a post-fact society, we must quickly regain our footing so that we can play a role as the public makes sense of shifting terrains of fact and truth.

The post-fact era is one of anti-intellectualism "a phenomenon that has become so intensified in the last two decades that even to try to correct someone on what might have once been considered the most basic of facts can open one to the charge of 'elitism'" (Swanger, 2017, p. 9).

We have seen the rise of 'alternative facts' that serve to undermine our efforts to understand and address material and symbolic inequities. Despite evidence that immigrants have lower crime rates, immigration policy decisions are based on the 'alternative fact' that immigrants are criminals. Despite scientific consensus that climate change is caused by human activity, energy policy is based on the 'alternative fact' that climate change is fabrication. We must understand how alternative facts are created and given power if we are to continue to serve our historic role as advocates for the vulnerable and caretakers of the social fabric.

Whether what is happening today is new or confluence of familiar phenomenon, the complexity of the current moment is clear. We need to understand what post-factual politics means so that we can decide how to retool ourselves and the next generation of social workers. To this end, I summarize contemporary thinking on what is happening and why. I explore key themes including the purpose and dangers of lying in politics; the erosion of facts in our media through false balance and fake news; the deliberate production of ignorance by state and corporate agents; the shifting balance of emotions, values, and facts in public discourse; and whether anything is new about alternate realities, or the ways that groups within a society have competing ideas about what is true. I will conclude with some thoughts on the implications of post-factual politics for social work practice and education.

Much more is written about "post-truth" than "post-fact." I will use them somewhat interchangeably, although they represent slightly different but connected phenomena. Post-truth refers to the idea that the concept of truth, which traditionally has referred to that which is in accordance with reality, no longer has the same meaning. Post-truth also refers to a shift in public consciousness, from Truth and truths (competing and multiple) to "truthiness" – basing ones sense of truth on feeling rather than evidence – and thruthlessness, or the complete separation of assertions of truth from factual evidence.

Post-fact refers to a loss of faith in the concept of fact itself. Information based on evidence no longer has the same influence on public debate, and the criteria for what can be called a fact are no longer respected. The attack on truth and facts frightens us because factual truth has long served as the basis for public discourse (Birmingham, 2010, citing Arendt, 1945). Members of a democratic society are able to share opinions and debate ideas when we respect factual truth. The fear is that without factual truth, we have no public sphere and no bulwark against totalitarianism (Birmingham, 2010).

Understanding Post-Fact

In the post-fact world, "virtually all authoritative information sources [are] called into question and challenged by contrary facts of dubious quality and provenance" (Fukuyama, 2017). The traditional solution – to put out good information and let it rise to the top – no longer works in our world of social media where new technologies are weaponized to spread misinformation through trolls, bots, and fake news stories. Trust in the impartial institutions we once relied on in the US to produce factual information (i.e., government agencies, newspapers of record) has eroded (Fukuyama, 2017). The rules of what constitutes a fact have changed, and we have "[moved] from a situation in which information find value through incorporation into meaningful collections on the basis of reasonably well-defined criteria to a situation where information find value through wide circulation..." (Laybatts & Tredinnick, 2016).

The idea that "facts" are in crisis is often linked to both postmodernism and the information society. "The problem is the oversupply of facts in the 21st century: There are too many sources, too many methods, with varying levels of credibility, depending on who funded a given study and how the eye-catching number was selected" (Davies, 2016). Factual truth, which requires credible testimony and witnessing, is challenged by the ability of anyone with a camera, computer, and ability to manipulate images to provide fake witness (Manjoo, 2008). The idea of 'fact' is a historical product, emerging in medieval times and increasing in power over centuries with the creation of modern governments, academic institutions, social sciences and management professions. Just as the rise of the fact was a transition period, "We are in the middle of a transition from a society of facts to a society of data. During this interim, confusion abounds surrounding the exact status of knowledge...in public life" (Davies, 2016).

With our experience in crisis intervention and trauma, the current climate of change, fear, and confusion is familiar terrain for social workers. Out of all of the disciplines and professions, we are one of the best suited to helping turn the fact crisis into an opportunity for healing and creating a potentially more socially just configuration of the public sphere.

Lying in Politics

Lying, spinning, mudslinging, and misleading are not new phenomenon in US politics. Trump is not the first to make untrue statements about an opponent to tarnish their image, knowing that fact-checkers could not completely undo the damage. But scholars and journalists distinguish two key features of the current moment. The first is the amount of false information that is easily proven to be not true spoken by people with enormous power and their representatives. Despite their obvious falsehood, it is almost impossible for anyone else diminish the lies' power. The second is the fact that lying no longer carries consequences for powerful actors. Being caught in a lie no longer requires an apology and no longer results in punishment (Boston, 2015). Totalitarian-style lying is not new in the world, but the amount of it happening in liberal democracies is alarming.

As Swanger (2017) explains, post-fact statements "are of a different order than that of plain lie or plain lie rendered more potent by the architecture of propaganda... [T]hese kinds of statements are constructed so as to be beyond the reach of evidentiary remedy...Unlike the lie and propaganda, these kinds of statements do not operate in relation to concealment....They are, instead, as public as one could wish..." (pp. 11-12). Questions about events that should have been easily answered by factual evidence remain disputed. Often cited examples of post-fact debates include whether Iraq had weapons of mass destruction, whether or not John Kerry was a war hero in Vietnam, and whether President Obama was born in the US.

The modern lie is dangerous for a variety of reasons. For one, it can distract from important issues and create disorientation among political opponents, journalists, and voters, impeding the democratic process. Political strategists have admitted to doing this on purpose. As Karl Rove famously said in an interview with the New York Times, "When we act, we create our own reality. And while you're studying that reality... we'll act again, creating other new realities." These tactics of disorientation create new challenges for policy advocates, organizers, and social movement leaders who may have a harder time identifying a target and keeping members engaged.

Another danger is the devaluation of the history in which the struggle for social justice is grounded. Several journalists and scholars have written about the way the modern lie, and Trump's use of lying in particular, represent efforts to rewrite history, to take away the power of leftist and centrist interpretation of history (e.g., McGranahan, 2017). Many scholars to have looked to Hannah Arendt's work on totalitarianism to understand the use of lies in contemporary politics. For Arendt, the modern political lie does not merely attempt to mislead but to rewrite history and thereby change reality (Caruth, 2010, citing Arendt, 1971). The modern lie goes beyond hiding; it destroys. "The violence of the modern lie in the absolute loss of the reality that it denies" (Birmingham, 2010, p. 83, citing Arendt, 1973).

A final danger is the ability of the post-fact lie to create division and incite violence. By creating and feeding stereotypes, lies facilitate the targeting of particular social groups. Modern lies create a sense of chaos, leaving us vulnerable to the liar's promise of certainty about who is the problem and what is the solution. We need to recognize the way that modern lies mimic domestic violence and its strategy of isolation. Our profession has decades of knowledge on working in family and community violence, and we have skills to offer. We can only do this effectively if we draw on the skills we have honed working in high-stress environments to recognize toxic dynamics and take care of our own mental and emotional health. We have the knowledge and skills needed to avoid disorientation and help others find ground.

Facts, Values, Emotions

Facts – ideas about reality with institutional support – have never been the most powerful player in politics. US politics is a messy mix of interests, values, ideology, symbols, stories, and emotions. As Stone (2011) explains, policy conflicts do not arise because of a lack of facts, or even a dispute over facts. Most conflicts are over values, with facts used to support a particular value-based claim. The ideal of policymaking through rational deliberation has always been somewhat of an illusion (Stone, 2011). Facts have always been intertwined with values and ideology in political truthmaking. It is already part of the social worker's skill set to provide policymakers with both data and stories to appeal on both rational and symbolic levels and to use common interests to build relationships across ideological divides.

We may, however, need to do some retooling. One characteristic of the post-fact period is the sense that emotions, particularly anger, are more important indicators of truth than facts (Suiter, 2016; Laybatts & Tredinnick, 2016). Truth is no longer judged by factual evidence but by emotional resonance. People want to be free from the traditional rules of truth, the labor of evidence, and the risk of authentic dialog. As Pomerantsev (2016) explains:

> The very point of Trump is to validate the pleasure of spouting shit, the joy of pure emotion, often anger, without any sense. And an audience which has already spent a decade living without facts can now indulge in a full, anarchic liberation from coherence.

People want to be free from truths that do not match their experience, truths that challenge their sense of self, and truths that feel too uncomfortable or painful to bear. As social workers, we can see that the devaluation of factual truth is connected to suffering, and finding a new balance between facts, values, and emotions in policymaking starts with a recognition of that suffering.

False Balance, Fake News, and the Production of Ignorance

In a large, complex, industrialized nation like the US, citizens need help gathering information outside of their direct experience in order to understand issues facing their city, state, and country. We have long relied on the press to keep us informed, and this has always been problematic, given that the press is beholden to advertisers and customers (Bybee, 1999, citing Lippman, 1922).

The relationship between media and corporate interests is well studied. In *Manufacturing Consent*, Herman & Chomsky (1992) describe the role of capital investment and profit-making in the production of news mass media outlets. Investors and advertisers influence content. Editors leave out content to avoid negative responses that could reduce revenue. These dangers of investor- and consumer-driven news were heightened with the advent of cable news stations and the super-sizing of media corporations.

The profit motive of today's large media corporations is deeply connected to our fact crisis. False balance is "the journalistic practice of giving equal weight to both sides of a story, regardless of an established truth on one side" (Sullivan, 2012) or "giving equal weight to unsupported or even discredited claims for the sake of appearing impartial" (vanden Heuvel, 2014). Driven by the need to market themselves as impartial, media outlets stretch to find two sides, even if it means presenting viewpoints with no substantiating evidence. The result is a devaluing of evidence-based knowledge, expertise, and facts.

Another hallmark of post-fact media is fake news. While a somewhat recent addition to our public vocabulary, fake news has roots in both propaganda and corporate campaigns to debunk unflattering science. A useful concept here is agnotology – the study of ignorance. While there are multiple forms of ignorance, the one most relevant for our discussion here is "strategic ploy" ignorance (Proctor, 2008, p. 3). Strategic ploy or active construct ignorance is deliberately engineered, and a group that does not want another group or members of the public to know certain things "actively work to organize doubt or uncertainty or misinformation to help maintain…ignorance (Proctor, 2008, p. 8). Examples include trade secrets, military secrecy, and corporate attempts to hide dangers associated with their products. Corporations and governments have long been involved in manipulating the facts by withholding information, providing incomplete or slanted information, and controlling what information is circulated by the media (Stone, 2011). Though today due to social media these entities may have less control over what is circulated, they have more means for spreading misleading information.

One key tactic of manufacturing ignorance is affirming the absence of definite proof. Proctor (2008) describes how the tobacco industry manufactured doubt about the hazards of smoking. When research began to accumulate showing a link between cigarettes and cancer, the tobacco industry launched a campaign to inject doubt into the public's understanding. "Through press releases, advertisements, and well-funded industry research fronts, epidemiology was denounced as 'mere statistics', animal experiments were said not to reflect the human condition, and lung pathologies revealed at autopsy were derided as anecdotes without 'sound science'" (Proctor, pp. 11-12). A related tactic is requiring high proof. An example of this tactic is the claim that here is not enough consensus on whether human activity is causing climate change for us to base policy decisions on it (Sismondo, 2017). Like tobacco, the fossil fuel industry has engaged in an agnotological project, "where any disagreement is amplified to try to create a picture of complete dissensus" (Sismondo, 2017 p. 5, citing Oreskes & Conway, 2010).

The goal is to muddy waters so that no clear truth exists. While state-sponsored propaganda is a familiar creature, we now also have a market-driven fake new industry. The fake-news industry is made up of outlets with ideological motives, but also those purely concerned with profit. Some fake news outlets are paid directly by business and ideological interests for the dissemination of fictitious "facts" (Rabin-Havt, 2016). Others make their money from advertising revenue, tailoring stories to readers. The result is a proliferation of fabricated "news" stories designed to satisfy not only political and corporate interests, but also consumer demand.

Activists, advocates, victims, and politicians fought back against big tobacco, eventually winning lawsuits and regulations. As social workers, we know how to collect data and stories; support victims; collaborate with lawyers, journalists, community leaders, and lawmakers; build networks and coalitions; and maintain a long-term vision. Responding to the marketization of ignorance does not require much retooling if we still have faith in the power of collective action and effectiveness of courts and legislatures.

Alternate Realities

Another aspect of post-fact society taking on new forms in the US is the coexistence of multiple realities. Throughout our history, dominant storylines have elided people's experiences, forcing many to live with a fractured sense of reality. Our entire project of nation-building was based on the viewpoint of a particular group claiming to be universal, for example that America was empty land waiting to be discovered by Europeans or that whites were a superior race justified in killing and enslaving non-whites (Mills, 2008). The legacy of racialized and classed hierarchies continues to shape lives and perspectives. Researchers have documented the role of segregated neighborhoods in the creation and maintenance of incongruent worldviews (e.g., Massey & Denton, 1993). Our country is also full of religious, ideological, and cultural groups who have created alternative institutions (i.e., schools, newspapers, publishing companies, housing developments, ritualized gatherings) to support their truth.

And yet, alarms sound today about social media is fostering unprecedented splintering in how we make sense of government, community, and ourselves. Social media bubbles allow groups to isolate themselves even further than physical and institutional segregation, tailoring media consumption in ways that exclude anything that could challenge ones worldview (Laybatts & Tredinnick, 2016). The election of Donald Trump was a shock to many liberal whites because it was nonsensical in their reality bubble.

As social workers, we know how much social context shapes people's experience, and how much experience shapes worldview. But we may need to enhance our understanding of digital contexts and the power of digital segregation. We know from Marx that exploitive socioeconomic relations fundamentally shape social ideation (Mills, 2008). We have a long history of helping communities bring those relations to light. We also know from post-modern theory that there are multiple truths, and from post-modern practice that the work is helping others sit with, not shut out, complex truth worlds. Social workers have the skills to help people dig into their worldviews on both individual and group levels.

Implications for Social Work Practice and Education

As Mair (2017) argues, most of the existing explanations for post-truth portray the public as passive victims of social media echo chambers, information overload, and clickbait. The image of the public as pawns is incomplete; we must also remember that humans are active, meaning-making beings who are engaging knowledge, skills, values, and reflection to make sense of contemporary contexts. As Mair (2017) explains,

> If the Enlightenment project can be thought of as an attempt to establish a new epistemological settlement, displacing an older one, then perhaps what we are witnessing is a new struggle – or a new phase in an ongoing struggle – over theories of truth, belief and knowledge, in the context of a radically altered information environment (p. 4).

Seeing the public as active gives advocates a toe-hold, a place to engage individuals and communities in activities that help develop a deeper understanding of their relationship to the whole.

I have already touched on above the various skills social workers have that are relevant in the post-fact context. In this section, I will discuss further the various ways we can draw on those skills to make change. These include: joining the effort to figure out the role facts can still play in today's struggles for justice, skilling ourselves and our students in media literacy for a post-truth media landscape, continuing to learn and teach reflection and introspection to help us stay grounded and avoid disorientation, and engaging in authentic and persistent community practice.

Adjusting our relationship to facts

We need to get really clear about the pros and cons of the traditional concept of fact, and what we want 'fact' to mean in the future. Peace studies scholar Swanger (2017) looks that the question of what post-fact means for social movements in the US. She wonders whether it is wise to wait for facts to rescue us:

> ...the Indisputables, as rare as precious gems but apparently not yet in any high demand. In fact, they appear quite useless: for example, '*The Graduate* was released in 1967'; 'The National Guard killed four white college students at Kent State in 1970'; 'Nixon was re-elected in 1972'... This smattering of plain-looking pebbles of indisputable facts is all that remains of any possible grounds on which to forge a consensus – if we continue to insist on sticking to the facts, on looking to the facts to rescue us. And what kind of 'consensus' would that be? (Swanger, 2017, p. 4).

The fear of letting go of facts, of letting fiction win out over facts, is that it will lead to totalitarianism. But it may not be wise or possible to return facts to their previous status. Instead of thinking about facts in terms of true and false, it may be more helpful to think of true – that which has historical, archival, investigative, empirical, and/or institutional support--and fictional – that which lacks that support but which still has 'meaning-giving discursive structure'" (Swanger, 2017, p. 13, citing White, 2010). Clinical social workers already know how to make space for facts that are not based on evidence but that clients hold dear. Those skills must be translated to community and policy practice.

Media literacy

"The traditional remedy for this malady of misinformation has been information literacy, digital literacy, and critical reasoning skills" (Laybatts & Tredinnick, 2016). We may need to partner with professionals outside in other professions and disciplines, including information technology and communications. Let us not leave our students to fend for themselves, believing their generation knows more about digital technologies, but instead focus specifically on identifying credible sources, avoiding information bubbles, and bridging digital communities.

Introspection and following one's conscience

To address the pull of totalitarianism, Arendt (1958) recommends a return to thinking, reflection, and dialogue with oneself. This involves honestly facing what is happening, enacting obstacles to oversimplification, and following not ideology but conscience. All of this should sound familiar to social workers well versed in reflection, supervision, and reflexive practice. We do not need to learn new skills but affirm out commitment to introspection. Post-truth feels post-conscience, like a time when people lie or mislead because truth is no longer required. When formal rules regulating lying weaken, we can help people, and be helped by others, to reflect on how lying feels and reject it (Berkowitz, 2010, citing Arendt, 1958).

Consciousness-raising and community organizing

Facts are the lifeblood of expert-driven policy making. While post-fact politics brings many challenges, it is also an opportunity to move beyond top-down models and to allow more voices into the policy process. This requires bottom-up movement building and community-based work. Social media tools can support but not supplant the shoulder-to-shoulder work that builds trust, relationships, and commitment. Let us also create opportunities for good old-fashioned consciousness-raising to expose corporate and government-sponsored realities that do not ring true to people's experiences.

Conclusion

Social workers have many relevant skills for addressing challenges faced in the post-fact political and social landscape. As our society makes sense of the shifting terrain of fact and truth, we have an opportunity to assert ourselves into public discourse to advocate for more equitable social relationships. We must start by clearly articulating a model for post-fact action. To do so, we must be ready to learn from other disciplines to acquire skills in digital literacy. But we must also acknowledge the relevance of our expertise in reflection, empathetic listening, trauma, family and group work, and community organizing.

References

Arendt, H. (1945). The seeds of a fascist international. Essays in understanding, 1930-1954: Formation, exile and totalitarianism. Schocken Books.
Arendt, H. (1951). The origins of totalitarianism. New York: Harcourt Brace.
Arendt, H. (1958). The human condition. Chicago: University of Chicago Press.
Arendt, H. (1971, November 18). Lying in politics: Reflections on the Pentagon Papers. New York Times Review of Books.
Berkowitz, R. (2010). Introduction. In R. Berkowitz, J. Katz, & T. Keenan (Eds). Thinking in dark Times (pp. 3-18). New York, NY: Fordham University Press.
Birmingham, P. (2010). A lying world order: Political deception and the threat of totalitarianism. In R. Berkowitz, J. Katz, & T. Keenan (Eds.), Thinking in dark Times (pp. 73-77). New York, NY: Fordham University Press.
Bray, J.N., Lee, J. (2000). Collaborative inquiry in practice: Action, reflection, and meaning making. Thousand Oaks, CA: Sage.
Bybee, C. (1999). Can democracy survive in the post-factual age?: A return to the Lippman-Dewey debate about the politics of news. Journalism and Communication Monographs.
Caruth, C (2010). Lying and history. In R. Berkowitz, J. Katz, & T. Keenan (Eds). Thinking in dark Times (pp. 79-92). New York, NY: Fordham University Press.
Davies, W. (2016, August 25). The Age of Post-Truth Politics, New York Times.
Finn, J. L., & Jacobson, M. (2003). Just practice: Steps toward a new social work paradigm. Journal of Social Work Education, 39, 57-78.
Herman, E., Chomsky, N. (1992). Manufacturing consent: The political economy of mass media, 2nd Ed. New York: Pantheon.
Keyes, R. (2004). The post-truth era: Dishonesty and deception in contemporary life. St. Martin's Press.
Laybatts, C., Tredinnick, L. (2016). Post-truth, information and emotion. Business Information Review, 33(4), 204-6.
Lippmann, W. (1922). Public opinion. New York: Harcourt Brace.
Mair, J. (2017). Post-truth anthropology. Anthropology Today. 33(3), 3-4.
Manjoo, F. (2008). True enough: Learning to live in a post-fact society. Hoboken, NJ: Wiley.
Massey, D., & Denton, N. (1993). American apartheid: Segregation and the making of the underclass. Cambridge, MA: Harvard University Press.
McGranahan, C. (2017). An anthropology of lying: Trump and the political sociality of moral outrage. American Ethnologist, 44(2), 1-6.
Mills, C. (2008). White ignorance. In R. Proctor & L. Schiebinger (Eds.), Agnotology: The making and unmaking of ignorance (pp. 230-249). Stanford, CA: Stanford University Press.
Pomerantsev, P. (2016, July 10). Why we're post fact. Granta.
Proctor, R. (2008). Agnotology: A missing term to describe the cultural production of ignorance (and its study). In R. Proctor & L. Schiebinger (Eds.), Agnotology:

The making and unmaking of ignorance (pp. 1-33). Stanford, CA: Stanford University Press.

Rabin-Hayt, R. (2016). Lies, incorporated: The world of post-truth politics. Anchor.

Sismondo, S. (2017). Post-truth? Social Studies of Science, 47, 3-6.

Stone, D. (2011). Policy paradox: The art of political decisionmaking, 3rd Ed. W.W. Norton and Co.

Swanger, J. (2017). Racial social change in the United States: Badiou's apostle and the post-factual moment. Palgrave.

Suiter, J. (2016). Post-Truth politics. Political Insight, 25-27.

White, H. (2010). The fiction of narrative: Essays on history, literature and theory, 1957-2007. Baltimore: Johns Hopkins University Press.

Worthen, M. (2017, April 13). The Evangelical Roots of Our Post-Truth Society, New York Times.

Human Rights Based Social Work and New Right Populism

Cheryl A. Hyde & Claire Galpern

> The General Assembly [of the United Nations] - Proclaims this Universal Declaration of Human Rights as a common standard of achievement for all peoples and all nations, to the end that every individual and every organ of society, keeping this Declaration constantly in mind, shall strive by teaching and education to promote respect for these rights and freedoms and by progressive measures, national and international, to secure their universal and effective recognition and observance, both among the peoples of Member States themselves and among the peoples of territories under their jurisdiction.
>
> The Universal Declaration of Human Rights

December 10, 2018 marks the 70th anniversary of the adoption of the Universal Declaration of Human Rights (UDHR) by the United Nations General Assembly. This historic document, produced in the shadow of the Holocaust, serves as the touchstone for the broad human rights movement, affirming the fundamental rights of all people to economic, political and cultural security. While not legally binding, it has been the basis for various international laws, covenants and treaties, and frames the ways in which organizations and movements protect and pursue human rights (http://www.un.org/en/universal-declaration-human-rights/). This includes the profession of social work.

In this chapter, we provide an overview of the basic human rights tenets and discuss how these principles relate to social work. We consider how social work's values and ethics dovetail with human rights, as well as social work initiatives and issues that are part of human rights campaigns. We then suggest that a human rights framework for social work is an essential component in confronting the rising challenge of right wing populism. Our primary emphasis is on the United States.

Principles of Human Rights

At first glance, it may seem obvious that a human rights perspective focuses on "human" and "rights" (Wronka, 2013). Yet as Ife (2009) suggests, these components are actually quite complex with commonly shared definitions often illusive. "Rights" are seen as encompassing three traditions: natural rights, state obligations, and constructed rights. Natural rights are believed to originate in human nature and as such, are universal. States-obligated rights are generated (or taken away) by legislative or deliberative bodies, and thus are contingent on the actions of these bodies. Constructed rights are derived from lived experiences and are framed by the context from which they arise (Douzinas, 2000; Ife, 2009; Orend, 2002). While philosophically the claim of universal rights is set forth often, human rights campaigns largely are shaped by states-obligated and constructed rights (Clapham, 2015; Donnelly, 2013).

Parsing what "human" means necessitates considering what types of groups or individuals, historically and currently, are not viewed as fully human (Clapham, 2015; Ife, 2009). Africans who were enslaved, indigenous people who were targeted with genocide in the Americas, Jews who were exterminated in Nazi Germany, people with mental illnesses who were locked away, and so forth, have been (and in some cases continue to be) designated as "not human" and therefore not worthy of society's protection but rather deserving of exploitation and destruction. To recognize that all individuals, regardless of gender, race, nationality, religion, age, health, citizenship and so forth should be ensured basic rights against abuse, torture, and genocide was and is an extraordinary claim (Buergenthal, Shelton & Steward, 2002; Wronka, 2013). As will be discussed below, this is a critical piece in refuting right wing ideology.

Essentially, human rights is a "legal mandate to fulfill human need" (Wronka, 2013), as articulated by the UDHR and subsequent documents such as Convention on the Elimination of All Forms of Racial Discrimination (1966), the Convention against Torture and other Cruel, Inhuman or Degrading Treatment or Punishment (1984) and the Convention on the Rights of Persons with Disabilities (2006) (for a list of human rights documents, see Ife, 2009). These articulations of human rights did not just spring forth in the 1940s; indeed, there is a rich history including such documents as the U.S. Declaration of Independence and France's Declaration of the Rights of Man and Citizen (Hunt, 2007). Generally, three waves, or generations, of human rights are recognized (Ife, 2009; Wronka, 2017; Mapp, 2014). First generation rights encompass political and civil rights that are individually based (e.g. freedom of speech, right to a fair trial). Human rights actions that focus on first generation rights usually involve the prevention of human rights abuse and the protection of exiting rights. Second generation rights social, cultural, and economic rights (e.g. right to education, employment, health care); these rights support individuals and groups in reaching their full potential. Collective rights (e.g. healthy environment, beneficial economic development for Global south countries, indigenous sovereignty) constitute third generation rights. This set of rights, which were recognized more recently and are not in reflected in any UN covenant, focuses on the rights of communities or populations and stand in contrast to the individual based first and second generation rights. Indeed most western democracies, including (especially) the United States, equates human rights with individual civil liberties rather than the broader range of societal level political, cultural and economic rights (Clayton & Hopps, 2013; Ife, 2016). This relatively narrow perspective has implications for how U.S. social work engages in human rights campaigns.

Human rights work tends to fall into three interconnected categories: the law, institutions, and social movements (Hunt, 2007; Limoncelli, 2017). It is through organizations such as Amnesty International, the Human Rights Campaign, Advocates for Human Rights, the International Labour Organization or Oxfam that most of us become familiar with human rights issues and initiatives. These non-government organizations (NGOs) provide infrastructure for human rights initiatives by serving as advocates and watchdogs, providing myriad resources, and litigating critical cases. Broader mobilizations to end human rights abuses and advance human rights to disenfranchised populations often directly challenge states and regimes from the "bottom up" in their pursuit of collective rights (Nussbaum, 2016; Shannon, 2016).

There is, however, an ongoing debate as to whether "human rights" is a useful framework for achieving social and economic justice. Other liberation and justice language and strategies may be more useful and can get excluded by the dominance of human rights, or at least first generation human rights (Ife, 2016; Wronka, 2017). The emphasis of the human rights framework on the relationship between the state and the individual may not leave room for taking into account economic forces and issues; nor does the state granting rights facilitate bottom-up empowerment (Kennedy, 2004, 2006, 2012; Ryckman, 2016). Framing individuals as "rights-holders" may reify ideas about entitlement and victimization, sentiments that are fundamental to right wing populism and deter cross-community coalitions and broader social change efforts (Cemlyn, 2008; Hochschild, 2016; Kennedy, 2004, 2006, 2012). There is the danger of justifying harmful or imperialistic military occupation in the name of "humanitarian intervention." And more powerful countries, such as the United States, tend to highlight human rights violations in the Global South while ignoring their own human rights abuses (Wronka, 2017). Nonetheless, human rights movements across the globe have brought attention to, and in some cases successfully mobilized interventions against, issues such as human trafficking, genocide and ethnic cleansing, war crimes, torture and corporal punishment, food scarcity and famine, and labor abuse and exploitation (Clapham, 2015; Mapp, 2014; Sikkink, 2017).

Social Work and Human Rights

The argument has been made that social work is a human rights profession (Clayton & Hopps, 2013; Healy, 2008; Ife, 2008; Meshelemiah, 2016; Murdach, 2011 Staub-Bernasconi, 2016; Witken, 1998), though it may be more accurate to suggest that components of the profession are congruent with a human rights framework. Clearly there is overlap, given social work's advancement, at least through various ethical codes, of social and economic justice, self-determination, and human dignity (Cemlyn, 2008; Davis & Reber, 2016; Lundy & van Wormer, 2007). In the US, the Council of Social Work Education mandates curriculum coverage of human rights through its accreditation standards; its Kendall Institute focuses on global education and provides resources on human rights issues. The National Association of Social Work has several sections that address human rights related issues, and has filed amicus curiae briefs in court cases seeking to protect human rights and challenge human rights violations (Davis & Reber, 2016; Meshelemiah. 2016. Not surprisingly international social work bodies have embraced and promoted human rights extensively: "advocating and upholding human rights and social justice is the motivation and justification for social work" (IFSW, n.d; see also Healy, 2011; Mapp, 2014).

Human rights based social work is manifested in several ways. Reichert (2011) suggests three key social work perspectives and practices that align with human rights: empowerment, the strengths-based perspective and challenging oppression. Further, principles of social work, specifically dignity and worth of individuals, cultural proficiency and humility, and self-determination, cohere with human rights (Cemlyn, 2008; Ife, 2008; Lundy, 2007; Meshelemiah, 2013; Wronka, 2017). Social work's person-in-environment or multi-system framework is particularly well suited for understanding the impact of human rights abuses on individuals, families and communities (Clayton & Hopps, 2013). In short, a human rights lens can be incorporated across social work intervention modalities, from micro to mezzo to macro practice (Ife, 2008, 2009; Wronka, 2017).

Social workers engage in human rights work in primarily two ways: by participating in broader human rights initiatives and by practicing social work through a human rights lens (Ife, 2016). As an example of the former, the Poor People's Economic Human Rights Campaign led by the Kensington (Philadelphia, USA) Welfare Rights Union, which included social workers and other advocates to challenge the increasingly punitive social welfare policies that targeted individuals and families in poverty (Clayton & Hopps, 2013; Poor People's ..., 2012). This mobilization linked issues of economic abuse with a human rights framework. In general, however, naming social work issues as human right concerns does not happen as often as it could. A notable exception is the edited volume of Hertel and Libal (2011); the chapters reflect clear connections between pivotal issues (e.g. domestic violence, child welfare, LGBTQ protection) and human rights. Similarly, Libal and Harding (2015) ground human rights in community practice, and distinguish this partnership from charity-based and needs-based social work approaches; they focus on mobilizing for affordable housing, food scarcity, and health care.

More typical is for social workers to do human rights based work in organizations that focus on issues that fall within the broad human rights spectrum even if the organizations don't explicitly identify as such. In clinical, group, community and policy arenas, social workers who assist human trafficking victims, advocate for immigrant and refugee rights, monitor police brutality, pursue educational access for women and girls, or more generally promote the principles of dignity and security in their work with marginalized populations, are implicitly engaged in human rights work (for examples, see Berthold & Libal, 2016; Cox & Pardasani, 2017; Hounmenou, 2012; Limoncelli, 2017; Weaver, 2016).

Combatting Right Wing Populism

Simply stated, right wing populism is antithetical to the values of a human rights perspective. With its nativist and authoritarian orientation, right wing populism contradicts the international or global perspectives of the human rights movement (Albertazzi & Mueller, 2017). Right wing populist strategies are inherently exclusionary, running counter to the universal ethos within human rights. At its core, right wing populism is about stripping any group deemed unacceptable of their humanity.

Right wing populism is a grassroots component of the broader New Right movement that also encompasses traditionalist Protestant and evangelical campaigns, hate groups, militias, anti-government efforts, conservative think tanks, and reactionary media outlets (Bertlett & Lyons (2000), Jimenez, 2017; Schmitz, 2016; Wodak, 2015). In the U.S., a considerable segment of the Republican Party is persuaded by, and beholden to, this right wing agenda; in a number of European countries radical right parties have become part of ruling coalitions. The core of right wing populism is nationalism, authoritarianism and anti-elitism, though myriad groups and the broader movement also espouse an amalgam of rigid gender roles, racial supremacy and anti-Semitism (Albertazzi & Mueller, 2017; Bertlett & Lyons, 2000; Mudde, 2017). Many of the groups and issues targeted by various right wing platforms are the same issues embraced by human rights advocates and social workers, thus it is critical when combatting right wing populism to understand the larger context that gives it support.

Right wing populism foments grievances and discord by scapegoating immigrant groups and communities of color; reinforces traditional and gendered authority by attacking reproductive rights, specifically, and women's rights, in general; blames elites for perceived disempowerment; and pursues deregulation in the name of jobs (that rarely materialize as promised) but at the expense of a healthy environment (Bertlett & Lyons, 2000; Bloch, 2016; Hochschild, 2016). Paradoxically, right wing populism undercuts labor unions and related economic organizing and supports corporate profits and power, even while appealing to a working class population. Attention is shifted from holding corporations and their allies as responsible for economic disparities to the blaming of "the other" (i.e. people of color, immigrants); right wing populists identify themselves as the victims of a government that allows everyone but them to get ahead (Bloch, 2016; Schmitz, 2016; Wodak, 2015). Right wing populism has a deep emotional hold on its followers.

Social workers involved with efforts that support, protect and empower women, immigrants, unions, people of color and other disenfranchised groups essentially are engaged in human rights based work in opposition to the New Right. What is less apparent is intentional human rights work by social workers aimed explicitly at countering right wing populism; as Fazzi (2015) notes, the profession has not analyzed or address rightwing populism. At least in the United States, social work seems to have focused attention on broader right wing political efforts primarily during the 1980s and 1990s, corresponding with the rise and extension of Reagan's anti-welfare, pro-corporate policies (e.g. Midgley & Jones, 1994; Withorn, 1982). While these analyses invoked social and economic justice, the inclusion of human rights is more assumed than asserted. Recent scholarship has focused on the debilitating impact of neoliberal, austerity policies on human services. As important as these writings are, they rarely specifically implicate rightwing populism in this broader conservative assault (Abramovitz & Zelnick, 2015; Cemlyn, 2008; Hasenfeld & Garrow, 2012; Hyslop, 2018; Lundy & van Wormer, 2007), though social work scholars have been critical of how corporate rights are granted precedence over human ones (DeLuca-Acconi, 2017; Pyles 2009). On the international stage, there are some examples of specifically challenging the far right nationalism and protecting immigrants and refugees though these are not social work initiatives per se (Sikkink, 2017). Of note, the September 2017 issue of

Social Dialogue (International Association of Schools of Social Work) featured several articles on social work's responsibilities in combatting rightwing populism.

It also is necessary to acknowledge that, unfortunately, social work is not always theorized or practiced from an empowerment or human rights (explicitly or not) perspective. Historically and currently, social workers have been involved in social control rather than liberatory efforts such as opposing union organizing or enforcing punitive welfare policies (Murdach, 2011; Piven & Cloward, 1993). A human rights ethos is undermined by approaches to practice that fail to consider broader economic and political contexts, which has implications primarily for clinical social work and agency protocols (Abramovitz & Zelnck, 2015; Meshelemiah, 2013; Specht & Courtney, 1994). On an even more disconcerting note, Noble (2017) suggests that "another challenge worthy of attention is the temptation of overworked and under resourced practitioners to use populist discourse as an easy 'escape route' to find answers to the almost unsolvable social issues stemming from rising wealth inequality and the profound changes transforming the workforce and society in post-industrial countries" (p. 8; also see Turtianinen, 2017). In other words, because of economic and political vulnerability social workers need to guard against being enticed by rightwing populist rhetoric and actions.

Yet just as social work is well positioned to embrace a human rights perspective, so to is it for addressing right wing populism. In order to do so, however, the profession needs to take a more politicized turn with greater attention paid to broader systemic contexts and concomitant dominant, neo-liberal ideologies (Berthold & Libal, 2016; DeLuca-Acconi, 2017; Hyslop, 2018; Pyles 2009). We conclude this chapter by identifying some key steps that human rights based social work needs to pursue order to combat right wing populism.

Social work needs to move toward a more explicit naming of issues as collective human rights. Failure to clearly frame social work concerns and initiatives as part of the larger human rights family and as societal rather than individual in nature dilutes our understanding of, and solutions to, them. A critical component is incorporating an understanding of the dynamics of oppression in order to secure needed rights of those who suffer from right wing efforts, including naming as "hate" the actions of right wing populism (Berthold & Libal, 2016; Ortiz, Garcia & Hernandez, 2012; Pewewardy & Alemida, 2014). It should go without saying that social workers should collectively protest right wing populist actions, such as hate rallies and marches.

Reframing in this way has implications for working directly with individuals and families who are victimized by right wing policies and initiatives. Trauma informed practice should be situated in a human rights framework. Specifically, clinicians need to work with clients to contextualize the "presenting issues" (e.g. PTSD, anti-social behaviors) as responses to right wing hate, help them understand and build resilience against right wing extremism and connect them with human rights resources. For example, immigrants facing the possible deportation live in constant fear and report difficulty finding or keeping a job, decreased hope, and increased unwillingness to report crimes such as domestic violence or sexual assault; all of which has serious implications for mental health and family functioning (Becerra, 2016; Perreira & Ornelas, 2013; Reina, Lohman & Maldonado, 2014). Social workers need to connect the dots between right wing nationalism, resulting anti-immigrant policies, state-sanctioned deportation raids, and the well-being of their affected clients; similar connections exist for tracing the impact of other right wing assaults.

While social work has been involved in advocacy since its inception, there needs to be greater engagement in policy work on national, state and local levels that monitors and challenges right wing populism and resulting legislative initiatives (DeLuca-Acconi, 2017; Duarte, 2017; Lundy, 2007). For example, in the U.S., a number of states have passed anti-immigrant measures designed to deny access to health, education and welfare systems; actions that constitute human rights violations. Social workers, in collaboration with immigrant rights groups, need to offer testimony and participate in lobbying efforts that denounce these measures. Clinicians are particularly well situated to document the harm of anti-immigrant laws; they need to bear witness through advocacy (Noble, 2017). Conversely, social workers need to support city and state initiatives that protect immigrants, such as sanctuary cities/states. Similar logic would apply to advocacy on other human rights issues, and in the process would counter right wing populism.

Related to this policy advocacy is the need to build more partnerships with the legal profession (Berthold & Libal, 2016). Because the pursuit of human rights, particularly seeking redress for violations and abuses, often are handled through the courts, social work should expand its relationships with law partners engaged in rights-based work including anti-hate litigation. In the U.S., examples include the American Immigration Lawyers Association, the Southern Poverty Law Center, or the Lambda Legal Fund; cooperative arrangements between social work and legal centers include the Asylum and Human Rights Clinic (University of Connecticut) or the Young Center for Immigrant Children's Rights (University of Chicago) (Berthold & Libal, 2016). Social work organizations and professional associations could join in lawsuits, provide expert witness testimony, and support clients by providing direct services and connecting them with additional resources.

Because right wing populism gains traction among those who are, or perceive to be, economically vulnerable, it also is important to engage in community and economic development that is rooted in human rights principles. Libal and Harding (2015) provide examples of mobilizing around human rights issues such as extreme poverty, health care, homelessness, and food security; successes in these areas counter right wing populist appeals (also see Davis &

Reber, 2016; DeLuca-Acconi, 2017; Pyles, 2009). Further, organizing efforts that meld human rights and economic issues, especially support for and promotion of union organizing, provides an alternative to the scapegoating platforms of rightwing populism (Duarte, 2017; Lundy, 2007). These more macro initiatives also would help social workers, many of whom are in financially precarious situations, align more proactively with their clients and constituents in pursuit of economic justice.

Finally, social workers may want to build bridges into the rightwing populist base in order to counter its ideological arguments and emotional pull. Social workers possess a unique skill set that recognizes the connections between broad structures, behaviors, and affect. Using a human rights framework would require social workers to not just recognize the grievance narratives of right wing populists, but also challenge the hatred and bigotry by naming the real victims of rightwing actions, a strategy that may undermine social work's commitment to self-determination and the "telling of one's own story." Social workers also need greater economic fluency in order to understand the root of these grievances while offering different strategies for addressing them. To be sure, this is a tall order but not impossible to guide rightwing populists into seeing "the other" as fully human and that the real threat is corporate greed, not the immigrant family next door.

Conclusion

In this chapter, we have provided an overview of human rights based social work and suggested ways in which the adoption of this framework could counter rightwing populism. Social work has an historical commitment to human rights issues. This commitment, however, currently is undermined by neo-liberal policies that force austerity measures on human services while at the same time creating conditions that lead to heightened economic vulnerability and sow the seeds for rightwing extremism. Social workers need to make a choice, and explicitly adopting a human rights framework may be a strategy that helps them combat the rising tide of rightwing populism.

References

Abramovitz, M. & Zelnick, J. (2015). Privatization in the human services: Implications for direct practice. Journal of Clinical Social Work, 43, 282-293.

Albertazzi, D. & Mueller, S. (2017). Populism and liberal democracy. In C. Mudde (Ed.), The populist radical right. New York: Routledge, pp. 507-525.

Becerra, D. (2016). Anti-immigration policies and fear of deportation: A human rights issue. Journal of Human Rights in Social Work, 1, 109-119.

Berthold, S. & Libal, K. (2016). Migrant children's rights to health and rehabilitation: A primer for US social workers. Journal of Human Rights in Social Work, 1, 85-95.

Bertlet, C. & Lyons, M. (2000). Right-wing populism in America: Too close for comfort. New York: Guilford Press.

Bloch, K. (2016). "It is just sickening": Emotions and discourse in an anti-immigrant discussion forum. Sociological Focus, 49, 257-270.

Buergenthal, T., Shelton, D., & Stewart, D. (2002). International human rights in a nutshell (3rd ed.). St. Paul, MN: West Publishing.

Caplan, M. & Ricciardelli, L. (2016). Institutionalizing neoliberalism: 21st century capitalism, market sprawl, and social policy in the United States. Poverty & Public Policy, 8, 20-38.

Cemlyn, S. (2008). Human rights practice: Possibilities and pitfalls for developing emancipatory social work. Ethics and Social Welfare, 2, 222-242.

Clapham, A. (2015). Human rights: A very short introduction (2nd ed.). New York: Oxford University Press.

Clayton, O. & Hopps, J. (2013). Human rights and social work in historical and contemporary perspectives. In the Encyclopedia of Social Work. DOI: 10.1093/acrefore/9780199975839.013.943.

Cox, C. & Pardasani, M. (2017). Aging and human rights: A rights-based approach to social work with older adults. Journal of Human Rights in Social Work, 2, 98-106.

Davis, A. & Reber, D. (2016). Advancing human rights and social and economic justice: Developing competence in field education. Journal of Human Rights in Social Work, 1, 143-153.

DeLuca-Acconi, R. (2017). Empowering social workers to transform the dominant narrative: Advocating for human rights over corporate profit. Journal of Human Rights Social Work, 2, 3-15.

Donnelly, J. (2013). Universal human rights in theory and practice (3rd ed.). Ithaca, NY: Cornell University Press.

Douzinas, C. (2000). The end of human rights. Oxford: Hart Publishing.

Duarte, F. (2017). The challenge of right-wing populism for social work. Social Dialogue, 17, 36-38.

Fazzi, L. (2015). Social work, exclusionary populism and xenophobia in Italy. International Social Work, 54, 595-605.

Ferguson, I. (2017). Hope over fear: Social work education towards 2025. European Journal of Social Work, 20, 322-332.

Hasenfeld, Y. & Garrow, E. (2012). Nonprofit, human-service organizations, social rights, and advocacy in a neoliberal welfare state. Social Service Review, 86, 295-322.

Healy, L. (2011). International social work. New York: Oxford University Press.

Healy, L. (2008). Exploring the history of social work as a human rights profession. International Social Work, 51, 735-748.
Hertel, S. & Libal, K. (Eds.) (2011). Human rights in the United States: Beyond exceptionalism. New York: Cambridge University Press.
Hochschild, A. (2016). Strangers in there own land: Anger and mourning on the American right. New York: The New Press.
Hounmenou, C. (2012). Monitoring human rights of persons in police lockups: Potential role of community-based organizations. Journal of Community Practice, 20, 274-292.
Hunt, L. (2007). Inventing human rights: A history. New York: W.W. Norton & Co.
Hyslop, I. (2018). Neoliberalism and social work identity. European Journal of Social Work, 21, 20-31.
Ife, J. (2016). Human rights and social work: Beyond conservative law. Journal of Human Rights in Social Work, 1, 3-8.
Ife, J. (2009). Human rights from below: Achieving rights through community development. New York: Cambridge University Press.
Ife, J. (2008). Human rights and social work: Towards rights-based practice, (rev. ed.). New York: Cambridge University Press.
International Federation of Social Work (IFSW). (n.d.). Core mandates. Retrieved from http://ifsw.org/get-involved/global-definition-of-social-work/.
Jimenez, J. (2017). The impact of the conservative Protestant movement on social policy. Journal of Progressive Human Services, 28, 91-106.
Kennedy, D. (2012). The international human rights regime: Still a part of the problem? In R. Dickinson, C. Murray, E. Kastelli & O. Pedersen (Eds.), Examining critical perspectives on human rights (pp. 19-34). Cambridge, UK: Cambridge University Press.
Kennedy, D. (2006). The humanities in Human Rights: Critique, language, politics. PMLA, 121(5), 1656-1657.
Kennedy, D. (2004). International humanitarianism: The dark sides. The International Journal of Not-for-Profit Law, 6(3). Retrieved from http://www.icnl.org/research/journal/vol6iss3/special_2.htm.
Libal, K. & Harding, S. (2015). Human rights-based community practice in the United States. New York: Spring.
Limoncelli, S. (2017). The global development of contemporary anti-human trafficking advocacy. International Sociology, 32, 814-834.
Lundy, C. (2007). Social and economic justice, human rights and peace: The challenge for social work in Canada and the USA. International Social Work, 50, 727-739.
Mapp, S. (2014). Human rights and social justice in a global perspective: An introduction to international social work (2nd ed). New York: Oxford University Press.
Meshelemiah, J. (2013). Human rights perspectives in social work education and practice. In Encyclopedia of Social Work. DOI: 10.1093/acrefore/9780199975839.013.1206

Midgley, J. & Jones, C. (1994). Social work and the radical right: Impact of developments in Britain and the United States. *International Social Work*, 37, 115-126.

Muchacha, M. (2016). Politically motivated violence (PMV) in Zimbabwe and the role of social work. *Journal of Human Rights in Social Work*, 1, 156-164.

Mudde, C. (2017). Introduction to the populist radical right. In C. Mudde (Ed.), *The populist radical right*. New York: Routledge, pp. 1-10.

Murdach, A. (2011). Is social work a human rights profession? *Social Work*, 56, 281-283.

Nelson, D., Price, E., & Zubrzycki. (2014). Integrating human rights and trauma frameworks in social work with people from refugee backgrounds. *Australian Social Work*, 67(4), 567-581.

Noble, C. (2017). What is this thing called "populism"? *Social Dialogue*, 17(September), 6-8.

Nussbaum, M. (2016). Women's progress and women's human rights. *Human Rights Quarterly*, 38(3), 589-622.

Orend, B. (2002). *Human rights: Concept and context*. Ontario: Broadview Press.

Ortiz, L., Garcia, B., & Hernández, S. (2012). Why it is important for social work educators to oppose racist-based anti-immigration legislation. *Journal of Social Work Education*, 48, 197–203.

Perreira, K. & Ornelas, I. (2013). Painful passages: Traumatic experiences and post-traumatic stress among immigrant Latino adolescents and their primary caregivers. *International Migration Review*, 47, 976-1005.

Pewewardy, N. & Almeida, R. (2014). Articulating the scaffolding of white supremacy: The act of naming in liberation. *Journal of Progressive Human Services*, 25, 230-253.

Piven, F. & Cloward, R. (1993). *Regulating the poor*, (Rev. ed.). New York: Vintage.

Poor People's Economic Human Rights Campaign (2012). About us. Retrieved from http://economichumanrights.org/?page_id=9.

Pyles, L. (2009). Where's the "freedom" in Free Trade? Framing practices and global economic justice. *Journal of Community Practice*, 17, 73–87.

Reina, A., Lohman, B., & Maldonado, M. (2014). "He said they'd deport me": Factors influencing domestic violence helpseeking practices among Latina immigrants. *Journal of Interpersonal Violence*, 29, 593-615.

Ryckman, K. (2016). Ratification as accommodation? Domestic dissent and human rights treaties. *Journal of Peace Research*, 53(4), 582-596.

Salmela, M. & von Scheve, C. (2017). Emotional roots of right-wing political populism. *Social Science Information*, 56, 567-595.

Schmitz, R. (2016). Intersections of hate: Exploring the transecting dimensions of race, religion, gender, and family in Ku Klux Klan web sites. *Sociological Focus*, 49, 200-214.

Shannon, D. (2016). Food justice, direct action, and the human rights enterprise. *Critical Sociology*, 42, 799-814.

Sikkink, K. (2017). *Evidence for hope: Making human rights work in the 21st century*. Princeton, NJ: Princeton University Press.
Specht, H. & Courtney, M. (1994). *Unfaithful angels*. New York: Free Press.
Staub-Bernasconi, S. (2016). Social work and human rights – Linking two traditions of human rights in social work. *Journal of Human Rights in Social Work, 1*, 40-49.
Tolliver, W., Hadden, B., Snowden, F., & Brown-Manning, R. (2016). Police killings of unarmed Black people: Centering race and racism in human behavior and the social environment content. Journal of Human Behavior in the Social Environment, 26, 279-286.
Turtianinen, K. (2017). Recognition as a moral yardstick against nationalistic social work practise. Social Dialogue, 17(September), 12-17.
Twill, S. & Buckheister, N. (2009). A descriptive research study of economic human rights violations in America. Journal of Poverty, 13, 365-383.
Wahl, R. (2017). No justice, no peace? The police, people of color, and the paradox of protecting human rights. Human Rights Quarterly, 39, 811-831.
Weaver, H. (2016). Between a rock and a hard place: A trauma-informed approach to documenting the traumatic experiences of Tamil refugees. Journal of Human Rights in Social Work, 1, 120-130.
Withorn, A. (1982). Beyond realism: Fighting for human services in the eighties. Catalyst, 4(2), 21-37.
Wodak, R. (2015). The politics of fear: What right-wing populist discourses mean. Los Angeles, CA: Sage.
Wronka, J. (2017). Human rights and social justice: Social action and service for the helping and health professions (2nd ed.). Thousand Oaks, California: SAGE Publications.
Wronka, J. (2013). Human rights. In Encyclopedia of social work. DOI: 10.1093/acrefore/9780199975839.013.190.

Remaining Professional, Taking a Stance: Social Work Strategies for Countering the Influence of Right-Wing Populist Politics

Barbara Schäuble
The author received a translation grant by DGSA, German Society of Social work. Translated by Ariane Baldus.

The social landscape is changing. Evidence of this includes not only the election of right-wing populist Alternative for Germany (AfD). The shift is also manifesting in recurring assaults on refugee housing (Bundeskriminalamt 2017), increasing homophobic violence (Spiegel online, 2017), arson attacks on the cars of anti-racist activists, hate speech against sex educators and pregnancy advice centers, and the muzzling of state-funded facilities regarding statements on AfD.

Considering the deteriorating climate, social work practitioners are called upon to remember that what they hold as self-evident has emanated from experiences of tyranny, from the struggles of social movements, and from partisan activities by professionals. They can have a significant impact by declaring their actions, even where institutionally self-evident, more explicitly than to date as against degradation, racism, and nationalism. In their work against the extreme right, social workers can draw on a broad spectrum of practice strategies. This article discusses the reach and effectiveness of these strategies.

Shifting baselines

First, the fundamental question that needs to be addressed is to what extent social work itself is changing. The range of tasks and self-image of social work depend largely on a social mandate, and that mandate is currently unclear as German society undergoes intense controversies in terms of its identity. The debate centers on whether the social agenda should be: a diverse society that champions democracy, equality, solidarity, and human rights, or a nationalistic, more inequality-oriented society, as claimed to be legitimate and commendable by right-wing populists?

In order to avoid further erosion of social accomplishments in the wake of a right-wing culture war, the consequences of right-wing populist interference with social work and how that interference can be countered remain to be evaluated. For the time being, a fairly strong perseverance can be assumed on the part of the profession and service providers. Social workers act within a socially-defined mandate, which is not merely governmental but also manifests itself in the demands and needs formulated explicitly and implicitly by its users. Professionals define their mandate based on historically-developed professional self-concepts. And perhaps even more importantly: Past definitions of social work are institutionalized in legal claims, organizations, methods and routines. They are expected to remain stable.

This also applies to the functions attributed to social work. Ideologies of exclusion and inequality are incompatible with humanist and rights-based self-concepts of the (younger) profession and with the range of contexts within which social work is practiced. Although a rapid shift towards inequality is not yet apparent, it could be expected in the long term. One reason for this: Exclusionary ideologies are resonating with right-wing populists who work in the social sector or are professionalizing in the field (Bitzan & Scherr, 2007). Even more importantly, populist social policies connect to "exclusive" tendencies in social work. They are facilitated by the fact that professionals–often coming from a different milieu and having never experienced poverty or racism themselves–do not always adopt their clients' issues as their own (Kuhlmann, 2017).

In the wake of an eroding welfare state, populist argumentations can also impact those active in social work, as they legitimize the retreat from service provision and from solidary communities. The latest incidents, such as the closing of a communal food bank for non-Germans, can also be seen as strategies to ease the workload on the part of overwhelmed volunteers. And there are historical precedents: Kuhlmann (2017) references the fact that reduced workload was one of the motives of welfare workers not to speak out more forcefully against National Socialist welfare policies during the 1930s.

Authoritarian standards and norms and naturalizing interpretations of social problems are not entirely foreign to social work. Normalizing (Kessl & Plößer, 2010) and disciplining logics of social work (Dollinger, 2011) are part of the historical legacy of the profession. Equally, social workers do not remain unaffected by a common perception of crisis and a sense of "raw bourgeois culture" (Heitmeyer 2011) as well as racist divisive discourses. Recent studies have been discussing to what extent punitive-restrictive concepts of support are gaining ground amongst social workers (Oelkers, 2011). Unambitious practice models, substandard training, unimaginative environments, and local cultures of dominance provide even more breeding ground for such tendencies.

Some of these aspects are taken up by Italian researcher Luca Fazzi (2015) in his 2013 study on how the electoral successes of the Lega Nord in Northern

Italy have influenced social work. The party propagated a nativist-clientelist realignment of the social sector. It demanded preferential treatment of "our people" and limiting access to welfare state provisions for social and ethnic minorities. As a consequence of such agitation, some social workers were unable to organize the support of volunteers for the disadvantaged groups they were assisting. Often quite isolated in small-city or rural environments, many of the social workers interviewed by Fazzi supported "exclusive" policies or, despite being critical of them, remained passive. In contrast, their metropolitan counterparts (Fazzi calls them "pragmatists" and "activists") and the staff of larger service providers, proved to be more capable of taking action.

Social work is situated amid a (socio-)political process of negotiation and change, which is reflected in the need to defend against challenges to social work itself. Already, in regional and local councils the right-wing party is inquiring whether girls-centered social work is too expensive and a sign of discrimination against boys. And AfD regional electoral programs are asking: 'Can we not do without academic migration and gender studies?'

The Populist Re-adjustment of Social Issues

The growth of right-wing populist and far right agendas and respective parliamentary activities are already contributing to the increasing precariousness of long-held notions of social work such as equal participation regardless of social-economic status, gender, sexual preference, nationality, and skin color. Chauvinist, nationalistic and "völkische" (biologistic-racist) argumentations weaken the ties of social work to social justice, democratic negotiations, protection of minorities and human rights. This leads to proposals for sweeping benefit restrictions for unaccompanied minors (Kooperationsverbund Jugendsozialarbeit, 2016), for an authoritarian criminal policy, hard-heartedness towards refugees, and denigration of solidary practices, as expressed in media attacks against "Gutmenschen" (or "do gooders," the German ugliest word of 2015). Social workers are confronted with exclusionary and derogatory counter-discourses, coming from both external sources as well as their clients, partner organizations, and co-workers. Professional bodies of knowledge that could act as bases from which to reject attacks on social work's mission do exist, such as laws, professional ethics (Otto et al., 2010; DBSH, 2014; IASSW, 2012), and traditional practice strategies. However, the urgency to explicitly draw on these, is only beginning to be recognized in the social work field, after having for decades neglected the justification and advocacy of social work values which were seen as self-evident.

The fact that right-wing populist positions have remained widely overlooked can most likely be attributed to the fact that those who claim such positions do not necessarily consider themselves right wingers but rather political "centrists," as their exclusionary attitudes are increasingly normalized. Partly the result of habituation, this can also be attributed to the fact that centrists generally approve of democratic governance, in contrast to far right nationalist and racist who do not. Surveys estimate the right-wing populist potential at 42% of the population. Around 20% are considered to be distinctly right-wing populist (Küpper et al., 2015).

Right-wing populist policy proposals are profiting from a sense of crisis, that is perceptions of an economic (post-industrialization, digitalization, tertiarization), distribution-related and democratic exigency (Priester, 2017). And they give direction to this sense of crisis: against the establishment, against migration, against liberal principles and the liberalization of lifestyles. Apart from a sense of belonging, such notions also offer protection, the securing of privileges, a self-perception as critic and victim, as well as strong emotions.

However, right-wing populist interpretations hold promises only for part of the population. For others they imply uncertainty, lack of appreciation, neglect, degradation, revoking of legal entitlements and existential threat. Yet, the agent-centered perception of right-wing extremism and populism is still quite popular. This approach not only blurs the historical and structural backgrounds of right-wing populist movements but also obscures the fact that exclusionary policies create social conditions which produce current inequalities.

Explanatory Approaches

Reactions to such developments require in-depth background analyses, which are far from concluded. The discussion of explanatory approaches in terms of an increased acceptance of right-wing populist interpretations and the debates on counter-strategies have so far only delivered preliminary insights. Social-scientific theories are accentuating diverse causal relationships.

1. Numerous authors point to the taking up of social and political orientations in socialization contexts such as families (Hopf et al., 1995), peer groups (Bohnsack et al., 1995) and the public sphere, which limits the impact of short-term educational efforts.
2. A potential but not necessarily determining background for an affinity to right-wing populist and right-wing extremist interpretations can be located in social and biographical challenges, such as experiences of disintegration and individualization (Heitmeyer,1989). Möller and colleagues (2016) have pointed out, amongst other things, a lack of sensual experience, which

finds an outlet in populist denigration and threats of violence. However, this in no way implies that the desire for agitation, hate speech, and practices of persecution always emanate from a place of deficiency (Dietze 2017; Sartre 1994). While experiences of disintegration might be causing an affinity toward right-wing positions, critical interventions can foster new interpretations of an individual's personal situation. Acquiring more coping strategies and exploiting new means of integration and inclusion can also be helpful, although the latter might be limited in areas with structural mass unemployment.

3. In addition to experiences of disintegration, over-integration in the sense of intense conformism can also provide the backdrop to right-wing and right-wing extremist orientations (Koppetsch, 2013). Accordingly, pedagogic opportunities (e. g. intracultural reflection) are designed to challenge normalizing perceptions and to bring to awareness differences in the supposedly homogenous.

4. Other theories highlight the political character of right-wing mindsets and problematize their demands of social closure. While criticizing the populist self-image of 'being normal', these theories also point out that not all populists are biographically fraught individuals (Bommes & Scherr, 1992; Scherr, 2003). These theorists identify social closure as strategy of safeguarding established privilege (Rommelspacher, 1995; Elias & Scotson, 1990). They recommend dialogue, human rights education, and strategies of confrontation, limitation, and interruption. This includes, for example, barring organized right-wing extremists from entering youth facilities or denying far right politicians a podium at social-work events.

5. Many authors emphasize the correlation between the mindsets of individuals and the social climate in general, including the promotion of exclusionary acts by far-right leaders, local structures of opportunity, elite discourses, the media, and targeted propaganda. They point to the inherited ideologemes of inequality, presenting racism and nationalism as part of a powerful civic culture, which marginalizes specific groups of people, partly through forms of systematic institutional discrimination. Right wing populism offers a feeling of legitimate dominance (Rommelspacher, 1995; Kimmel, 2015). In response, social work should return to its mission to reinforce weakened positions, make available equality-based spaces, and provide opportunities for reflection.

6. Theories-of-power-oriented research indicate that systematic inequalities prevent those being attacked from asserting themselves adequately and from developing counterforces. Accordingly, counter strategies should focus on self-help, empowerment, and lobbying.

7. Ultimately, socio-theoretical conceptions emphasize that the basic social structure and its associated shared principles of competition and (economic) evaluation and devaluation form the central background for the emergence of right-wing extremism and right-wing populism (Bauman, 2007; Koppetsch, 2013). Here, educational strategies have a limited effect,

but they may support the development of different cultural and reflexive spaces. Thus, the impact of these structural dimensions can be diminished at the local level, creating free spaces or 'peninsulas' and 'germ forms' (Habermann 2009) for solidary developments.

Specific Practice Strategies for Social Work

Within professional social-work discourse, the "work against the far right" plays a fairly insignificant role. This might be explained by the fact that integration and inclusion as well as equality and democracy represent general objectives of the profession. Since the problem of right-wing oriented youth gained broader attention during the 1990s, a whole range of methods for dealing with populist affinities have been developed in the social work field. As local, pragmatic, and partly funding-oriented strategies, they are not entirely consistent with the above theories (Scherr, 2003, p. 254). Practical measures never respond directly to research findings. The latter would require full-scale promotion of pluralistic and equality-oriented social spaces in order to diminish populism. Scherr (2003) points out that public funding programs primarily pursue the paradoxical objective to "prevent unwanted escalations and radicalizations of prosperity- and location-oriented nationalism as well as of fears, prejudices and enemy stereotypes, which in diluted form might represent acceptable elements of democratic positions" (p. 254).

During the past 20 years diverse methods against right-wing extremism have been developed, thus expanding the range of strategies for civic, human rights, and holocaust education. Recent approaches include individual, group, and community work. Many of these measures were nationally funded programs, which in their wide range surely represent a German peculiarity. The following section introduces relevant strategies and discusses them in the light of causal theories.

Initially, during the 1990s, when the far right began to be noticed and discussed, a social education action plan–the concept of "accepting youth work"–received state funding. Implemented between 1992 and 1996, the intention of the "action program against aggression and violence" was to handle problems of right-wing-leaning youth by means of individual and group work. In this context, right-wing extremism was treated as though it were a symptom of biographical issues and social processes of disintegration. At the same time, the political significance of the young peoples' mindsets was not given top priority. The "accepting youth work" approach thus came under criticism as a reward system and "skin care at state cost" (Buderus, 1998), characterized by work overload and a lack of competence on the part of professionals.

The program was followed by a process of stagnation, in part because the topic was kept under wraps and in part because repressive solutions were being endorsed. Initiated by political activists and local agents, eventually civic and community-oriented approaches such as "mobile advice" and "victim counseling" were developed (Jaschke & Wendel, 2013). These were aimed at activating and advising civic society, at reinforcing and connecting those affected, and at incorporating the perspective of victims into broader society's consciousness.

In 2000, a state-funded support program ("Jugend für Toleranz und Demokratie") was set up, which initially took up these locally-developed action strategies and which also promoted civic education in and outside of schools. Both strategies conceptualized right-wing extremism as more political than the initial program had and displayed correlations to political-cultural theories of right-wing extremism. The funded political measures were aiming to shed light on populist slogans and far right ideology. At the same time, they were also striving to facilitate debates amongst politically diverse mindsets, while researchers were working to clarify the meaning and functionality of individual right-wing extremist interpretations (Möller et. al., 2016). Victim counseling for those who suffered fascist attacks also encompassed lobbying with and for vulnerable groups such as persons of color, refugees, the homeless, juvenile punks, and other members of local democratic counter-cultures. Mobile advice teams were counseling mayors and hotel owners on what to do when far right demonstrations or festivals were announced, and committed citizens were shown how to lobby against the right. By promoting democratic milieus, the mobile advice teams were putting theories of political socialization into practice, without identifying as such, arguably because most of these initiatives remained small-scale.

During the following 10 years, national action plans were again implemented, this time in new funded schemes structured differently than earlier efforts. For one, selective priority funding was initiated; secondly, instead of specifically targeting right-wing extremism, the focus was placed on a more general fight against "extremism" or "de-radicalization." Greater attention was once again given to perpetrator-orientated work. Exit-oriented work and strategies to work with the parents of right-wing extremist kids were extended. Currently, there is also a boom in "argumentation training against populism" or "against racism," a reaction to the combination of the rise of exclusionary rhetoric in public discourse and the perceived lack of response by active citizens and helping professionals. Argumentation trainings are intended to analyze right-wing populist argumentation patterns and discourse strategies, to broaden the communicative repertoire and, not least, to sharpen one's own concepts and values.

The creative scope and limits of social work

A considerable spectrum of measures has emerged, taking up various causal assumptions and corresponding to the range of anti-violence work in other fields, such as violence against women. In spite of their diversity, educational settings have had little success in establishing comprehensive and longer-term spaces for socialization and education, which might provide opportunities to experience a culture of equality, solidarity, and negotiation (Scherr, 2014, p. 63). In view of a paradoxical mission, tight budgets, and project-bound structures, these measures are incapable of effectively counterbalancing larger societal distortions and far right interpretations. In addition, the measures against right-wing populism are not necessarily adequate to address the problem (Lynen von Berg & Roth, 2003) or are not executed by qualified staff, and thus might lose support.

Remaining professional and taking a stance

Fazzi's study with Northern Italian social workers shows how important professionalism, self-confidence, and persistence are in order for social workers not to yield to the right-wing populist re-encoding of social matters. Too many social workers are unaware of their own professionalism and social position, or they fail to classify the concepts on which the profession is based as liberal institutionalizations of socio-political conflicts. In fact, they might themselves need orientation and perhaps also external counseling. They also need to know that many legal rights, institutions, paradigms, and competencies of social work were hard won though struggle and must not be relinquished carelessly. Therefore, the concept of "open" institutions, for instance, does not imply a lack of purpose but rather a lack of barriers for the disadvantaged and minorities. The exclusion of neo-Nazis does not violate the principle of openness. Openness means creating opportunities for access, communication, and education for heterogeneous youth groups, which might be driven off when right-wing groups are allowed to take hold. When your own facility is under siege, an alternative to making concessions can be to draw on and affirm social work concepts and methods. External advice can be helpful, as can self-empowering labels such as "social work as a human rights profession" and the development a mission statement, to support staff in taking a stand against discrimination. Therefore, prior to developing measures for third parties to confront right-wing populism, a process of self-reflection and self-empowerment on the part of professionals is required.

Everyday social work practice and 'cultivating the social sphere'

The special measures described in paragraph 4 are not the only contribution of social work against right-wing populism. They complement the standard program of "everyday social work," which perhaps plays the most significant role in the fight against right-wing populism und right-wing extremism. Social work in general strives for integration, inclusion, and an experience of equality; creating and expanding participatory, educational, and empowerment spaces for individuals and groups; and overcoming deprivation, all based on inclusive humanist and human-rights-oriented assumptions. They also contribute towards "cultivating the social sphere" (Kunstreich, 2013). Scherr (2014) rightly points out the idealism of such formulations. In many settings, heterogeneity is not a given and not always do social workers pro-actively confront the creation and stabilization of dominance relationships. Solidary social spaces, which clients can actively experience, are far too few in number. For Scherr, only long-term, well-conceived, and inclusive settings such as youth work and schools are promising socialization and education spaces for supporting the development of critical and democratic individuals.

The ability of social work to prevent the development of derogatory attitudes is of an everyday nature, but it should not be overestimated. Specific measures designed to increase solidary spaces should be integrated more explicitly into regular activities. What does this imply?

Everyday social work practice as politicizing educational work

Social workers can explain their day-to-day activities towards clients and third parties as solidary, humanistic, human rights-oriented in nature and thus combine their practice with stronger educational impulses. Also, contributions of social workers to, as well as the reliance of the profession on, the achievements of social movements, social rights, and social transfers can be highlighted. Residential youth communities are the product of the 1970s movement for the rights of institutionalized children, and youth centers can be linked to the youth center movement.

Everyday social work as support for professional and solidary networks

Additionally, social workers can work to strengthen solidary counter-cultural spaces. With a stronger focus on empowerment, they can advance the opening up of social work to the interest of migrants, which means reinforcing their self-organization and self-representation and supporting antifascist and anti-racist initiatives.

Social workers can network with each other to remain true to their own objectives and, in the field of multi-case work and advocacy, to defend their aims politically. Those who are socially committed rely on solidary spaces and professionally competent co-workers who enable them to let go of their fears of being attacked for their activities as pregnancy advisors, sexual educators, and refugee social workers. In the wake of increasing Internet agitation, journalist Kübra Gümüşay (n.d.) demands: "We must organize love, because hate is organized." This implies uniting more strongly in terms of professional objectives and to seek political influence by means of associations and networking.

Social work as a form of organized political influence on an everyday basis

Despite a changing zeitgeist, social workers are not powerless. For one, it is a creative profession; social workers are capable of co-creating social worlds, not least due to their role as "street level bureaucrats" who mediate authority between social policy and people's needs. At the same time, the reach of the profession is limited and part of a de-politicizing dynamic, which can also be attributed to a lack of awareness of how much its tools are the achievements of radical grass-roots movements and the liberal institutionalization of claims formulated by these movements. There is little reason to assume that this will change in the near future. Still, in view of this situation the question must be addressed how social work can exert its potential influence on everyday educational processes and the sociopolitical field more forcefully. In her works on

Alice Salomon, the pioneer of German social work exiled in 1937, Kuhlmann (2017) exposes how Salomon, in looking back on her work, struggled with the question if whether, instead of focusing on social work, she should have exerted more political influence to counteract the National Socialist takeover.

We are facing a similar question today, and I propose social workers can do the former without failing to do the latter. For this, we need to understand the starting points of right-wing populist social reorganization and to work on spreading the available counter-strategies.

References

Bauman, Z. (2008). Flüchtige Zeiten: Leben in der Ungewissheit. Hamburg: Hamburger Edition.
Bitzan, R. & Scherr, A. (2007). Rechtsextreme Studierende und JugendarbeiterInnen. In: Sozial Extra 31/ H 1, pp. 8-10.
Bohnsack, R., Loos, P., & Schaeffer, B. (1995). Die Suche nach Gemeinsamkeit und Gewalt in der Gruppe. Hooligans, Musikgruppen und andere Jugendcliquen. Opladen: VS Verlag.
Bommes, M. & Scherr, A. (1992). Rechtsextremismus. Ein Angebot für ganz gewöhnliche Jugendliche. In J. Mansel (Ed.), Reaktionen Jugendlicher auf gesellschaftliche Bedrohungen, (pp. 210-227). Weinheim und München: Beltz Juventa.
Bundeskriminalamt (2017). Bundeslagebild. Kriminalität im Kontext von Zuwanderung. Retrieved from http://www.bka.de/SharedDocs/Downloads/DE/Publikationen/JahresberichteUndLagebilder/KriminalitaetImKontextVonZuwanderung/KriminalitaetImKontextVonZuwanderung_2016.html.
DBSH (2014). Berufsethik des DBSH. Ethik und Werte. Forum Sozial, 4, www.dbsh.de/downloads/DBSH-Berufsethik-2015-02-08.pdf
Dietze, G. (2017): Ethnomasochismus und Androsadismus. Bausteine einer geschlechtersensiblen Affekttheorie des Rassismus. In B. Bargetz, E. Kreisky] G. Ludwig (Eds.), Dauerkämpfe. Feministische Gegenwartsanalysen. Frankfurt/M.: Campus, pp. 229-238.
Dollinger, B. (2011). Punitivität in der Diskussion. Konzeptionelle, theoretische und empirische Referenzen. In B. Dollinger, & H. Schmidt-Semisch (Eds.), Gerechte Ausgrenzung? Wohlfahrtsproduktion und die neue Lust am Strafen. Wiesbaden: VS Verlag für Sozialwissenschaften, pp. 25-73
Elias, N., & Scotson, J. L. (1990). Etablierte und Außenseiter. Frankfurt a. M.
Gümüşay, K. (n.d.). Organisierte Liebe [video]. Retrieved from https://www.youtube.com/watch?v=BNLhT5hZaV8
Habermann, F. (2009). Halbinseln gegen den Strom. Roßdorf: Helmer
Heiner, M. (2010). Soziale Arbeit als Beruf. München: Reinhardt

Heitmeyer, W. (1989). Rechtsextremistische Orientierungen bei Jugendlichen. Weinheim: Beltz Juventa.
Heitmeyer, W. (2011). Rohe Bürgerlichkeit. In: Zeit 22.09.2011, www.zeit.de/2011/39/Verteilungdebatte-Klassenkampf/komplettansicht
Hopf, C., Rieker, P., Sanden-Marcus, M. & Schmidt, C. (1995). Familie und Rechtsextremismus. Familiale Organisation und rechtsextreme Orientierungen junger Männer. Weinheim und München: Juventa.
IFSW/IASSW (2012). Statement of Ethical Principles. Retrieved from https://www.ifsw.org/policies/statement-of-ethical-principles/.
Jaschke, G. & Wendel, K. (2013). Wie alles anfing. In: Opferperspektive e.V. (Ed.), Rassistische Diskriminierung und rechte Gewalt. Münster: Dampfboot, pp. 216-226.
Kessl, F. & Plößer, M. (2010). Differenzierung, Normalisierung, Andersheit. Soziale Arbeit als Arbeit mit den Anderen – eine Einleitung. In. F. Kessl, M. Plößer (Ed.), Differenzierung, Normalisierung, Andersheit. Wiesbaden: VS, pp. 7-17.
Kimmel, M. (2015). Angry white men. Zürich: Orell Füssli.
Kooperationsverbund Jugendsozialarbeit (2016). „In erster Linie junge Menschen". Das Recht auf individuelle Förderung und passende Hilfen für junge Geflüchtete sicherstellen. Retrieved from http://www.b-umf.de/images/Kooperationsverbund-Jugendsozialarbeit_Stellungnahme-Jugendwohnen-umF.PDF
Koppetsch, C. (2013). Die Wiederkehr der Konformität. Streifzüge durch die gefährdete Mitte. Frankfurt a.M.: Campus.
Kuhlmann, C. (2017). Soziale Arbeit im nationalsozialistischen Herrschaftssystem. Zur Notwendigkeit von Widerstand gegen menschenverachtende Zwangsmaßnahmen im Bereich der „Volkspflege". In R.-E. Amthor (Ed.), Soziale Arbeit im Widerstand! Fragen, Erkenntnisse und Reflexionen zum Nationalsozialismus. Weinheim, pp. 40-57.
Kunstreich, T. (2013). Transversale Bildung - Versuch einer Konkretisierung. In R. Braches-Chyrek, D. Nelles, G. Oelerich & A. Schaarschuch (Eds.), Bildung, Gesellschaftstheorie und Soziale Arbeit. Opladen: Budrich, pp. 121-131.
Küpper, B., Zick, A. & Krause, D. (2015). PEGIDA in den Köpfen. Wie rechtspopulistisch ist Deutschland? In A. Zick & B. Küpper (Eds.), Wut, Verachtung, Abwertung. Rechtspopulismus in Deutschland. Bonn: Dietz, pp. 21-43.
Lynen von Berg, H. & Roth, R. (Eds.). Maßnahmen und Programme gegen Rechtsextremismus wissenschaftlich begleitet. Aufgaben, Konzepte und Erfahrungen. Opladen: Leske und Budrich.
Mackert, J. (2004). Die Theorie sozialer Schließung. Tradition, Analysen, Perspektiven. Wiesbaden, VS Verlag für Sozialwissenschaften
Möller, K., Grote, J., Nolde, K. & Schuhmacher, N. (2016). „Die kann ich nicht ab!" Ablehnung, Diskriminierung und Gewalt bei Jugendlichen in der (Post-)Migrationsgesellschaft. Wiesbaden: Springer VS.

Oelkers, N. (2013). Punitive Haltungen in der Sozialen Arbeit. Kontroll- und Straforientierung im Umgang mit Abweichenden und Wohlfahrtsempfängern bei Studierenden der Sozialen Arbeit. Sozial Extra 37, H. 9/10, pp. 34-38

Otto, H.-U., Ziegler, H. & Scherr, A. (2012). Wie viel und welche Normativität benötigt die Soziale Arbeit? In H.-U. Otto & H. Ziegler (Eds.), Das Normativitätsproblem der Sozialen Arbeit. Neue Praxis. Sonderheft 10, pp. 11-23.

Priester, K. (2016). Rechtspopulismus – ein umstrittenes theoretisches und politisches Phänomen. In F. Virchow, M. Langebach & A. Häusler (Eds.): Handbuch Rechtsextremismus. Springer VS, pp. 533-559.

Rommelspacher, B. (1995). Dominanzkultur. Texte zu Fremdheit und Macht. Berlin: Orlanda.

Sartre, J.-P. (1994): Überlegungen zur Judenfrage. Hamburg: Rowohlt

Scherr, A. (2003). Pädagogische Konzepte gegen Rechts – was hat sich bewährt, was ist umstritten, was sollte vermieden werden? In H. Lynen von Berg & R. Roth, Roland (Eds.), Maßnahmen und Programme gegen Rechtsextremismus wissenschaftlich begleitet. Aufgaben, Konzepte und Erfahrungen. Opladen: Leske und Budrich. pp. 249-264.

Scherr, A. (2014). Jugendarbeit und Rechtsextremismus: Was kann und was sollte Jugendarbeit zur Aneignung menschenrechtlicher und demokratischer Überzeugungen beitragen? In Kulturbüro Sachsen (Ed.), Politische Jugendarbeit vom Kopf auf die Füße. Zum anwaltschaftlichen Arbeiten mit menschenrechtsorientierten Jugendlichen im ländlichen Raum, www.kulturbuero-sachsen.de/images/PDF/WJD-Abschlussdoku.pdf

Spiegel, H. v. (2012). Die Last der großen Ansprüche und die Mühen der Ebene. In Widersprüche 32 (2012), S. 13–31

Spiegel online 09.08.2017. Hasskriminalität gegen Schwule und Lesben nimmt zu. www.spiegel.de/politik/deutschland/schwule-und-lesben-behoerden-registrieren-mehr-homophobe-straftaten-a-1161925.html

Conclusion: Right-Wing Populism as Continuing Challenge to Social Work

Kerry Dunn & Jörg Fischer

Each of our authors provides another piece of the puzzle of the rise of right populism and its implications for the social work profession. Here, we summarize key ideas in order to pull together the overall picture produced across the chapters and what they mean together as a whole. We also identify the pieces that need further elucidation in order to continue the conversation on what social work is in today's political climate.

Implications for Practice

Instead of seeing the ascendance of right-wing populism only as a threat, social workers can see it as an opportunity to re-engage with our professional values and redefine our role and position in society. Some of our authors see the current political climate as a call for the profession to adopt specific approaches: Hyde and Galpern propose we use a human rights framework to more explicitly connect the profession to broader human rights struggles and align with the economically and socially vulnerable, and Leidinger and Radvan suggest that a feminist lens can help social workers be more strongly attuned to current threats to democracy and equality. Some suggest moving into new terrain: Reisch explains it is time for social workers to get braver, face difficult truths, take more risks, ask new questions, and finally address the profession's micro-macro divide. Others urge us to reconnect to historic values and strategies: Schäuble reminds us pay attention to the political nature of the everyday role we already play in co-creating social worlds with clients, and Dunn connects our strategies for intervening with interpersonal trauma to the abusive nature of right-populist rhetoric. We need forums for social workers to hash out which practice frameworks and strategies are best suited for protecting our profession and stakeholders today.

As many of our authors describe, right populism is a symptom of deeper issues, including widespread dissatisfaction with the process of modernization. Hyde and Galpern, Meyer, Richter and Quent, and others discuss the connection of right-wing populism to neoliberal and austerity policies that have increased inequality, hurt working people, and eroded faith in government. They suggest that part of the solution must be to engage in policy advocacy and economic development. Social workers can play a role in developing and moving forward the kinds of policies that help to economically, politically, and socially reintegrate people left out of the prosperity created by globalization.

In addition, social workers must help people find more constructive ways for people to voice disillusionment. Möller proposes a specific intervention, the KISS model, which is a form of groupwork that helps young people address not only the ideas but also emotional states associated with extreme-right belonging. More exploration is needed on existing groupwork models that can help to facilitate healing of marginalized and perceived marginalized identities, intergroup understanding, and trust.

We also see the current moment as an impetus for social work to do more to address the lack of communication between social groups in democratic societies. Social work has always had as part of its mission to strengthen public welfare and protect individual and community rights. From an empowerment perspective, we do not force people into a particular ideology but instead help them find answers for themselves. We now must do more to create spaces where members of society can come together to ask new questions and start new conversations, which reinforce the belonging of vulnerable groups in the political community. The chapters by Bürgin and Schäuble provide concrete steps for how social workers can use civic education to help people grapple with democracy's potential as well as its limits.

Creating democratizing spaces will require a return to social work's foundational skill: listening. This is no small task in a world where the dominant modus operandi is to maximize one's opinion, demand easy answers, and distrust those who disagree. Social workers push back against the forces driving populism by listening and giving people the opportunity to tell their story. As Hyde and Galpern point out, we do not have to accept all opinions voiced in the public sphere, but we have to remember that being ready to listen to people's perspectives is the starting point of our job. Additional work may be needed on how to train new social workers to listen in ideologically-polarized contexts.

Responding to right-wing populism also requires us to be aware of the strategies used by its proponents so we do not get drawn in by them. Leidinger and Radvan, Häusler, Meyer, Dunn and Schäuble all write about specific rhetorical strategies that social workers must be alert to in order to challenge the erosion of human rights victories. They remind us to teach new social workers how to stand firm and have faith in our profession's values and methods in order to avoid disorientation and cooption. As Reisch and others point out, in order for social work to be effective in this new landscape, we have to get really clear about who we are as a profession, our relationship to government and the political system, and our vision for the just society we are working toward.

There are also new skill sets to acquire. Dunn and Reisch both highlight the need for more media literacy so that social workers can identify and effectively challenge inaccurate or distorted statements by public figures. Richter and Quent mention the necessity to increase participation in policy making, which would require social workers to get more training in participatory policy making models. Hyde and Galpern suggest social workers need to learn more about economics so they can more fully understand the grievances of right-populist supporters, offer strategies to address them, and help people move beyond scapegoating groups to understanding structural forces.

Whatever happens next, the power of right-populism, and the damage it has done to the standing of social work values and democratic institutions, will not be reversed overnight. Kazmierczak reminds us that as the standards upon which social work is based regress, social workers will continue to face a growing crisis of conscience and new ethical dilemmas. We need to continue to train new social workers to engage in ethical decisionmaking and to draw on supervisors and colleagues for support and advice. Schäuble brings to mind the role of social work during the Nazi era and the danger of focusing merely on protecting the profession versus engaging in larger struggles against oppression.

The various solutions proposed by out authors can be brought together to produce a comprehensive approach. While our readers are free to pick and choose the strategies proposed by our authors, we recommend thinking about how they can be combined. Using a framework that combines human rights and feminist theories will ensure that efforts at civic education are both inclusive and do not reproduce dehumanizing and oppressive discourses. Recognizing the ways that the traditional skills and tools of social work are directly relevant to the work needed today will help us stand firm in the face of attacks on our profession and constituents.

Implications for Research

Our authors have pointed to several areas that require additional exploration. In addition to evaluating the approaches described in the previous section, we identify three key areas for social work research: (1) analyzing right-populist discourse in order to bring its dangers to light, (2) assessing the impact of right-populist policies on people's lives, and (3) documenting the ways that social work practitioners are challenging or succumbing to right-populist worldviews. Our authors provide models for research on these topics, which we will discuss in turn.

Critical discourse analysis

One area for social workers to do additional research is studying right-wing populist discourse to uncover its meaning and impact. The chapter by Meyer provides an example of this form of analysis, with a focus on gender. Using transcripts of speeches of and official party documents, Meyer tracks how women leaders of the National Front and AfD talk about gender in ways that attack feminist ideals and harken back to traditional gender roles. This method could be extended to other threatened forms of progress toward equality.

It may also be helpful to look at the emotional weight of particular ideas that have a spatial component, such as the German word 'Heimat', which partially translates in English to homeland. Heimat is broader than homeland, conjuring up images of German history and culture to which people have an emotional connection. Likewise, in the US the word America is broader than a geographical location, and can have multiple meanings and evoke a variety of emotions connected deeply to people's identities. Social work research could uncover how the meaning of these words, and their use by right-wing populists, is impacting the people and communities with whom we work.

Policy analysis

More work is also needed to assess the impact of policies created by right-wing populist governments on people's lives and on the social work profession. Kazmierczak and Borodkina both provide models for linking official discourse, policy, and real-world impacts. Populism claims to represent the will of the people and to fight for the common person against the elites of society. Social work researchers should engage in projects that investigate the truth of these claims by documenting whether right-wing populist policies improve social and economic outcomes for non-elites.

Social Work's response

Additional research is also needed on how social workers are responding, whether they are being coopted by populist social policy, and under what conditions they are standing firm to protect social work values, the profession, their clients, and our communities. Subtopics here include whether social workers' ideas about their role in politics are changing in the new political environment and how the historical micro-macro split is shaping the profession's engagement with new right populism. Social worker research could also look at how social work practitioners are engaging with 'alternative facts' and clients and community groups who have worldviews based on polarized news sources as well as a defensive attitude toward empirical knowlege and rationally-based thought processes. This includes working with constituents for whom their right-wing populist ideology is connected to religious faith and particular forms of Christianity. The lack of attention to religion in this volume is a shortcoming.

In the chapter by Reisch, he outlines the challenges that social work faces in societies that are directed by illiberal heads of state, such as the US under Trump, and explores how social work is responding to these challenges. He does so by analyzing the official statements by national and local professional social work organizations, editorials published by social workers, and other media where practitioners are describing their efforts around the country. Using these sources he is able to analyze the position taken by elements of the profession and where more forceful rebuke of harmful rhetoric and policies are needed. Such documentation of social work's response must continue in the US as well as in every country where right-wing populists are influencing social policy.

Authors

Olga Borodkina, PhD, Professor, Department of Social Work, Faculty of Sociology at Saint Petersburg University/Russia, e-mail: o.borodkina@spbu.ru

Julika Bürgin, Prof. Dr., Professor for education/transformation and social research at the University of Applied Sciences Darmstadt/Germany, Department of Social Work, e-mail: julika.buergin@h-da.de

Kerry Dunn, JD, PhD, Assistant Professor, Department of Social Work Education, California State University, Fresno/USA. email: kerryd@csufresno.edu

Jörg Fischer, Prof. Dr., Professor for Educational Concepts at the University of Applied Sciences in Erfurt/Germany and Director of the Institute for Local Planning and Development, e-mail: joerg.fischer@fh-erfurt.de

Claire Galpern, MSW, Organizer at UNITE HERE Local 247 Philadelphia/USA, email: cgalpern@gmail.com

Alexander Häusler, Dipl. Soz.Wiss., Senior researcher of the research unit on right wing extremism, University of Applied Sciences Düsseldorf/Germany, e-mail: alexander.haeusler@hs-duesseldorf.de

Cheryl A. Hyde, Dr., Associate Professor at the Temple University School of Social Work Philadelphia/USA, email: chyde@temple.edu

Tomasz Kaźmierczak, PhD, Assistant Professor, Head of the Department of Social Work Methods and Theories, Institute of Social Prevention and Resocialisation at University of Warsaw/Poland, e-mail: kazmierczak@uw.edu.pl

Christiane Leidinger, Prof. Dr., Professor of Sociology and Gender Studies at University of Applied Sciences Duesseldorf/Germany, e-mail:christiane.leidinger@hs-duesseldorf.de

Birgit Meyer, Prof. Dr., Professor for Family Politics and Gender Studies at Esslingen University of Applied Sciences/Germany, e-mail: birgit.meyer@hs-esslingen.de

Kurt Möller, Prof. Dr., Professor for Theories and Conceptions of Social Work at Esslingen University of Applied Sciences/Germany, e-mail: Kurt.Moeller@hs-esslingen.de

Matthias Quent, Dr. phil., Director of the Institute for Democracy and Civil Society in Jena/Germany, e-mail: matthias.quent@idz-jena.de

Heike Radvan, Prof. Dr., Professor for Theory and Methods of Social Work at Brandenburg Technical University Cottbus/Germany, e-mail: radvan@b-tu.de

Michael Reisch, MSW, Ph.D., Daniel Thursz Distinguished Professor of Social Justice at the School of Social Work, University of Maryland/USA email: mreisch@ssw.umaryland.edu

Christoph Richter, MA Sociology, Anthropology and Journalism. Research Assistant at the Institute for Democracy and Civil Society in Jena/Germany, e-mail: christoph.richter@idz-jena.de

Samuel Salzborn, Prof. Dr., Visiting Professor for Research on Antisemitism at the Technical University Berlin/Germany, e-mail: salzborn@tu-berlin.de

Barbara Schäuble, Prof. Dr., Professor for Diversity-Sensitive Social Work at Alice Salomon Hochschule Berlin/Germany, e-mail: schaeuble@ash-berlin.eu

Fabian Virchow, Prof. Dr., Professor for Social Theory and for Theories of Collective Action at Hochschule Duesseldorf/Germany, e-mail: fabian.virchow@hs-duesseldorf.de

Index

anti-immigrant 8ff., 65, 75, 91, 96, 198
civic education 12, 169-172, 174, 176, 211, 220f.
class 10, 20, 22, 24f., 46, 54, 60f., 64, 94, 100, 115, 118f., 151, 162, 196
democracy 9, 10, 23, 36ff., 44, 46f., 50, 52, 56, 62f., 89f., 127, 134f., 139, 141f., 144, 160, 170, 173-176, 205, 210, 219ff.
disability policy 11, 107, 109, 111ff.
empowerment 112, 124, 193f., 197, 209, 213f., 220
ethnonationalism 35-38
familyism 11, 117-120, 126
fear 9, 22, 52, 66, 73, 75, 82f., 143, 148, 150, 159, 170, 180f., 187, 198, 210, 214
feminism 24, 72f., 79, 115f., 120, 127, 148
gender 9, 24, 71f., 75, 78f., 82f., 115ff., 119f., 125ff., 148, 151, 160, 171, 192, 196, 207, 222
Germany 8f., 13, 17, 19, 22, 24, 25ff., 37f., 41ff., 49, 62, 64f., 72, 74, 77-83, 122f., 133f., 169, 171, 175
globalization 9, 55, 59, 63ff., 82, 148, 150, 220
human rights 7, 10, 12f., 35, 71, 83, 106, 111, 116, 121, 126, 172, 191-199, 205, 207, 209f., 212f., 219ff.
ideology 8f., 11, 18, 24, 26, 34-37, 45, 60f., 64, 79, 97, 111, 118, 125, 134, 183, 188, 192, 211, 220, 223
illiberal democracy 94, 96f.
inequality 8f., 11, 24, 34-37, 50, 66, 76, 94, 111, 120, 127, 134, 148, 151, 160, 176, 197, 205f., 209, 220
neoliberalism 9, 104, 150
NGOs 94f., 105f., 111, 113, 193
non-voters 9, 42, 44, 45, 47, 49-55
Poland 11, 13, 59, 89ff., 93-97
policy advocacy 151, 158, 161f., 198, 220
political parties 23, 61f., 65
post-fact 12, 179f., 182-188
post-truth 12, 180, 186, 188
prejudice 136, 140, 210
producerism 62
propaganda 22, 25f., 37, 91, 182, 184f., 209
right-wing populism 7-13, 18, 33, 37, 46, 59, 61ff., 71, 73, 82, 115, 126, 133, 134f., 138, 140, 142, 144, 148, 151, 209, 212f., 219f.
Russia 11, 13, 60, 99-112, 154
self-empowerment 213
sensory experience 141f.
social justice 7, 10, 25, 71, 96, 99f., 104, 116, 150, 156, 159-162, 172, 176, 182, 194, 207
social mandate 205
social policy 7, 11, 42, 56, 89, 96, 99ff., 104f., 107, 112f., 148, 214, 222f.
USA 13f., 147, 194
youth 12, 153, 171-174, 209f., 212ff.
youth work 171-174, 210, 213

Budrich Journals

European Review of International Studies	International Journal for Research on Extended Education	Journal of the International Network for Sexual Ethics & Politics	Politics, Culture and Socialization
ISSN: 2196-6923	ISSN: 2196-3673	ISSN: 2196-6931	ISSN: 1866-3427
eISSN: 2196-7415	eISSN: 2196-7423	eISSN: 2196-694X	eISSN: 2196-1417
volume 5, 2018	volume 6, 2018	volume 6, 2018	volume 9, 2018
3 x per annum	2 x per annum	2 x per annum	2 x per annum
approx. 150 pp./issue	approx. 120 pp./issue	approx. 120 pp./issue	approx. 200 pp./issue
Language: English	Language: English	Language: English	Language: English

- Available Print + Online -
- Single Article Downloads -
- Various Subscription Types for Individuals and Institutions -
- Free Contents (ToCs, Editorials, Book Reviews, Open Access Contents) -
- Online Access by Campus Licence via IP for Institutions -
- Archival Rights for Institutions -
- Permission for Interlibrary Loan -
- VPN access permitted -
- No Limitations on Number of Users at Budrich Journals -

www.budrich-journals.com